SACRAMENTO PUBLIC LIBRARY

N. High

D0960034

XL
love

XL
love

How the Obesity Crisis Is Complicating America's Love Life

Sarah Varney

RODALE.

Mention of specific companies, organizations, or authorities in this book does not imply
endorsement by the author or publisher, nor does mention of specific companies,
organizations, or authorities imply that they endorse this book, its author, or the publisher.
Internet addresses and telephone numbers given in this book were accurate
at the time it went to press.

© 2014 by Sarah Varney
All rights reserved. No part of this publication may be reproduced or transmitted in any form
or by any means, electronic or mechanical, including photocopying, recording, or any other
information storage and retrieval system, without the written permission of the publisher.

Rodale books may be purchased for business or promotional use or for special sales.
For information, please write to:

Special Markets Department, Rodale Inc., 733 Third Avenue, New York, NY 10017

Printed in the United States of America
Rodale Inc. makes every effort to use acid-free ∞, recycled paper ♻

Book design by Kara Plikaitis

Library of Congress Cataloging-in-Publication Data is on file with the publisher.

ISBN 978-1-60961-483-6   hardcover

Distributed to the trade by Macmillan

2 4 6 8 10 9 7 5 3 1   hardcover

We inspire and enable people to improve their lives and the world around them.
rodalebooks.com

For Fountain, Jake, and Jesse

And for Nana, whose generous spirit warms us still

"Overweight bodies will soon be the modal human form."
—Alexandra Brewis, "Obesity and Human Biology:
Toward a Global Perspective," *American Journal of Human Biology,*
24, no. 3 (May/June 2012): 258–60.

"Sex is not fundamentally democratic or kind."
—Alain de Botton

CONTENTS

PROLOGUE

The helium balloons turn slowly in the still, warm air. One balloon is a crouching green frog; another, a smiling monkey printed with "Hang In There"; another, a 3-foot-tall pink foot announcing, "It's a girl!"

The balloons are tied with string to rows of incubators, and in those incubators are rows of newborns the size of kittens. The vast hall—nearly a football field long—beeps and pulses in the muted southern spring light. And yet, amid the machines, there are no sounds of babies crying. In their incubators, where the humidity reaches 97 percent to replenish the water they lose through their translucent skin, the babies wince and constrict, but no sound emerges from their mouths. Born months early, their lungs are so underdeveloped or their bodies so riddled with tubes that they cannot cry aloud.

Tied to one of the beds is a Minnie Mouse balloon with a bright pink bow and earnest, expectant brown eyes. Inside the isolette is a wisp of bone and skin and hair—the human form as it looks inside a mother's womb. Next to this baby girl is a boy whose legs and arms are no thicker than a crayon; a blue tube snakes into his nose and delivers oxygen, while a second colorless tube clears out carbon dioxide. Another tube—this one orange—delivers breast milk directly to his miniature stomach. He weighs just over a pound and a half.

Curiously, in between some of the tiny babies are exceptionally large ones—babies who weigh 12 pounds or more at birth and yet lie here with breathing tubes. A nurse in lilac scrubs asks another nurse, "Is he IDM?" The nurse nods back. *Infant of diabetic mother.* The newborn's rapid breathing signals immature lungs. He came into being amid a flood of glucose; his own pancreas tried to compensate by producing even more insulin, thus fueling such rapid growth in the womb that certain organs couldn't keep pace.

The neonatal intensive care unit at the University of Mississippi Medical Center in Jackson is one of the largest in the nation; it's a puzzling distinction given the Magnolia State's small population. Yet Mississippians, who in just a generation have become the nation's heaviest Americans, live in a future that the rest of the United States is just now catching up to. These rows of underdeveloped and overgrown babies—many born to extremely heavy mothers whose chronic hypertension and diabetes forced them into premature birth—are signs of the ultimate collision of fat and sex, a collision that can have profound consequences for the physical health of these babies and confound their journey into sexual beings as they grow up.

CHAPTER ONE

Beginnings: Puberty, Puppy Love, and the Prom

North of Jackson, the Mississippi Delta opens into a flat stretch of saturated, fertile earth between the Yazoo and Mississippi Rivers. In the winter and early spring, the fields along the country roads here are covered with snarled, dormant kudzu vines. The eerie gray vines are everywhere, and the totality of the takeover is startling: They hang in a brittle mop from trees; they turn hillsides into resting Snuffleupaguses with unruly coats of gray fur; they threaten to overtake dirt driveways. Kudzu has become the curse of the Delta: Farmers have tried to burn it, only to witness the irrepressible vines roaring back to life with lush leaves in summer. Entrepreneurs have tried to turn it into an earth-friendly biofuel, with little success. Livestock producers have set ravenous goats afield, only to find their four-chambered stomachs no match for the invasive plant's virility.

Like the impressively resistant kudzu, the disease of obesity, too, has crept into the Delta and the nation beyond. A rarity just a few decades ago, it is overtaking everything in its way—spreading through homes and schools, across cotton fields and catfish farms; altering the genes that parents pass down to their children; and disrupting how and when the very stages of life are marked, including the awkward progression from childhood to the sexual self.

The Delta town of Belzoni—70 miles from Jackson—owes its existence to the slithering path of the Yazoo River and the tenacious and ugly catfish that bathe in its waters. The river forms the southern border of the town and provides the water for the area's fabled catfish farmers. Some 40,000 acres are underwater, sunken to provide vast pools for farm-raised bottom-dwellers. The small town has dwindled in size in the last decade, but Belzoni persists in its claim as "Catfish Capital of the World." On the town's main thoroughfare, 5-foot-tall painted catfish sculptures stand on their tails: a Superman with a curious brown fedora; a farmer in blue overalls; a whiskered dandy in a green bow tie.

Propped up on the tidy brick sidewalk next to one of the sculptures is a handwritten chalkboard announcing the day's lunchtime special at the Greasy Row Grill: fried pork chops. Inside the diner's kitchen, a vat of grease crackles with a new order of fries. Just about anything goes into the fryer to be encased in a crispy, high-calorie coat of oil: green beans, mushrooms, cheese sticks, tamales, pickles, crawfish tails, and, of course, catfish.

Yet even in a state that leads the nation in obesity, towns like Belzoni—and the bodily changes in their children and teens—stand out.

A team of researchers from the state health department descended upon nearly a dozen public elementary schools in the Delta during the winter of 2009–2010 and precisely measured the height, weight, and waist circumference of some 1,100 children between the ages of 6 and 11. Researchers determine body mass index—a common measurement of body fat—by dividing one's weight in kilograms by the square of one's height in meters, and for adults, BMI is widely viewed as a reliable indicator.[1] But these researchers were even more concerned about the risks to children with rounded bellies and excess abdominal fat.

Why? This type of fat puts them at greater risk for chronic diseases, such as type 2 diabetes and heart disease, than fat that sits on the hips and buttocks. The lead researcher, Abigail Gamble, PhD, and her colleagues suspected that the "normal," "overweight," and "obese" standards set by the Centers for Disease Control and Prevention were less reliable for children, and particularly for African American children, since the location of body fat in different racial groups can vary even when BMI is the same.[2]

Instead, Dr. Gamble and her researchers would measure the children's waist circumferences and determine their waist-to-height ratios. Those measurements, in addition to BMI, would give a more complete picture of the health of kids in the Delta.

What they found was troubling even for a region in the Deep South used to bad news about big bodies: Based on BMI, nearly half of the elementary children were overweight or obese (18.3 percent were overweight and 28.8 percent obese).[3] However, when they looked at the waist circumference measurements, *almost 60 percent* had enough fat around their bellies to put them at risk for weight-related chronic diseases, and 42 percent were at risk based on the waist-height ratio. And reflecting nationwide trends, the rate of obesity by BMI in the nearly all-black school districts was higher (31.9 percent), as were the percentages of children at risk for chronic diseases.

A big belly is a dangerous thing, and to call the abdominal adipose tissue merely "fat" is to underestimate its power. Children as young as 9 have been found to be in a constant state of low-grade, systemic inflammation.[4] As *Health Affairs* senior editor Jonathan Bor explained in his excellent piece, "The Science of Childhood Obesity," "Adipose tissues that gather around the waist contain not only fat, but immune-system cells called macrophages. These normally work to remove pathogens and dead cell debris from the body. But when secreted by fat, they can inflame arteries and trigger cancers."[5] These same white blood cells release chemicals that can lead to insulin resistance; as these children get older, they are more likely to face type 2 diabetes. Indeed, researchers now estimate that one out of every three boys and two out of every five girls born in the

United States in the year 2000 will be diagnosed with diabetes during their lifetime.[6]

Obesity and its perils now start almost as life begins, and its degree is becoming more extreme: One in eight preschoolers in the United States is now obese, and the percentage of obese children ages 6 to 11 years old increased from 7 percent in 1980 to nearly 18 percent in 2010. More children are pushing the boundaries of severe weight gain;[7] the proportion of boys and girls with extreme waist circumferences and waist-to-height ratios has been increasing nationwide.[8] And the heaviest children are becoming even heavier.

Once the weight is on, it often stays on. Fatness in childhood is destiny later in life: 80 percent of obese teen boys and 92 percent of obese teen girls will remain obese during adulthood and will face far higher risks for heart disease, kidney failure, cancer, and stroke at younger ages.[9] All of this excess weight on American children is enough, experts say, to reduce the average life expectancy in the United States by 5 years or more over the next several decades.[10] Even if current obesity rates remain steady, the country's health care system is headed toward a cost crisis: By 2030, epidemiologists predict medical expenses alone could increase by up to $66 billion a year.[11]

Public health advocates have been buoyed by signs that the surging national childhood obesity rate is beginning to level off and perhaps even decline for toddlers. But these fledgling declines have been uneven across the country, and poverty-stricken areas and those with large black and Latino populations have seen little improvement.

And nowhere is that pattern more apparent than in the Deep South. Dr. Gamble's findings[12] were a reminder of the tenacious hold that obesity has there. She suggested in her findings that despite a Mississippi state policy that directs schools to increase physical activity and promote healthy eating, obesity was manifesting "in minority children of low socioeconomic status at an increasingly younger age." And obesity wasn't merely showing up on arms, legs, and tummies. It was making its presence known in more private places, too.

* * *

THIS was not news to Carlton Gorton, MD, of Belzoni, who has been treating young girls—fans of Dora the Explorer and Curious George—who are growing pubic hair.

Out the back door of the Greasy Row Grill and across a dirt courtyard is the Gorton Rural Health Clinic, where Dr. Gorton and his father, Mack, have been taking care of generations of families. Carlton's grandfather owned a drugstore in Belzoni, and his father set up his practice more than 4 decades ago. Most of the clinic's patients—young and old—are overweight; many are morbidly obese, Dr. Gorton told me when we met one afternoon at the clinic. They arrive with a Medicaid or Medicare card, or no insurance at all, and pay what they can.

Dr. Gorton was sitting at a stately wooden desk when I walked into his office. The walls were covered with football memorabilia and photographs from Ole Miss, where Dr. Gorton attended medical school. He is handsome and unassuming, and he speaks in a mellifluous tone that makes even unpleasant facts tolerable to the ear.

With deep concern in his voice, he told me that during routine exams in his clinic, he has discovered girls as young as 5 and 6 years old who are developing pubic hair. These alarming signs of puberty are usually related to his patients' ample body fat. "They're usually off the growth chart," said Dr. Gorton. A few of the girls come to the clinic each month for a hormone shot prescribed by a pediatric endocrinologist. "It's holding them off from going through puberty," he said plainly.

Kindergartners with pubic hair are discomforting proof of obesity's powers over the unfolding human body. To Dr. Gorton, it was part of life in the Delta.

* * *

AND yet, the chemical tide of hormones and synthetic compounds that scientists believe is prematurely ripening girls' bodies continues to surge forward both here and elsewhere. Some 15 percent of American girls now begin puberty by first or second grade,[13] and over the last quarter century, the age when American girls begin menstruating has decreased by 2.5 months.[14]

The subtle shift has been enough to attract the attention of Kotex. The brand that has shepherded generations of girls through their first periods has begun offering "U by Kotex Tween," a shorter and narrower pad marketed to girls as young as 8 that comes neatly folded in colorful plastic pouches decorated with stars and hearts.

The hastening of girls' periods has been more pronounced among African American girls for reasons not entirely understood. In what is widely considered the most reliable data showing differences by race, researchers led by Frank Biro, MD, the director of adolescent medicine at the Cincinnati Children's Hospital Medical Center, followed more than one thousand 9-year-old girls for a decade. They found that black girls begin puberty at about 9½ years old—third-graders—and begin their periods at age 12, 6 months before white girls for both events.[15]

But what has concerned pediatricians and pediatric endocrinologists more than the earlier start to menarche—the first menstrual cycle—is what Dr. Gorton has seen in Belzoni: the much earlier onset of breast development and pubic hair. It is now well established that girls' breasts are "budding" earlier in the United States, something borne out by a 2010 study that tracked 1,239 girls in East Harlem, New York; Cincinnati; and the San Francisco Bay Area.[16] Again led by Dr. Biro, the researchers found significant differences in the percentages of girls who are developing breasts by the time they turn 7 years old: 23 percent of black girls; 15 percent of Hispanic girls; 10 percent of white girls; and 2 percent of Asian girls.

This was epidemiological evidence of what local pediatricians had been seeing in clinics around the country. "The proportion of girls who had breast development at ages 7 and 8 years, particularly among white girls," the researchers concluded, "is greater than that reported from studies of girls who were born 10 to 30 years earlier."

The big question is: Why? Why are American girls—more so than girls in other developed countries—shedding their puerile bodies and stepping into their sexual selves earlier? And what might obesity have to do with it? Anecdotal evidence like that seen in Belzoni suggested a profound shift was under way, but stronger scientific proof came from an unlikely source: rhesus monkeys.

* * *

IN Madison, Wisconsin, a group of young female rhesus monkeys born and raised at the Wisconsin National Primate Research Center must have been delighted to find their caregivers giving them extra snacks and sweet treats 7 days a week. Their relatives from the same colony, also prepubescent females, were getting the same old monkey diet of Purina chow and fresh fruits and vegetables. After a year of eating 30 percent more calories than their relatives but getting the same amount of physical activity, the female monkeys on the high-calorie diet had not only gotten fatter, but they had also started menstruating.

* * *

SCIENTISTS who are trying to understand why American girls are coming into their sexual selves earlier see a bewildering chemical kaleidoscope. Some researchers argue that environmental toxins like bisphenol-A, which can mimic estrogen, lead to earlier puberty; others point to difficult home environments where the stress of poverty, alcoholism, violence, and single-parent households unleashes other hormones like cortisol that could usher in early-onset puberty.

But the rhesus monkeys in the wintry climes of the Badger State offered a novel view into one of the leading theories: that body fat and menarche are linked. The researchers were able to control the environment the monkeys lived in and the synthetic chemicals they came in contact with;

they created two sterile bubbles where the only difference was how many calories the monkeys—all from the same family and with similar genetic proclivities—consumed.

Something curious had already been happening with the monkeys in Wisconsin. Ei Terasawa, Joseph Kurian, and their colleagues at the primate research center had noticed the age at menarche for their experimental rhesus monkeys had been declining for the past 3 decades, coinciding with changes made to enhance the monkeys' environment, including increased caloric intake.

The monkeys, it seemed, were experiencing similar phenomena as the young American girls: Their high-calorie diet led them to have more fat cells, and those cells were producing a critical hormone called leptin that, along with other hormones and neurotransmitters, helps trigger puberty. Pediatricians had long believed that girls begin their periods when they reach about 17 percent body fat,[17] and scientists began to ascertain the interplay between body fat, the brain, and critical signaling pathways.

There was other, older evidence of the link between fat and early puberty as well: An analysis that compared the body mass index and age of menarche of girls in the 1960s to girls in the late 1980s and early 1990s found that, when comparing two girls of the same age and race, an overweight girl was 2.4 times more likely to have started her first menstrual cycle.[18]

It now seems quite clear that the earlier a girl gains weight, the more likely she will get her period earlier, and the more likely she will remain heavy throughout her life.

* * *

OBESITY appears to be fundamentally altering adolescent sexual development, but this new normal is hardly without risks and may be a harbinger of serious health problems. Among girls who go through early puberty, there is an increased incidence of depression;[19] alcohol, tobacco, and substance abuse; riskier sexual adventures; teen pregnancy;[20] and even suicide attempts.[21] Developmental scientists have found, not surprisingly, that girls who physically develop before their peers are apt to gain weight and are more dissatisfied with their bodies.[22] That might seem less a concern among African American girls, who live in communities more accepting of larger body sizes and where precocious puberty is hardly exceptional. (Nearly one in four black girls has developed breasts by the age of 7.) Yet, scientists who study human development have not found that heavy black girls are shielded from depression as they progress into early adulthood. Even after controlling for economic hardship and parental education—factors that can fuel depression—girls who are obese as teens, regardless of their race or ethnicity, display more symptoms of depression than normal-weight girls as they age.[23]

All of which keeps Naznin Dixit, MD, chief of pediatric endocrinology and diabetes at Batson Children's Hospital at the University of Mississippi Medical Center in Jackson, very busy. Like it or not, Dr. Dixit is in a growth field. After all, pediatric endocrinologists are called in to solve hormonal mysteries when something has gone seriously awry with a child's development: a child who is abnormally short or extraordinarily tall; a child brought to the emergency room unconscious due to hypoglycemia; and what used to be called precocious puberty, defined as a girl who develops breasts and pubic hair before the age of 8 or a boy who develops pubic or facial hair, or an enlarged penis or testicles, before the age of 9.

And Dr. Dixit continues to be stunned by the remarkable number of referrals for her expertise, including obese children with hormonal complications. "The degree of obesity in these kids is really massive," she told me in her medical office in Jackson.

Boys are not immune: The turbulent hormonal chemistry at play in obese boys' bodies, in which enzymes present in belly fat are busily converting testosterone into estrogen, can lead to embarrassment for boys and concern for endocrine scientists.

"We see the development of breasts and massive breast enlargement [among boys]," Dr. Dixit said. "It's not just fat. It's breast tissue." Obesity is associated with a significantly higher risk of breast cancer in women, according to a study sponsored by the National Cancer Institute,[24] but the future risks to boys who develop breast tissue aren't well known.

The risks don't stop at the physical. "Clearly we know that if kids start puberty early, their childhood is shortened," she said.

And that is Dr. Dixit's main worry, that these new patterns of obesity and sexual maturation are ripening young bodies faster than their minds can keep up. Early adolescence is a critical window for emotional and behavioral development, and yet, Dr. Dixit said glumly, "it suddenly gets impacted with this early puberty and so-called rage of hormones."[25]

There's also the trickier and potentially more treacherous issue of other people's perceptions. "These kids look older than they actually are," Dr. Dixit explained. "Psychologically, they haven't emotionally developed to the same extent as their bodies."

The tween and young teen girls Dr. Dixit sees often have adult breasts and curves, yet they've had little time to adjust to their bodies and understand why their families and friends have begun treating them differently. Dr. Dixit fears that these girls, walking around in sensual bodies, could become targets for sexual abuse. And her worries have a proven basis: One of the most recent studies, published in 2013, and which drew from 68,505 adult women, found that women who had early periods had an elevated risk for unwanted sexual touching and an even greater risk for forced sexual activity.[26]

Studies show that girls who experience an earlier age of menarche, not all of whom are overweight, are more likely to be sexually active sooner than girls the same age and are more likely to become pregnant and contract sexually transmitted diseases.[27] These girls may be sought after by older boys and, in some cases, preyed upon by young men or male family members.

By one estimate, one out of three junior high students and high school freshmen report having sexual intercourse,[28] which seemed to track with the remarks I heard from a dozen middle school girls who gathered to talk with me about weight and boys one afternoon in Jackson. All of the girls were African American, and most were overweight or obese and buxom.

Echoing academic findings,[29] the girls were curious about kissing, touching, and sex, and many expressed strong attractions of their own.

And while they sometimes laughed riotously at my questions about weight, dating, and sex, they didn't seem shy about answering my two major queries: How did boys in their seventh- and eighth-grade classes—or older boys in high school or in their neighborhoods—treat heavier or more developed girls? And even though many students in Jackson public schools are heavy, did bigger girls still get teased?

Soon, their stories tumbled out in a fast-moving river of southern patter. They talked over each other—often elbowing and high-fiving—and were eager to offer their opinions. What quickly became clear was that the standard for "normal" weight was not at all how pediatricians defined it: It was only the girls sitting around the table who were severely obese who spoke about being called names; those who, by all measures, were overweight simply considered themselves standard weight, or, the accepted term for curvy girls, "thick." From that cacophony of voices, here are some of the more poignant comments.

> "Some boys are probably trying to go with girls that got big boobs."
>
> "I like my shape the way it is."
>
> "Well, some are calling me fat."
>
> "They be talkin' about her, but I'd be tellin' her to say somethin' back to 'em because somebody call me fat, I'd . . . "
>
> "There's a girl, well, she in my classroom, and she real huge. And people talk about her all the time. She real big. Every time she walks, they make noise like, 'Boom Boom Boom' and call her 'obesity' and stuff. But she my friend. I stick up for her."
>
> "People call me fat. I say I'm phat with a P."
>
> "I don't say pretty, hot, and thick. I say, pretty hot, and tempting."
>
> "'Cause she ain't thick."
>
> "They say big girls get all the love."
>
> "They got them big ol' badonkadonk." [The girls laugh. Someone clarifies—big butts.]
>
> "Some skinny girls got that curve, that shape, and all that too."

"She gettin' offended."

"No, I'm not getting offended, I'm saying . . . "

"Yes, you is . . . "

"You were sayin' 'cause I'm not thick. Okay, but, I still be pullin', though."

"So you actually had sex with him?"

"Yup."

"My mom told me, when you first do it, it's gonna hurt. That's why I ain't doin' it, 'cause I scared."

"It ain't gonna hurt!"

✹ ✹ ✹

THESE girls will soon enter an even more fraught period of their lives: high school, the swirling, formative 4 years that couple intense emotional development with a surging sexual awakening. It is a time when friendships, personal beliefs, and tastes and preferences—sexual and otherwise—are often cemented.

Like high school itself, the study of teen sexuality can be vexing, confusing, and sometimes contradictory. And adding obesity to the mix makes the answers to questions about teen sex all the muddier.

To take just one example of why conclusions can be tough to find, consider this: Although sexual development is beginning at a younger age in the United States and the pervasive image of today's teenagers is of hookup-happy, selfie-shooting, casual sex fans, teens are, paradoxically, less sexually active than they once were.

Indeed, national surveys of youth behavior that researchers have long used to decipher teenage sexual behaviors have recorded sharp drops over the last 2 decades. In 1991, 54 percent of high school students reported that they had ever had sexual intercourse; by 2011, this figure had fallen to 47 percent.[30] (Over about the same period, teenage obesity more than tripled.)

That decrease crosses racial lines, too. Although the proportion of teen girls ages 15 through 19 who had ever had sex decreased for all racial and ethnic groups from 1995 to 2006 through 2010, the drop was greatest for blacks (34 percent) and Hispanics (29 percent) compared with whites (15 percent). For the first time, the proportion of teenage girls ages 15 through 19 who have never had sex is similar across all racial and ethnic groups.[31]

If puberty is taking place earlier, why is sex happening later? Perhaps these trends—one causing concern among public health officials, the other lauded—have something to do with each other. Obesity certainly appears to play a role in ushering in early puberty. Could it also be altering teens' romantic prospects and when they begin having sex?

* * *

THE sexual and romantic life of the American teenager has been scrutinized for decades, tracked in a long-running nationwide survey of thousands of American tweens and teens who reflect the racial and ethnic makeup of the United States. Yet, the extent to which weight has shaped teen dating and the teenage sexual experience has been somewhat of a mystery. There have now been several waves of junior high and high school students who have dutifully filled out nosy surveys about their private lives. And as these students have gotten older—and many of their waistlines bigger—researchers have begun to discern how the increased prevalence of obesity is influencing teen romance and early sexual activity and whether the degree of influence varies for black, Latino, white, and Asian teens.

Just as the era of childhood obesity was beginning, in the early and mid-1990s, surveys of youth attitudes about overweight classmates were unambiguous: Teenagers and young adults were reluctant to pair off with a heavy girlfriend or boyfriend.[32, 33] But since those surveys were taken, adolescent obesity has tripled: Nearly one in five 12- to 19-year-olds is obese, and more than a third are overweight or obese. The question now

is: In the new era of obesity, how does being overweight influence a teenager's sexual experience?

An intriguing study was published in the *Journal of Research on Adolescence* in 2005 that seemed to offer some clues, at least for girls, as to whether
obesity's pervasiveness somehow eased the costs of being a heavy teen in the
high school dating market. Carolyn Tucker Halpern, a professor of mater-
nal and child health at the University of North Carolina at Chapel Hill, and
her fellow investigators found that a teenage girl's odds for a romantic relationship, irrespective of her race or ethnicity, dropped 6 to 7 percent for
every one-point increase in her body mass index.[34, 35] In other words, the
heavier a girl became, the worse her chances at romance.

* * *

A line of ordinary family sedans and hulking pickup trucks, looking freshly
polished, turns into an empty parking lot off North State Street in Jackson,
Mississippi, just a few blocks from the grand Beaux Arts state capitol building. The car doors open and into the spring night air step young men in
tuxedos and young women in strapless gowns, layers of airy chiffon and
tightly stretched sateen glittering in the headlights. Squads of teenagers
yip and yowl at the sight of each other's finery; their call-and-response
echoes off nearby buildings.

The young women step onto the sidewalk and link arms. Tottering
in high heels, they balance on the arm of a date or brace against each
other, two and three across. Bare shoulders rising in protest against the
cool evening temperature, they cup their forearms beneath exuberant
breasts that spill out of expertly constructed strapless bodices.

It soon becomes apparent that this parade will be led, unabashedly it
seems, by a new generation of teens many sizes bigger than the ones who
marched along these streets in previous decades. An elegant, obese young
woman brushes across the sidewalk in a floor-length gown; a morbidly
obese girl, wearing a bracelet of flowers on her wrist, is a shimmering mass

of silver sequins. A boy holding the arms of two heavy girls in strapless teal dresses pronounces to no one in particular, "Hello! We are here!"

These are hefty teenagers, full of vitality and eager anticipation, who have chosen not to lose.

* * *

IF you're going to be a fat teen, there is no better place to fit in than Mississippi. The me-too world of high school that traffics in status has recalibrated to the new order: About 40 percent of teens here are overweight or obese,[36] and among black teens, the rate is even higher. When they turn 18, they'll earn a new distinction: They'll join the three out of four black adults here who are overweight or obese. For white adults, two out of three are beyond a normal weight.[37]

Preparations for the Murrah High School prom began weeks, or even months, ago, depending on whom you ask. Girls eyed potential candidates—both dresses and dates—at the local mall. At Once Upon a Dress, Puttin' on the Glitz, and Prom Dream, shop owners stocked feathered and sequined creations that hung limply from plastic hangers by strips of ribbon.

The local newspaper, the *Clarion-Ledger,* published a story in late March, "Dream Dresses: Prom Season Punctuated with Color." It featured advice from prom shop owner Susan Nash, the owner of Susan's Shoppe Formals. Ms. Nash predicted high-low dresses, jersey styles with cut-outs, and volcano stone embellishments. "High-lows are dresses that are short in the front and long in the back," she explained. "Jersey knit dresses are so comfy and forgive the wearer to gain or lose a couple of pounds without compromising the fit."

The girls featured in the article—all but one were white—looked nothing like the teens prepping for the "Harlem Nights"–themed prom for Murrah High School. Slender and narrow-hipped, their breasts were tucked neatly behind shirred bodices. The look: Chaste Siren.

At a local mall, a salesperson had spent the lead-up to prom advising more buxom girls to stay away from strapless dresses. "Go with straps," the clerk suggested. They often declined, so instead the shop had to make accommodations for heavier teens with their very adult busts.

On a Friday afternoon in April, a few hours before prom would begin, swarms of boys fill the food court en route to pick up their tuxedos at the Northpark Mall in nearby Ridgeland. The food court atrium is painted robin's-egg blue and soft butter yellow, and a children's play area lines one wall. All around the room, flat-screened television monitors play raunchy music videos. On the screen above the Chick-fil-A, a chain gang of sweaty women in bikinis is hard at work in a metal salvage yard. They stop and stare as a BMW motorcycle comes to a screeching stop. The synth beats begin, and hip-hop artist Taio Cruz dismounts from his bike, removes his red helmet, and launches into his strip club anthem "Dynamite." The women trail behind him in an orgiastic line.

Other entertainments, meanwhile, are aimed at other appetites: The Chick-fil-A, the StirFry 88, the Cajun Grill, and the Steak Escape are doing a brisk business. Several women sit at a table in front of the video screens, their cellulite unrestrained by tired black leggings. After a few sips of their fountain drinks, the women casually glance at the pulsing video screens.

Around the corner from the food court, a line has formed at Tuxedo Junction. The salespeople are trying to bring order to chaos: "Picking Up and Trying On," says one handwritten sign, while another implores, "Fittings Plus Picking Up and NOT Trying On."

The boys stare absently at their phones and listen to earbuds, tapping and bouncing, and try not to back into a rack of pastel-colored vests hanging behind them. One obese boy is dressed in gray sweatpants. He wears a white T-shirt and white high-top sneakers that he has left strategically untied.

But despite his carefully edited displays of masculinity—the cool stance, the gleaming white kicks—his body is surging with a very essential hormone—estrogen. The visceral fat accumulating inside his abdominal cavity, which stretches his rounded belly outward, is a lumpy, buttery yellow. Filled with an enzyme called aromatase that is busy converting testosterone into estrogen,[38] the fat rests snugly against his stomach, liver, and other organs. The tissue is not a harmless, lifeless blob, but instead is almost an active gland secreting its own chemicals and sending messages to the boy's brain. Unlike the less troublesome subcutaneous fat around the hips and thighs, visceral fat can lead boys like him to develop pendulous breasts and disrupt the chain of events that produces healthy sexual development.

Just how does this misfiring of hormones—this new chemical order in which the balance of estrogen and testosterone is altered—play out in puberty? As obese teenagers find themselves tumbling into the maw of adolescent sexual development, will their bodies be able to respond to the sights and sounds of teenage girls spilling out of their cantilevered dresses on prom night?

* * *

"ADOLESCENCE is a period in life that begins in biology and ends in society," wrote Anne C. Petersen, PhD, the renowned child development expert.[39] Indeed, as much as parents might like to imagine they are the primary influence in their child's life, by high school that is no longer the case. Adolescent psychologists say with certainty that teens value their relationships with friends more than any other type of relationship.[40]

Young teens arrive at high school as partially solved equations and then triangulate off each other to fill in the rest. Identity. Self-esteem. Romantic prospects. The dictatorship is total. In fact, while pediatricians, endocrinologists, and parents worry incessantly over the earlier age of puberty among American adolescents, peer relationships are a more accurate predictor of whether or not tweens or teenagers are dating than whether they have reached puberty.[41] That suggests adolescents may be more attuned to their friends than their bodies when deciding when to date.

While girls who physically mature earlier are more likely to become sexually active at a younger age, that doesn't appear to be the driving force in when—or whether—they start to date. Those first romantic relationships that begin as daylong love affairs ending with the last bell to inseparable high school sweethearts are an awkward and vital human ritual; they are the building blocks for interpersonal skills crucial in adulthood. And the best chance at getting started—the best predictor of young romance—is who your friends are. That raises questions for bigger girls' social and emotional development, and for their romantic success later in life.

Studies have found that obese adolescents are about half as likely to begin dating as healthy-weight teens.[42] That leaves heavy girls—and to a lesser extent heavy boys—with fewer opportunities to forge romantic relationships during adolescence and develop the relationship skills they'll need later on, when couples face very adult demands.

All of which raises the question: If heavy teens are shunned from crucial friendship networks, how do they get their start as novice daters?

* * *

If a visitor were to look down from a balcony at the Murrah High School prom, the extremely obese girls would come into focus, and the pattern—precisely where those who are fat fit into the school cliques—would begin to appear. The elegantly dressed girl in the silver sequined top with a fuchsia pleated skirt swings back and forth in a mob of exuberant dancers; a girl in a strapless turquoise dress grinds against a stocky boy in a white tuxedo and laughs as she tugs on her bodice to keep it from falling down. Another heavy girl sings and pumps her hands in the air, shouting, "Just gonna work!"

None of the extremely heavy girls is dancing near another. But they have not been exiled and left to form a group of their own or retreat from the playfully erotic vibe. Instead, they are spread out among the different social networks that are critical, researchers contend, for teen dating and for what one sociologist calls "the teen sex market."

* * *

IF you are a big teenage girl in a state like Mississippi, where heavy bodies are commonplace, your best bet at having a boyfriend is to fit into a group of friends who will broker romantic deals on your behalf.

At Murrah High School, for example, there are a number of options: the football players, the engineers, the popular girls who prize fashionable, curated outfits—midriff shirts in the winter—and the "sneaker heads," whose fashion style runs to quilted Jordans, LeBrons, KDs, and Kobes.

A straight-talking senior named DesTenee, who described the dating world one afternoon, fell in with the nerds and said, laughing. "But I'm a fun nerd."

Poised and confident, DesTenee is practical and not at all judgmental when it comes to the question of where fat kids fit in at her school. The taxonomy was similar to what the tweens across town described: Obese or severely obese kids were "fat" or "of size"; girls who were curvy and "borderline of being overweight," DesTenee said, were "thick."

But again, what students here considered normal weight, most pediatricians would deem unhealthy. Up in Belzoni, Dr. Gorton had said African American parents routinely walked into his clinic worried that their children weren't gaining enough weight when, in fact, they were perfectly aligned on the growth chart.

"I have some patients whose weight is literally normal," Dr. Gorton said in a calm, southern drawl. "But they've been told there's somethin' wrong with 'em. They sick. They must have cancer 'cause they too little. So I address it from, 'You're perfect. You're completely healthy.'"

A week before her high school prom night, DesTenee looked statuesque walking into the library. She wore a Hello Kitty shirt featuring the cartoonish white cat in black-rimmed glasses. At the bottom, the shirt read "Available for Study Dates."

She had been astonished when her doctor chimed in about her weight. "I didn't know this that my doctor told me that for my size and my height and my age, I was overweight. I did not know that!" She was animated when recalling the moment and, seeming unwounded, laughed. She thought girls often looked around and thought, "Well, I'm not as big as her, so I'm not fat."

To be sure, comparative assessment is an important part of how cliques form and membership is assessed; many of the popular girls at her school are themselves "thick" and accept obese girls into their clique so long as they meet the group's exacting standards. "There is always one girl 'of size' who carries herself well," DesTenee said. She "has a certain confidence that she can be in that popular clique, and she has this fashion sense" that flatters her size. "She can pull it off."

But there are limits to this calculated generosity; the biggest of the big kids can stick around only as long as they have some utility. "I wouldn't see those popular girls or popular boys hanging out with someone of size if they didn't meet their standards. It's like, if you were of size or don't fit in, you have to try extra, extra hard," was how DesTenee put it.

The bigger kids need something special, some advantage that can buttress them against the hierarchy of cruelty and the elemental teenage impulse to ridicule.

"If you are 'of size' in this school, you have to have something to back you up with that size. Because if not," DesTenee warned, "you're just going to be tossed, like, to the wayside." The students who walk around seeming cowed, with their heads down and their shoulders slumped, get teased the most. Students will "throw shade," casting an indirect insult like, "I bet you wanna eat that hamburger!" The best defense is a puffed-up persona and swagger: "Like nose in the air. No one can tell me any-thing. 'I. *Own*. These. Hallways.'"

DesTenee echoed what other overweight and obese teens around the country said during interviews. From California to New Hampshire, Michigan to Mississippi, in small towns and suburbs and cities, heavy teens in high school today said that a sunny personality, one filled with confidence and bravado, is necessary for climbing social ladders.[43] Heavy people can be popular as long as they show no fear.

Having grown up in schools and homes more concerned with

emotional well-being than in previous generations, nonetheless, today's teens are still seeped in prejudice against bigger bodies.

Fatass. Big Dora. Big Mac. Fat bitch.

The prejudice might be scalable, but it remains, set in the filament of teenage social order and guiding youthful attraction.

"Whatever we see as true, we're going to idolize that. Whoever doesn't fit that standard of what society has picked for us, that's what we're gonna do. We're gonna bully that person," DesTenee said matter-of-factly.

*   *   *

JOE K entered high school in Michigan as one of those big kids, unsure of where he fit in. At 14, he already weighed 270 pounds. He was never the *only* fat kid; several of his friends weighed more than 300 pounds, and many others were overweight. But being bigger didn't preclude Joe from making friends with other guys; he felt equally at home with the football players on his team and snowboarders on the slopes as he did with friends in calculus class and band. For boys, at least, it seemed to Joe that personality and interests earned him entry into certain social groups, instead of his weight keeping him out. His school was no fat utopia, though; in middle school a heavy student was transferred out of Joe's class after some horrific teasing, and he suspected that kids ridiculed him behind his back. "If anything," he said, "my size carries an intimidating factor, and because of that, people don't tease me or pick on me."[44]

His size earned him respect on the football field, but it left him at sea when it came to girls. "Weight may not have played as large a role while making friends," he wrote in an e-mail, but "when it came to romantic relationships, it became much more important."

*   *   *

IT seems that when it comes to a teen's romantic prospects, size still matters. Being big and popular among status-hungry teens is one thing; getting someone to date you is another venture entirely. Yes, it was true that the obese girls at Murrah High School hadn't been sidelined and a freshman named Joe had a nest of friends, but would their social networks deliver romance?

Not reliably, particularly for girls.

"I don't date fat chicks." That's how boys responded to Katelyn, an 18-year-old from Texas, when she finally got up the nerve to ask them out in high school. NFC: No. Fat. Chicks. One overweight 17-year-old boy in California whose grandparents own a burger joint said, "'NFC' are words to live by for many males at my school."

Katelyn's school in Texas is decidedly cliquey; the social groups are sharply divided. "The cheerleaders hang out with other cheerleaders," Katelyn said. "The football players hang out with the football players, and if they're dating a cheerleader, they're hanging out with the cheerleader's friends."

Katelyn gave up on dating during most of high school. At 5-foot-1 and at times 180 pounds, "I always thought, 'Well, I'm the ugly, fat one.'" Her friends would take her shopping at the local mall, but her size was in a different part of the store. "I'm over here like, 'Oh, gotta go over here to the bigger side to get clothes while they look at bikinis or shorts or whatever.'"

It wasn't only that Katelyn envied her thinner friends. She felt hopeless in putting together the fashionable outfits that might attract a boy's eye.

* * *

YOUNG teenagers are shallow, brutal brokers of love and status, in part because they are just beginning to discern which personal attributes they find attractive. It's less about compatibility in early adolescence, and more about sneakers. Around age 12 or 13, the amorous focus of most girls—and boys—is often celebrity crushes; it's an experience of infatuation and wholesome cravings that is entirely fantasy.

"I always tell my students that you'll never be in love the way you are during adolescence because you've never had your heart broken before," said Lisa Medoff, PhD, a lecturer in adolescent development and sexuality at Stanford University.

In terms of cognitive development, young adolescents are beginning to practice abstract thinking—pondering things that are not right in front of them—"and so because of that, they begin to think about the ideal. The ideal world. The ideal relationship." And so, said Dr. Medoff, they "focus on the celebrity obsession and looking at celebrity relationships."

In their first attempts at developing the interpersonal skills that will become critical for successful adult romantic relationships, girls and boys select dates based on superficial features, like social status and stylish clothes, that will increase their popularity,[45] and for this they depend on the hive: those roaming bands of girls and boys at malls and movie theaters—sociologists call them cross-sex peer groups—in which the leader of the girls dates the leader of the boys, and everyone else pairs off, just as Katelyn described.

This is why adolescents value their friends more than their families or teachers or mentors: Their friends are the neural networks that spread the information that connects them with dates, often using their own social capital to broker their friends' romantic relationships. Teenagers who have more opposite-sex friends have greater odds of coupling up,[46] and they are more likely to lose their virginity within a romantic relationship.[47]

These aren't abstractions: Friends are the intermediaries and the messengers of first love. In the end, in fact, it was Katelyn's social group that rescued her from dating oblivion. "We're going to the movies," is what her friends told her, and they were bringing a mystery date. After they met at the film, the young man messaged Katelyn on Facebook, and they started dating. She was getting a late start compared to other girls, but at least she was off and running.

Yet even with success stories like Katelyn's, the delayed start in the essential task of human intimacy for some overweight teens worries child development experts.

During adolescence, the body grows upward and outward, the brain expands in unimaginable ways, and we begin to make choices about our beliefs and identity. These early romantic ventures are a critical part of cultivating a positive sense of self during the teen years. It's not surprising, then, that teens who date are more likely to describe feeling worthy and attractive,[48] and those relationships—as immature and fleeting as they might seem to adults—are profoundly formative. They shape our expectations of love; they refine our sense of sexuality; and they are the arenas in which we practice how to communicate and handle our emotions.[49]

"Puppy love allows you to develop romantic relationship skills," Holly Rose Fee, a sociologist at Bowling Green State University in Ohio, told me. Those skills allow teenagers to learn how "to balance another person's needs with your own needs. It helps with your own verbal communication. It helps you practice social skills that are critical to getting into college and getting a job. They do have a cumulative effect. They set people's life course trajectories off in different directions."

The more practice we have in romance, it turns out, the better our relationships with future Mr. and Mrs. Rights will be. Teenagers, after all, are lovers, husbands, and wives in training.

*   *   *

"ONE of the major tasks of adolescence is to develop your identity," said Dr. Medoff. "And incorporating your sexuality and your sexual identity into the larger sense of who you are is incredibly important." Teens who feel like they're not attractive to other people are missing out on the core formation of their identity and being able to practice intimacy and sexuality, she said. "If they're not given the opportunity to do that—if they feel that they're left out, they can't participate, and nobody's attracted to them, due to their weight—then they really are missing out on a key aspect of development."

How would the rising generations of obese teens fare in managing the stress and complications of adult unions if they had little practice at starter relationships during high school?

But first, social scientists wanted to pinpoint where the breakdown occurred for overweight and obese adolescents. Katelyn's friends had brokered a match for her at the movie theater, but were teenage girls, on the whole, willing to risk their reputations to help their heavier friends find love?

Clearly, Dr. Halpern's work suggested that girls were excluded from romantic relationships in proportion to their weight; heavy girls paid the highest price, and slender girls the least. The exclusion, if that was indeed the critical driver, was happening along a scale.

Some social scientists have homed in not on fickle teenage girls, but instead on teenage boys unwilling to risk their own reputations by dating girls who are considered unattractive. An obese teen with a sunny personality and heaps of confidence may get voted vice president of her class or have lots of friends, but she remains handicapped when it comes to landing a boyfriend, even in this new era of obesity.

"Weight plays a role in what you want your partner to look like," said Ethan, an 18-year-old who recently graduated from high school in Phoenix. "It's not being shallow. It's just what you like as a person. I personally wouldn't date someone who's very overweight."

This, of course, seems a little rich when you consider that, around his sophomore year, Ethan hit his heaviest weight at 234 pounds. At that weight, his dating options were limited to dating bigger girls or not dating at all. That was the main reason he lost 60 pounds by graduation: "I wanted to date, so I lost weight."

Yet, although heavy teenagers date less, they are not sexually inexperienced. There is a long-held myth and a more recent theoretical model, espoused by certain researchers, that bigger girls may have a niche in the teen sex market.

* * *

To figure out whether teens—healthy weight, overweight, or obese—are having sex, an economist and his colleagues proposed a "rational action theory," perhaps the least sexy approach to sex I encountered in my travels.

It looks like this:

**Utility = U (sex [appearance of partner], dating [appearance of date],
own appearance, own reputation [sex])**[50]

As boggling as it looks, the theory distills a common social belief
likely familiar to anyone who remembers the often cruel and unusual ways
of high school hookups: Boys pay a social price (represented as "Utility")
for dating girls who are considered unattractive, including heavy girls, but
not for having sex with them.

It's a theory confirmed by the anecdotes of some young men, too.
"Many guys will have sex with an overweight girl but won't date them,"
said Mason, a high school student in upstate New York, who at his heaviest weighed 215 pounds and stood just 5-foot-5.

The same isn't the case for girls, whose reputations—the theory and
rumor mills suggest—are penalized for having sex with too many boys.[51]
That creates an "opportunity," in economic terms, for heavy girls.

"Since unattractive girls are disadvantaged in the dating market," the
economist John Cawley, PhD, and his colleagues hypothesized, "they may
be especially eager for intimacy, and therefore more willing to accept a
loss of reputation in exchange for sex."

Sure enough, the perception that heavier girls—even though there
are many more of them today—make eager lovers remains common lore
among teenage boys.

"Overweight girls are generally more willing to participate in sexual
activities" than thinner girls, wrote Braden, a 15-year-old sophomore from
Colorado, in an e-mail. "And they generally do it with guys that are older
than them."

But hearsay is hardly science, and stark economic theories struggle to
capture the subtleties of the human experience. The prediction that heavy
girls had a niche in the teen sex market rested on bigger girls deciding to
take advantage of the so-called opportunity afforded to them by boys
eager to bolster their stature with more sexual conquests.

Yet, when Dr. Cawley and his colleagues analyzed thousands of responses from two different nationally representative data sets, they didn't find evidence for the widely held myth that fat girls were easy, after all. One data set showed no relationship between weight and the likelihood of sex, while another data set suggested overweight *and* obese girls—and, to a lesser degree, heavy boys—were much less likely to engage in sexual intercourse than healthy-weight girls. Compared to healthy-weight girls, overweight girls had 60 percent odds of starting sexual intercourse during the survey period, and obese girls had only a 32 percent chance. (Overweight and obese boys were less likely to have had sexual intercourse compared to healthy-weight boys, but not by as much.)

The results confirmed what Mason, Katelyn, and other heavy, and formerly heavy, teens described: Boys and girls weren't willing to simply pair up based on appearance—heavy girls with heavy boys, for example. If that had been the case, then heavy boys and girls would be just as likely to date and have sex as healthy-weight adolescents. "Instead, we find that obese individuals are less likely to date and have sex," Dr. Cawley and his colleagues wrote, "which indicates that such individuals would likely rather remain unattached and chaste than partner with someone of a similar size."

This association of a higher BMI and lower odds of being in a sexual relationship seemed to be the pattern that most researchers were detecting. Dr. Halpern found evidence of the connection in 2001 and in 2005, and other investigators did so as well in studies published in 2010 and 2011.[52]

Indeed, economists Joseph J. Sabia and Daniel I. Rees found that, for girls, with every additional pound of weight, the odds of sexual activity decreased. And still another research team found that overweight girls and boys lost their virginity significantly later than healthy-weight peers, and were more likely to enter early adulthood without any intimate relationship experience.[53] Even as the prevalence of obesity increased dramatically, bigger teens—or those who perceived themselves as overweight—lagged behind in sexual experience.[54]

Paradoxically, that delay offers heavy youth protection[55] from the risks of sex, but it isn't necessarily their choice. (Obese teens aren't all that content to sit on the sidelines: Obese boys and girls have been found to be more dissatisfied with their dating status than other teens.[56])

According to Yen-hsin Alice Cheng, a sociologist and demographer at the Institute of Sociology, Academia Sinica, in Taipei, Taiwan, the reason they put off sex wasn't "due to a delay of gratification, but to the undesirable situation in which they are excluded by friends."

Arrested sexual development, if deferred for too long, could interrupt the essential adolescent task of becoming what human sexuality professor Deborah Tolman, DSW, EdD, calls a "self-motivated sexual actor," capable of making responsible sexual choices.[57] Teen sexual exile could profoundly hinder intimate relationships in the future.[58] The accumulating evidence left little doubt that weight remained a powerful force in the teenage sexual experience.

But there are indications of a more upsetting reality for those heavy teens who do have sexual experience. Sociologists, economists, and public health researchers had paid scant attention to the role of weight in predicting other types of risky sexual behaviors, including anal sex and contraceptive use.

Abigail, a 17-year-old in Ohio who spent much of her childhood severely overweight, recounted how "this one girl decided that she would go and sleep with a guy that already had a girlfriend, so that she would be known as something other than the 'Overweight One.'"

From what Abigail witnessed at her school, the heavier girls are "more open to different things. Like, they'll try to work on their technique, I guess. They'll be more open to other styles. Like, they will often try anal [sex] earlier. And they'll brag about how good they give head."

Were heavy girls who had been shut out of the dating market more willing to engage in other types of risky sexual play? And were overweight and obese girls who did have sex more reckless than other teens?

As often is the case with unfolding changes to sexual patterns, the spread of sexually transmitted diseases provided the first clues. An assistant professor of obstetrics and gynecology at the Medical University of South

Carolina in Charleston, Margaret Villers, MD, was curious why doctors were seeing a remarkably high number of chlamydia cases in overweight teenage girls. Dr. Villers and her colleagues pored over surveys from more than 20,000 teenage girls who were part of the Centers for Disease Control and Prevention's long-running Youth Risk Behavior Survey.[59] She found that when obese girls did have sex, they were

* three times as likely as healthy-weight girls to have had sex by the age of 13;

* 30 percent more likely to have sex with more than three boys by the end of high school; and

* less likely to use condoms.

It wasn't the case that fat girls were easy when viewed as a group, but when researchers looked at the subset of heavy teen girls who did have sex, they found troubling evidence that suggested girls who believed they were less attractive engaged in riskier sexual behaviors than did healthy-weight adolescents.

Therapists say that overweight teenage girls can be reluctant to refuse any advances out of fear that they'll have few chances in the future for romantic and sexual attention. "Is their self-esteem so low that they're more likely to submit to things that are against their values and beliefs?" asks Drew Jackson, a licensed counselor in Jackson, Mississippi, who treats overweight and obese adolescents. "They're so . . . excited to have this connection, they don't want to jeopardize it."

* * *

A group of economists—Susan Averett, PhD, Hope Corman, PhD, and Nancy Reichman, PhD—asked an intriguing question: Are overweight and obese girls who attend schools with lots of heavy peers less likely to engage in risky sex than heavy girls who might stick out more at so-called light schools? After analyzing a nationally representative youth survey, the economists found that overweight and obese girls were 16 percent more likely to have had anal intercourse than healthy-weight teens, and that the effect was stronger when they considered the girl's weight relative to that of other girls in her school. The heaviest girls—those in the top 15 percent for BMI—are about 26 percent more likely than their lighter peers to engage in anal intercourse. The prevalence of risky behaviors became even clearer when the researchers looked at the subset of heavy girls who had lost their virginity: Those girls were 30 percent more likely to have anal sex, and heavy girls at "light schools" were 43 percent more likely.

The economists concluded that the findings were "consistent with a scenario in which an overweight (or less attractive) girl would be willing to incur greater risks in order to attract a partner, and boys would move to less physically attractive matches in order to find willing partners for risky sex. . . . The fact that we found stronger effects for relative weight (compared to other girls in the same school) than an individual's absolute weight provides further support for this scenario."

Extremely obese teens—those with BMIs at or beyond the 99th percentile—are a particular worry, say adolescent development experts.[60] Jennie Noll, PhD, professor of human development and family studies at Penn State, was part of a research team that published the first study, in 2011, to look at the sex lives of extremely obese high school girls.[61] Consistent with other findings, these girls were less likely to have sexual intercourse overall. But when they did have a sexual encounter, 42 percent reported using drugs or alcohol—*four times* the rate of healthy-weight girls.

That troubled Dr. Noll and her colleagues, since girls who were drunk or high often "did more" sexually than they originally intended, and were more likely to have sex without birth control. Combine drinking with abysmal self-esteem, and these girls are exceptionally vulnerable.

"If you have the kind of trauma that a severely obese girl goes through in her childhood, and your self-worth is dismal," Dr. Noll told me, "you don't believe you have any negotiating power. If you're at a party and you're drinking, and this skanky guy wants to have sex without a condom, you don't have the same capacity to get up and leave."

Dr. Noll worries that heavy girls who become sexually active aren't developing a mature sexual identity that will serve them well on their journey to adulthood; they're just stuck in a cycle. "He's gonna call her beautiful," said Dr. Noll, and then she thinks, "'It felt good when that kid came on to me at the party. I slept with him.' But it doesn't do anything to move [her] on in a developmental fashion."

Obese girls who feel isolated from their peers might not have trusted friends to turn to either. "They're missing out on the friendship group," said Stanford's Dr. Medoff, "and other people to bounce ideas off of, and say, 'Hey, is this normal? . . . Is it okay to be treated this way or not?'"

The picture that is emerging of heavy teen girls and sex is one of extremes: girls who enter adulthood romantically and sexually *in*experienced, and those who begin sex very early, by the age of 13, and pursue sexual encounters more recklessly. "I don't think either of those cases is going to have healthy relationships unless they've found Prince Charming," Dr. Noll told me. "Starting early has different ramifications from starting too late or not at all."

* * *

THE ramifications of weight on dating and sex grow murkier when other factors like race and ethnicity come into play. We are still in the early days of parsing how being overweight shapes youthful sexual experiences; researchers often turn to the same well-regarded national surveys, but they ask different questions about sexual activity and take varying approaches. For example, some control for confounding factors that are well understood to influence teen sexual activity—including how many parents are in the home and their education level—while others do not.

To that end, scholars investigating the romantic and sexual lives of overweight and obese teenagers in the United States have found conflicting evidence about whether these experiences vary among Latino, black, white, and Asian students.[62] Dr. Halpern, in her study in 2005, and others since have found that heavy black and Latino teens are just as handicapped when it comes to romance and sexual activity as whites. Others have found no differences between obese and nonobese African American girls.[63, 64]

Still, the lack of clarity, particularly with black and Latino youth, has been surprising, given the strong embrace of bigger bodies by African American and Latino culture.[65, 66] Black adults consistently report being the most satisfied with their bodies, despite the fact that four out of five African American women are overweight, and the prevalence of extreme obesity is highest among black men and women. Not only are they happier with their shape, overweight black women and Latinas often view themselves as normal weight.[67] Why haven't social scientists then found consistent empirical evidence that heavy black teens, who have been more widely studied in the sociology and economics literature than Latinos and other racial and ethnic minorities, are not disadvantaged in love and sex?

* * *

RASHEEDA Russell, a shy and graceful 23-year-old black woman who lives in Berkeley, California, doesn't remember any aspect of her childhood without recalling her surging breasts and thick thighs.

She felt the thrill of her first crush when she was 14. He was an older man—in his late twenties—in her neighborhood whose confidence she admired. Rasheeda kept her crush to herself, and began to believe that she was drawn to older men. Sometime later that year, still a reserved girl who spent her time writing song lyrics and poetry, she and her best friend were walking through a local park when an older boy called out to her.

"He just kind of said that I was beautiful. And I'm like, Whoa!" Rasheeda smiles softly, recalling the moment. "I've never heard that before."

Up until then, Rasheeda was the trusted friend at school. She was a quiet and private person whom people came to for advice, but she had never thought of herself as pretty. When this boy named Jeremiah called her beautiful, she smiled and politely thanked him. He was short, to be sure—2 inches shorter than her 5-foot-5 frame—but he had fetching light brown eyes, brown skin, and buzzed hair, and Rasheeda thought God had somehow answered her prayers.

"Prior to meeting him, I would always pray. I always wanted to be in a relationship, and I would pray like, *Send me someone*." When Jeremiah approached her at the park that day, she said to God, "*This must be who you sent for me*."

Her mother had died from kidney failure when Rasheeda was 4, and Rasheeda's new boyfriend became a welcome distraction from a house full of sisters and brothers, governed by a father who didn't seem to know how to deal with Rasheeda's changing body. She was a big girl, well past puberty, and with breasts that seemed to overtake her. "I don't even remember before they were this big," she says. Young men in her neighborhood assayed her breasts. "They didn't stare at my face, and I'm like, 'I'm up here!'"

During high school, Rasheeda says men in their twenties and thirties would often try to talk to her, commenting that she looked much older than her age. She took it to be a compliment. "That's when I started realizing that I may not be built like your normal ideal [teenager]."

Rasheeda didn't think much about her weight until she entered high school, when she began to notice that playing sports left her out of breath. Many of her friends were heavy, too, but her breathlessness turned her gaze to her body with fresh, critical eyes: "Yeah, that right there needs to go," she would say to herself, looking in the mirror.

She knew her shape was prized by the African American boys and men in her neighborhood, but it dawned on her—as other black women said in interviews—that black women still needed to meet certain expectations. Black men did not fully embrace women of all shapes and sizes; there was an ideal form. Black girls and women could be heavy—Rasheeda could see this all around her neighborhood—but they needed to have "the right curves in the right places." These were the girls that the boys called thick. ("If you have a Beyoncé body or a Jennifer Hudson body, then you're more likely to get a boyfriend," echoed Quanesia, a soft-spoken overweight sophomore in the Mississippi Delta.)

A less desirous shape, though, was called something else: booty do. "It's like your stomach sticks out more than your booty do," Rasheeda told me one afternoon in Berkeley. "You don't want to have that going on too much. Like your stomach is out there, [farther] than your butt. They prefer if your butt is bigger and not too much rolls going on." The ideal form might not be cover girls for the *uber*-white *Seventeen* magazine, but Rasheeda knew she had to keep her curves in line when she began dating. In the back of her mind, she worried that her Jack in the Box habit could sink her nascent romantic adventures.

The girls with the biggest bellies, like the brassy teens in Jackson, Mississippi, were often full of bravado, Rasheeda said. And although she liked them and was friends with them, she didn't totally buy their story: The confident persona shielded them from attack. "They struggle," she said. "You don't want to let no one see how it really is. 'Cause when someone see how vulnerable you are, then they pick at that and . . . it breaks you down even more, so you just don't even want to take it there."

Freshly embarked on her first teenage love affair, Rasheeda could lose herself in Jeremiah's kisses. When she complained to him about her bulging belly, she remembers him saying, "I like you for what you are and how you are." Through his eyes, she was, for the first time, a beautiful girl. It was then, when she saw his desirous gaze, that she began replacing her shapeless hoodie sweatshirts with more form-fitting clothes. Men had made her an unwitting sexual object for years, but now she was choosing to put her body in play. "I wore hoodies and big clothes that I didn't know what was underneath there. And soon as I started peeling away, I started noticing these curves, and it was a whole different ball game after that."

She had let her new boyfriend believe that she wasn't a virgin, since at 14, "if you were a virgin, that was a bad thing." She liked the fact that Jeremiah, who was two grades older, had waited to have sex. Most of her male friends had had sex by then, and she took comfort, pride even, in Jeremiah's virginity: "Oh, I found one that is. That's good. He waited," she told herself.

When her own sexual urges came on, Rasheeda wasn't sure what to make of them. "At first, I didn't know what the hell it was." She enjoyed pleasing her boyfriend during sex—she was, after all, someone who took care of other people—and she said she could be present during their intimate moments, and the voice that criticized her stomach rolls quieted.

Rasheeda and Jeremiah eventually split up. He left high school, and she had bigger dreams: to graduate and become a social worker. "I would have these conversations with him about where did he see himself, and I don't think he really had a clue. I think he was just going to wing it, and that wasn't cool with me." She was reticent about finding another man who would love her, but not enough to stay in the relationship. "I've always stuck with this saying that I can do way better than that. There's something out there for me. This is not what I'm supposed to be going through."

* * *

WHILE science has its hands full coming up with definitive answers on many of these questions, there have been some fascinating findings. Yen-hsin Alice Cheng, the Taiwanese demographer, has asked some of the most intriguing questions about overweight American youth and how their sexual experiences might vary, depending on gender and race and ethnicity. Dr. Cheng, who studies the transition between adolescence and adulthood, decided to focus on one critical measure of sexual development—the age at which heavy teens first had sex—and she sought to uncover the social mechanisms that influenced the timing. When taken as a group, across racial categories, heavy kids were marginalized from the peer networks so vital to early romance and intimacy. But Dr. Cheng wanted to test whether these networks were as crucial to African American teens, who, she suggested, operated with more generous social norms regarding body size. When African American men and teenage boys were asked to look at silhouettes of women's bodies, for example, they had a preference for large buttocks.[68] (Less is known about the body types idealized by Asian Americans and Latinos.)

Dr. Cheng and her colleague Nancy Landale, PhD, professor of sociology and demography at Penn State, began by asking some 8,200 teenagers across the United States how often they felt lonely, how often people were unfriendly to them, and if they felt disliked by people.[69] The students nominated up to five male friends and five female friends, and then these "friend nominations" were tallied up in order to discern the authenticity of the teens' relationships; two students might act chummy with each other, but one might discount the friendship, while the other cherished it. Drs. Cheng and Landale then calculated a number representing each student's closeness with same-sex and opposite-sex friends. The nominations provided a map of friendship networks, linking boys and girls together. Each student represented a point on the map, along with a trove of data about his or her weight, height, racial and ethnic background; whether he or she lived in a single-parent household; family income and education; and romantic and sexual experiences.

What the researchers saw were fascinating variations between boys and girls and blacks, Latinos, and whites. First off, overweight boys were just as likely to become sexually active as normal-weight boys. It was instead *underweight* boys who seemed to pay a price: They lost their virginity later than normal-weight and heavy boys, no matter how many well-meaning friendships they had.

For girls, they found that being overweight did seem to matter: They more often felt alienated among their peers, were less likely to have close friends, and, as other researchers had found, were less likely to have romantic relationships. As a result, heavy girls were 20 percent less likely to have had their first sexual intercourse than normal-weight girls during the time period of the study. (The researchers controlled for other variables known to affect the timing of first sex.)

It wasn't for lack of want, though: Overweight adolescents reported that they were *more motivated* to have sex than normal-weight peers. They believed "having intercourse would make their friends 'respect' them more, would give them 'a great deal of physical pleasure,' would 'relax' them, would make them 'feel more attractive,' and would make them 'feel less lonely.'"

But that wasn't the end of the story. Next, Drs. Cheng and Landale looked at the impact of friendship and found a different pattern: Heavy girls enmeshed in tight friendship networks had the *same rate* of first sex as normal-weight girls. This was the case even though classmates rated overweight girls as less attractive. The relationship between weight and first sex, wrote the authors, is no longer statistically significant when social relationship variables, i.e., circles of friends, are taken into account. When it comes to having those first sexual experiences—those early experiments so critical to healthy sexual development—it proved worth the extra effort to make friends.

These overall findings largely reflect the experience of white girls and boys who represented a majority of the teens surveyed (which reflects the racial and ethnic makeup of the United States).

But the results for black, Latino, and other racial categories were quite different: Being overweight, Dr. Cheng found, in contrast to a number of other studies, played no role in when these teens lost their virginity, nor did being socially alienated or the most popular kid in school. Overweight black and Latino outcasts—boys and girls—had the same odds of first sex as popular, normal-weight kids.

Dr. Cheng's maps of teenage sexual debut didn't make a distinction between those who were merely overweight and those who were obese. While there seemed to be evidence that black and Latino youth were successful pursuers of romance and sex, and they benefited from a culture that made allowances for certain bigger shapes, what of those girls who Rasheeda described—the "booty dos" with big bellies and rolls of fat? The girl at the prom in downtown Jackson who danced joyously in her silver sequined top, and the one holding on to her strapless teal gown on the dance floor? These were not curvy girls with prized shapes; they were severely, extremely—physicians would say morbidly—obese.

Dr. Cheng's study wasn't the definitive answer on how obesity and race influence the teenage sexual experience, but it did add another intriguing way to understand the role of weight in adolescent lives, and the variations in sexual development.

* * *

FOR heavy white teenagers, especially girls, the picture has slowly come into focus: These girls are less likely to have romantic and sexual relationships during their teenage years. As the number of heavy white girls continues to grow, it seems plausible that the spread of obesity is contributing to the decrease in adolescent sexual activity detected by national surveys. And while heavy African American girls don't seem to be disadvantaged in terms of dating and sex, the prevalence of *extreme* obesity is much higher among black teens than other racial and ethnic groups, and continues to rise sharply. It's unclear if severely heavy African American girls are finding as much success in dating.

* * *

AND yet, on that night in the ballroom at the Old Capitol Inn in downtown Jackson, the room was practically vibrating with hormones. On the wooden dance floor, surrounded by clusters of black balloons stirred by the rising heat, hundreds of teenagers moved their bodies in buoyant unison to the thumping beats of the rap trio Travis Porter, rapping about "top-notch bitches."

In interlocking circles that tilted and pitched across the floor, throngs of young women in their bejeweled strapless bodices lunged from side to side, raising their arms above their heads and joyously shouting the lyrics to the strip club anthem with absolute conviction. The rappers made their preference for "real thick" women—big, busty, and curvy—known.

The DJ stood up on a stage behind a bank of amplifiers and computers. He wore a white dress shirt and loose tie over his willowy frame; oversize white headphones were propped awkwardly over his ears. He was playful and commanding with the crowd. "Put your hands up!" he ordered, and waves of arms reached toward the ceiling. The determined teenagers eyed one another brightly, their smiles growing wider, and they celebrated this golden moment in a chorus of delight.

The end of high school was near.

* * *

OVERWEIGHT and obese teenagers were once a rarity in the United States; now they are common in every state. And although there are variations among different racial and ethnic groups, the overall trend suggests that weight gain is impacting when American children physically develop, when they first have sex, and the opportunities they have to form their first romantic and sexual relationships. Adolescent therapists contend that heavy teenagers who face repeated rejection (beyond the normal teenage infatuations and heartbreak), or who turn sharply inward during crucial windows of psychological development, can find it difficult to trust others with their loves and wants. Even girls and boys whose personalities have grown as big as their bodies can miss out on the most essential human experience: intimacy.

"The key to intimacy is vulnerability," said Drew Jackson, the therapist in Mississippi who works with teens. Teenagers who determine being vulnerable is too risky and too hurtful can find themselves in "surface relationships."

It's a precarious place; perched at the edge of adolescence, they are leaving childhood behind and reaching into a future in which the nectar at the center of human connectedness is elusive. With adolescence coming to a close, the progress for many is incomplete. The development of the Self is cumulative; what comes before sets the stage for what happens next. Insults to the Self, like those to delicate organs, are absorbed and assimilated, and affect the patterns of unfolding lives.

These are not isolated cases of damaged youth. There are now millions of teenagers who, come spring, shop for prom dresses and hunt for dates, and who are barreling toward adulthood with little experience in the art of human intimacy.

CHAPTER TWO

Dating: Failure to Launch

There is nothing quite like the anxiety of asking a potential love interest out on a date. There is the first gesture—that first outward sign that a private thought has been put publicly, perhaps impulsively, into motion. An eyebrow rises. A cheek blushes. The mouth inhales slightly and the lungs swell just before the proposal—even the most purposefully blasé or inexpertly bungled—can be made.

If we spend our adolescence and early adult years erecting the scaffolding of our identity, draping it with clothes and sneakers and music and practiced affectations that we have come to believe signal coolness, then why are we undone—all those cautiously edited displays stripped away— by one simple question: *Would you like to have dinner with me?*

It's even awkward to watch wild animals begin their courtship. To see them preen and perform in such an obvious way is an embarrassing reminder that we are not so very different. When a peahen takes a pass on an eager peacock, instead choosing a partner with larger, more iridescent tail feathers, the rejection stings our hearts, too. But what if that peacock didn't just have larger feathers, but a larger girth as well? If his strut turned into a waddle, how would he fare in seducing a mate?

There is perhaps no other species that has come close to matching the sudden and severe population-wide weight gain as humans in the United States. Wild animals can—and do—fatten up when there is an abundant supply of food. Given a plate of nachos and a super-size Coca-Cola, even the fiercest and fittest beasts would likely binge. In their essay on the similarities between animal and human health, Barbara Natterson-Horowitz, MD, a cardiology professor at UCLA, and author Kathryn Bowers observe, "Tamarin monkeys have been seen to eat so many berries in one sitting that their intestines are overwhelmed and they soon excrete the same whole fruits they recently gobbled down."[1]

And yet, animals can't stay stuffed for long. "Nature imposes its own 'weight-maintenance plan' on wild animals," Dr. Natterson-Horowitz and Bowers write. "Cyclical periods of food scarcity are typical. Threats from predators limit access to food. Weight goes up, but it also comes down."

It's not just predators who carry out these life-or-death directives; it is picky females—evolutionary enforcers working over evolutionary time—who punish aspiring mates that are too heavy. "Females recoil from signs of disease, parasites, or infirmity," writes Diane Ackerman in her singularly crafted *A Natural History of Love.*

> *An exhausting courtship display doesn't just impress a female with a male's seriousness, it tells her if the male is hardy, if his cardiovascular system is strong, if he has the stamina to be her mate. She could also learn this through athletics, spirited play, or sending him out on quests. Or she could make him serenade her. Female gray tree frogs are attracted to operatic males that will sing sprightly numbers long into the Caribbean night. The males use vast amounts of oxygen in the process and tire themselves; but that suits the female fine. She wants a robust, vigorous crooner who will sire hearty offspring.*[2]

Since wild animals do not, for the most part, stay overweight for long, scientists can't know how they would fare in the dating market. Evolutionary biologists would suggest an answer: not well. For the primates known as humans, modern social scientists have been trying to figure out whom we *aspire* to date and whom we *actually* date now that our families, tribes, and kingdoms no longer (for the most part) make those decisions for us.[3]

The leading ideas that have emerged, including something called the matching hypothesis, have become central tenets of social psychology, and those principles are not unlike the rules that govern courtship for gray tree frogs. Evolutionary theorists would say the rules were put into motion eons ago by persistent and cunning forces that direct our genes like puppets. But what happens when the majority of those in the dating market—courter and courted alike—suddenly, in a blink in evolutionary time, become severely overweight? When the dating pool becomes filled with suitors who might tire at physical tests and "spirited play," will the females recoil?

* * *

"How 'bout we go out to dinner?" As the question hung in uncertain, hopeful suspense, Rob Gaughan wasn't sure what he would do if Tamara said "Yes." At the time, Rob was in his early thirties, and he had never been on a proper date. Rob towered over the world around him: He was 6-foot-8 and weighed more than 350 pounds. It had been almost a decade since he'd had sex, with a vivacious blonde-haired woman from his improvisational comedy troupe in Chicago, and now he was living in Los Angeles, a few years into sobriety and successfully losing the weight that he once feared would lead him into the same crippling existence it had led his mother.

Rob had made a promise to himself: Once he lost 98 pounds, he would start to date. (He worried about jinxing his weight loss goal if he needed to reach 100.) He had seen Tamara (not her real name) at Alcoholics Anonymous meetings in Los Angeles every Friday night for months, and he decided he would ask her out. But how should he approach her? What should he say? He had no idea how to woo her; he had never had a girlfriend.

Rob told his sponsor in Overeaters Anonymous, Kenny Lombino, that he thought Tamara might be interested in him.

"Ask her out," Kenny told him. "That's how it starts."

"But what do I talk about?" Rob asked Kenny. Where should he take her if she agreed to dinner? And, perhaps more urgently, when should he try to kiss her?

Rob was eager to have sex. As a portly single man who had spent his life so far without a girlfriend, Rob knew how to tip at strip clubs. But he was unpracticed in courtship.

Rob faced a challenge that befalls many men and women who begin their romantic lives as obese: He never had the "starter" relationships that teenagers and young adults use as training grounds for adult romantic relationships. He had missed out on those delirious flings that help us learn how to move in tandem with another person, in which we begin to sketch the outlines of the kind of relationship we want to be in, where we break another person's heart and have our own broken and survive. It seems decidedly unromantic, but the tester relationships and love affairs of our teens and twenties are skill-building exercises that ready us for committed, long-term unions. There is utilitarian value in a broken heart.

Rob's best friend, Gabe Cuevas—the men had been in Boy Scouts together growing up in Chicago—suggested he wear slacks and a shirt with a collar, and when he got up the courage, he should take his date to Luna Park, a restaurant in West Hollywood, and then he should make sure that over dinner, they only talked about *her*.

But first, Rob had to ask Tamara out. Like a boxer headed into the ring, he tried to psych himself up. "I've been stabbed before," he told himself. "I can do this."

At the end of the AA meeting, as they were turning off the lights, he looked at her, full of anxiety and lust, and said, "How 'bout we go out to dinner?" And she said *Yes*. There would be a lot of details to work out, including which night of the week they would go out and at what time, and if he should bring flowers and exactly which slacks he should wear, and, of course, the problem of all his hanging skin.

Rob Gaughan was a garrulous, sarcastic, and thoughtful obese man who had jumped—reluctantly, awkwardly, and by necessity—into the dating ring. Would he fare better than an overweight gray tree frog?

* * *

DURING the past 20 years, the average weight of those in the dating pool has changed dramatically. A time-lapse series of maps from the Centers for Disease Control and Prevention shows how abruptly our bodies have transformed:[4] A map of obesity rates in 1985 shows only eight states, shaded dark blue, where 10 to 14 percent of adults are obese; as the maps roll over from year to year, more states turn blue, including Illinois, where Rob Gaughan was already a hefty high schooler. Then in 1997, the CDC adds a new color—beige—to show an emerging phenomenon: Obesity rates in Mississippi, Kentucky, and Indiana had hit 20 percent. As the clock starts ticking again and the years flip over, more states change from dark blue to beige until 2001, when Mississippi needs a new color—red—to signify that 25 percent of adults living there are obese. As the map speeds through 2002, 2003, 2004, more states turn red, first across the South and the Midwest, and then in 2006, Mississippi and West Virginia need yet another designation—dotted, dark red—showing that 30 percent of the adults who live there are obese. (At about that time, Rob Gaughan had gotten up the nerve to ask Tamara out on a date in Los Angeles.) By 2007, the Pacific Northwest turns red, and in the next few years, so do Nevada, Idaho, Wyoming, and most of the Eastern Seaboard. The South and Midwest— from Texas to Alabama, Missouri to West Virginia—close out 2010 with one in three adults severely overweight. By 2012, two out of three American adults would be overweight or obese.[5]

It's as if over just 2 decades, a majority of adults in the United States became a foot or more taller. How would those evolutionary enforcers— those picky females shopping around for a mate or those eager males strutting their tail feathers—respond to such a sudden alteration in body statistics? Would this new class of towering women and men, like Rob Gaughan, be prized catches or castoffs?

The stakes are high. Whether we sense it or not, the sifting and sorting and pairing off that happen during courtship set our lives in motion. The process answers, for a time at least, one of the most awesome and terrifying questions: Whom should I love? Intimate relationships are an integral part of human existence, and their effect is total: Whether we feel loved and cared for, whether we feel fulfilled and hopeful, they become our story, providing order and meaning. These close relationships, gay or straight, are a natural human virtue. They are the most primitive beginnings of moving man out of nature into society.

The French anthropologist Claude Levi-Strauss observed that the coupling of human beings expresses a fundamental human need.[6] Social connection is vital not only to the survival of the species,[7] but to human well-being, because it bolsters our psychological development and gives us a sense of belonging.[8] The psychologists who study the value of close relationships among adults can sound like poets:

Perhaps the most potent form of approval occurs when one is loved.[9]

And yet, those who emerge into their sexual selves as obese are less likely to find love in adulthood. The trend is especially stark, the research shows us, for women.[10]

* * *

IN the collection of essays *The Body Beautiful: Evolutionary and Sociocultural Perspectives*, the psychologists Viren Swami, PhD, and Adrian Furnham, DPhil, DSc, introduce us to the "Science of Bodily Beauty." They explore the question "What is beauty?" beginning with Pythagoras and the ancient Greeks, who found an answer in elegant proportions—"golden ratios" that were universal and objective, an unwavering Platonic ideal shared by all. That Pythagorean explanation of beauty stayed in place, they write, until the late 18th century, when philosophers such as David Hume and Edmund Burke raised the prospect that beauty could be based on one's own individual emotions and preferences. "Beauty is no quality in things themselves; it exists merely in the mind which contemplates them; and each mind perceives a different beauty," wrote Hume in 1757. It was then, Drs. Swami and Furnham observe, that "beauty had firmly been placed in the proverbial eye of the beholder."

That made beauty preferences—*Why* are you attracted to *this* person?—scientifically unquantifiable, and explains why the psychological sciences have been relative latecomers to the beauty debates.

As late as the 1960s, the scholarly pursuit of passionate love and sexual desire was considered frivolous and senseless. "It wasn't a respectable topic of study," recalled the famed psychologist Elaine Walster, PhD, in an interview with the Human Behavior and Evolution Society. "It wasn't amenable to scientific investigation; there wasn't any hope of finding out very much about love in my lifetime. And it wasn't 'hot'—the hot topic in the 1960s was mathematical modeling."[11]

Walster was undeterred.

Around that time, she and a group of researchers advertised a "Computer Dance" to incoming freshmen at the University of Minnesota that would give science a foothold in divining physical attraction. The Computer Dance, the results of which were published in 1966, would become, declared Drs. Swami and Furnham, "the catalyst for interest in physical attractiveness within the psychological sciences." Nearly a half century later, Dr. Walster's "serendipitous finding" could predict the fate of fat people trying to date on the Internet.

"Here's your chance to meet someone who has the same expressed interests as yourself," read the ad in the new student handbook at the University of Minnesota. Freshmen "Gophers" who purchased tickets were told that an IBM computer—a futuristic novelty at the time—would match them on a blind date based on their personality and interests. What the students didn't know was that as they moved through the ticket line, Walster's collaborators were rating the students' physical attractiveness, and they would be sorted into categories that might seem insensitive by today's standards: *Ugly, Average,* and *Attractive.* The Computer Dance was a big ruse.

Two days later, hundreds of freshmen were paired up, not based on their similarities, as they had been told, but randomly, with one exception: Men weren't matched with taller women.

The Computer Dance was staged at a large nearby armory. Around 8 o'clock in the evening, newly paired freshmen began arriving, completely unaware that they were part of a grand experiment that would swing the beauty pendulum away from the eye of the beholder and once more toward Pythagoras (and evolutionary psychology). The students and their dates danced and talked in the armory for more than 2 hours until an intermission was called and the students, some rounded up from restrooms and fire escapes, were asked to rate their dates. Dr. Walster and her colleagues imagined that personality, intelligence, or similar interests would best predict whether dates liked each other. Instead, they found the best predictor of whether two dates liked each other, and were still dating 6 months later, was their physical attractiveness.

Dr. Walster's work launched a frenzy of studies over the ensuing decades that sought to chronicle the rewards and penalties of physical attractiveness in nearly every aspect of our lives: its surreptitious and subtle— or blatant and brutal—imprint on hiring and salaries, first impressions and character judgments, and swooning hearts. "A wealth of evidence suggests that, despite the exhortations of received wisdom and age-old maxims," wrote Drs. Furnham and Swami, "physical beauty has both an immediate and predictable effect on social interactions."

That this was a revelation shows how far the pendulum has swung.

The attributes that people assign to physical attractiveness are strikingly consistent, even across cultures and across generations. When it comes to weight, the belief that the physically fit warrant higher status was firmly lodged in the American psyche. In a 1968 experiment, slim or normal-weight men and women were seen as more physically attractive than people who were very overweight or extremely thin.[12] Heavy people were less common then, but they were regarded as out-of-control social miscreants. In 1968, the sociologist Werner J. Cahnman, then a professor at Rutgers University, observed rather bleakly in his essay "The Stigma of Obesity":

Clearly, in our kind of society, with its stress on affluence and upward mobility, being overweight is considered to be detrimental to health, a blemish to appearance, and a social disgrace. What is much less obvious is that it is held to be morally reprehensible.[13]

* * *

STEPHANIE Nelson had no idea what was in store for her. As the majority of Americans tipped the scales into overweight at the close of the 1980s, Stephanie was tucked away in Seattle, Washington, surrounded by a group of friends who seemed not to care that she was far bigger than everyone else. She was smart, friendly, and capable, and that seemed like enough. From grade school on, Stephanie had steadily become obese. One boy in seventh grade had teased her about her weight, but the insult was so alien that she remembers having to ask someone else what exactly he meant. "I never once had the idea that anything about my body was bad or shameful," Stephanie told me. "But I also never once got the idea that there was anything about [it] that was good or attractive." She had a high school "boyfriend," but they didn't even hold hands.

Across the country, in Georgia, a psychologist was at work on an experiment that would paint a grim picture of what Stephanie would face when she left the confines of home and jumped into an entirely different dating pool in college.

* * *

MARY Harris, PhD, was a visiting professor in the psychology department at the University of Georgia when she posed an intriguing question: Did Americans believe that people who are obese experience a different kind of love?[14]

She recruited 222 college students to complete an anonymous questionnaire about their own dating histories and their feelings about love.[15]

The students had been told the experiment sought to understand whether it was possible to gauge a person's experience of love simply by looking at him or her. (At around that time, in 1990, the percentage of obese adult Georgians surpassed 10 percent of the state's population.) Each student viewed one of a dozen photographs that had been taken of six actors (three men and three women) posing as "Chris P." Each actor posed for two different pictures: one at his or her normal weight, and another dressed in extra layers of clothes to look obese. (Dr. Harris had run an earlier pilot study to ensure that the bulked-up Chris P. looked authentically heavy.) The students were asked to imagine what kind of love experiences Chris had had. What was remarkable about this experiment was that the "normal" and "fat" pictures of Chris P. were the *same person,* and yet Dr. Harris found marked differences in the love lives that students conjured up.

* 84 percent believed that a normal-weight Chris would be dating, whereas 48 percent believed a fat Chris would not be dating.

* A normal-weight Chris was seen as having been in love significantly more often than a fat Chris.

* Chris was seen as feeling significantly lower self-esteem when fat than when normal weight.

But Dr. Harris wasn't just interested in whether fat Chris was viewed as a sad sack, unlucky in love. She wanted to know if the college students believed that fat Chris would *experience* love in a different way, and what kind of romantic partner he or she deserved.

It might seem implausible that we could all agree on a singular definition of love: Are there certain criteria that must be met before someone can move definitively beyond liking into love? Or is it good enough if a person simply believes she's caught the bug?

Researchers have, in fact, designed a classification system for love that includes six different types of romance. Based on the "love styles" developed by John Lee in his famous 1973 book *Colours of Love,* two experimental psychologists, Susan Hendrick, PhD, and Clyde Hendrick, PhD, devised a Love Attitudes Scale to scientifically measure which type of love you're in—or in the case of the Chris P. experiment, which type of love you think an obese person might experience. Dr. Harris describes the six styles as follows:

> *The first love style,* **Eros,** *represents sensual, passionate, romantic love, characterized by physical intensity, honesty, openness, and high self-esteem. The love style entitled* **Ludus** *is one in which love is viewed as a game; no deep emotional commitments are made, and multiple partners are common.* **Storge,** *the third love style, develops from friendship and shared activities, and emphasizes companionship rather than intense emotions. Persons who score high on* **Pragma** *choose a lover based on careful consideration of what qualities might be suitable and take a rational, logical approach to selection of a partner. The love style* **Mania** *involves a possessive, dependent type of love characterized by mood swings, jealousy, and physical symptoms. Finally the last love style,* **Agape,** *reflects an altruistic, unconditional kind of love which focuses on the other's happiness and needs rather than on one's own.*

Dr. Harris wanted to know if heavy people were seen as restricted to certain styles of love. Discouraged by the stigma of being big, considered to be "a social disgrace," as the sociologist Cahnman had observed decades earlier, did they, in a sense, have to be more "rational" in their choices?

After analyzing the responses, Dr. Harris found that when Chris P. was dressed to look obese, both the female and male photographs were judged to be less Erotic and less Ludic, and more Manic. That heavy people were viewed as less arousing fell in line with widely held stereotypes: Dr. Harris surmised that "a fatter person would be expected to be less erotic, as his or her physique might be expected to preclude or at least reduce passion. A fat person might also be expected to score lower on Ludus, since the resources to attract numerous others and to lure them into casual relationships would be lacking." And what about the high scores for

Manic love? Why would obese people be seen as loving to the point of obsession, pinging incessantly between jealousy, insecurity, and bliss? A growing body of social research on close relationships suggested obese people were seen as having fewer attributes to exchange when they went looking for love.[16] Dr. Harris suspected that a bigger person, aware that she had few alternative romantic options, "might become more possessive and dependent in any relationship." Dr. Harris wasn't out to celebrate these findings; she merely set out to document them.

What was perhaps most disheartening about the results of the Chris P. study was that the college students saw no reason to live by the Golden Rule: They did not think they needed to treat others as they treated themselves, even those who were themselves overweight. While those filling out the survey wanted a love partner who was attractive, smart, and had a good sense of humor, they didn't think fat Chris needed the same. Chris P., bulked up in so many layers of clothing, deserved a heavier and uglier paramour.

* * *

STEPHANIE Nelson was completely unaware that this would be her fate when she left Seattle in the late summer of 1993 for the long car ride with her father across Canada down into Williamstown, Massachusetts, a quaint and wooded town in the Berkshires. The first person in her family to attend college, she anticipated starting a new life as a freshman at Williams College.

When she walked into her dorm room—a single room converted to a double overlooking a bucolic residential quad—Stephanie's roommate, the daughter of two doctors from New Jersey, had already plastered the walls with fine art posters, and in the dresser the two women would share, she had laid claim to the middle two drawers. "We got along for approximately a day and a half," Stephanie told me wryly when we met at a café along the main street in Williamstown.

The roommates settled into a routine by keeping different hours, but

Stephanie could see right away that she was different. "It was very clear to me that everyone here was prettier and had more money," she recalled. Her roommate shared clothes with other girls—J. Crew was the must-have label—and the girls would turn to Stephanie, she remembers, and say, "Oh, it's too bad that you can't do that."

Stephanie was undaunted. If she couldn't swap clothes with the girls, she could watch ice hockey in the common room of her coed dorm with the guys. Although there had been few sparks with her high school boyfriend, she was confident she knew how to flirt. Back in Seattle, Stephanie says, "guys would be friendly towards me, and I would think, 'Oh, they want to be friends with me or maybe want to date me.'"

So it didn't seem improbable to Stephanie that she could find a date for her very first "Sadie Hawkins" dance, and she had her eyes firmly set on a boy who often came to her room for as-of-yet wholesome visits. A month into her first semester at Williams, not long before the dance, Stephanie and her crush were in the library together. Her face lights up as she recalls the memory: "I think we were actually reading poetry to each other, something ridiculous like that," and he asked,

Do you know if people are going to the dance?

"And I was like, 'Yes.'"

Isn't everybody going to kind of go as a big group?

"And I was like, 'Yes.'"

So the fact that girls are supposed to ask the guys, maybe if that didn't happen, that wouldn't be that big of a deal?

Stephanie couldn't figure out what he was trying to say, until the words came spilling over his lips.

So do you think that the girl who lives next door to you would want to go with me?

She answered as best she could, and then wandered off and cried. It seemed to happen over and over during her 4 years at Williams. Men would befriend her or she would befriend them; her heart would start to flutter; and then, as if under some cruel hex, they would ask for one of her friends' phone numbers. "Most of the time I got the sense they were sort of clueless," Stephanie said. "They really didn't think of me as a woman, a girl, or as a dating partner. It was like they were just asking the RA if one of her students might be interested in dating. They just didn't see me as that, and I don't think they ever considered my feelings."

Stephanie had not, up until this point, been cowed by the limitations of her beauty—that she was somehow supposed to know that she was physically unattractive and ratchet down her expectations.[17] Stephanie had let herself believe she was good enough to pursue attractive men. "I've just been overweight my whole life," she said, "so it never occurred to me."

Instead, it seemed, she should have been walking around the leafy Williams campus with "I'm Fat Chris P." emblazoned on her sweatshirt.

*　*　*

How do people who are overweight or obese seem to learn the stupefying customs that direct human courtship? How do they come to see the rules of the game? By running headfirst into them. If the results from the Chris P. experiment held up, Stephanie's college classmates—including her unrequited poet—saw her as less sensual, passionate, and warm and deserving a heavy, unattractive boyfriend. Stephanie just didn't know it yet. The same would be true for Rob Gaughan years later as he chased women around Los Angeles. When Rob was at his heaviest, some 450 pounds, he told his best friend Gabe that he wouldn't date "fatties." Gabe would often shake his head in disbelief.

If the rejection was so painful, though, why did people like Stephanie and Rob, who were overweight or obese and thus considered unattractive, keep pursuing better-looking crushes? In experiments in the decades after the Computer Dance, including a restaging of the dance itself,[18] most people chose the most attractive dates even if they themselves were seen as undesirable. The real-life findings were at odds with a central tenet of social psychology dubbed the matching hypothesis, which held that romance seekers are realists when it comes to their dating chances. According to the hypothesis, men and women, fearful of rejection and their swooning hearts tempered by the odds, would seek out partners in the dating market who are as socially desirous as they are, but not more and probably not less.

The hypothesis was an extension of social exchange theory and equity theory, which proposed that romantic love was still largely a strategic game in which utility and economics set the rules. "A proposal of marriage in our society," wrote the sociologist Erving Goffman, PhD, in 1952, "tends to be a way in which a man sums up his social attributes and suggests to a woman that hers are not so much better as to preclude a merger or a partnership in these matters."[19] This is not the stuff of arias and sonnets; this is brass tacks.

So how could it be that researchers continued to find a similar strong bias against the obese like the one Dr. Harris had found with her photographs of "Chris P.," and yet in experiment after experiment, those seen as less physically attractive remained daring daters, heading hari-kari-like into the maelstrom? What had truly hindered discoveries about courtship behavior in the still nascent field of love research, some suggested, was that it was nearly impossible to replicate a realistic dating ecosystem. A group of inventive researchers from the University of California, Berkeley, said they needed "a dynamic dating situation in which individuals choose partners from a large pool of candidates."[20]

To truly divine courtship, they needed the Internet.

* * *

THE Internet suddenly allowed researchers to see tens of thousands, even millions, of social interactions that had previously been invisible to the human eye. They could cull through the data trails left by legions of searching hearts and watch as daters scrolled through potential matches, weighed options, passed over candidates, or made a pick. At the same time, scientists could see how the candidates judged those who judged them. The Internet had become an anthropological tool that could be used to observe humans as they sniffed around and sought out a mate. Perhaps it could be used to explain why a polite freshman at Williams would read poetry in the library with Stephanie Nelson and then proceed unthinkingly to break her heart.

Social psychologists know how the sniffing begins: Most daters—"ugly," "average," or "attractive"—seek out the best-looking candidates. And they have evidence of where daters end up: Couples in established romantic relationships tend to be similarly attractive. While other desirable attributes could be traded in the mating market—a younger woman might exchange her youth for an older man's wealth—researchers have consistently found that good-looking men are more likely to pair with good-looking women, and the plain or uncomely end up with each other.[21]

But what happens in between the first step and the last? That's what puzzled social psychologists: When did the sorting occur? If the matching hypothesis is truly about how individuals *select* a romantic partner, the UC Berkeley researchers needed to directly investigate the selection process. It is one thing to have a *preference* for a good-looking date, but *initiating* a relationship is a much riskier venture.

The researchers picked a random sample of profiles from a popular online dating site and called them "the initiators." Then, using the Web site's activity logs from 2009,[22] they pulled out the profiles and photos of the people "the initiators" contacted and separated them into love interests who responded and those who didn't. Next, a group of independent judges rated each photo for physical attractiveness, which allowed the researchers to compute a mean attractiveness score for the initiators, the nonreciprocating contacts, and the reciprocating contacts. It was the modern-day version of *Ugly, Average,* or *Attractive* from the 1960s' Computer Dance.

As in previous experiments, "initiators" contacted people who were more physically attractive, but when the researchers looked at who *returned* an initiator's advances, they saw evidence of matching.[23] When they divided the total number of contacts an initiator made by the replies received, they determined that "individuals who contacted others whose physical attractiveness was similar to their own were more likely to receive replies." In other words, a pragmatic realist found more success than an ambitious dreamer and faced far less rejection. It was not unlike sociologist Erving Goffman's rather unromantic assessment of marriage in 1952: You're not much better than me, so how about we get together?

In another study, some 3,000 heterosexual Internet daters were asked to rate their own self-esteem and describe the dates they met online whom they intended to meet in person. The daters were awarded a popularity score based on how often other users sought them out. What emerged from the data was the first evidence that matching occurred in the "real world." Women who had the lowest self-worth were much more likely to contact the least popular men, and unpopular men tended to reach out to women with low self-worth. This might sound rather obvious, but as in other fields of study that seek to understand everyday phenomena, social psychologists had made a basic scientific discovery. The results showed, the researchers wrote, "direct evidence that individuals in the earliest stages of dating will actually select relatively undesirable partners if they, too, have low social desirability." The researchers could have added: "The daters are self-aware enough to know where they stand."

Their findings challenged the notion that physically unattractive people end up with each other because that's who is left after all the highly desirable people pair off.[24] The findings suggested that those who are keener judges of their station and looks will have better odds of finding romance.

In that sense, Stephanie Nelson's mistake, according to the cruel dictates of modern American dating, may simply have been that she didn't see herself as her poet friend saw her. "It felt like a slow, horrible learning process," Stephanie said of coming to understand romantic rejection. "It was kind of like a bunch of little cuts." She delved into academics and decided, for now, that love was not for her.

* * *

CARLOS Romero spent much of his time on the planet of Azeroth. Inside the World of Warcraft, an online role-playing game with millions of subscribers, Carlos was known as a gifted warrior who garnered respect from the planet's other inhabitants. On Azeroth, he knew how to flirt with the female avatars and the women who played them.

The off-line world—the world where he was 22 and living in a tiny coastal town in North Carolina under layers of sweating flesh—was decidedly harsher than Azeroth and his romantic prospects grimmer. Carlos's father was a marine, and his mother worked at the local hospital. Growing up, he remembers that he was constantly looking in the refrigerator for leftovers. By eighth grade, he was obese: His knees hurt him during gym class, and he was embarrassed by how much he sweated even with the slightest physical exertion. He dated a muscular gymnast who broke up with him in front of everyone at the lunch table and remembers going back to class, folding his arms over his head, and crying into his book. "I was so upset," Carlos recalled.

The attacks came on two fronts: racial slurs aimed at his darker Cuban skin and taunts about his sagging breasts. "I remember to this day someone joking around about how I could fit into D-cups," Carlos said. In high school, the cliques started to coalesce, and Carlos began playing Dungeons and Dragons, an early fantasy role-playing game, and befriended other kids who seemed somehow not to fit in—the "nerdy outcasts," he called them. He remembers other heavy kids in school. But being morbidly obese made him feel isolated and alone, so much so that even when his few friends were unkind, he stuck with them. As he described it, "You're going to take more crap from someone because you need to have a friend in your life." In high school, Carlos began devising a set of rules.

He used those rules—rules also devised by evolutionary theorists—to navigate his new life as an obese young adult. If he was going to successfully nab a date, he needed to be pragmatic. Since one in three Americans was, like him, obese, Carlos had decided, "When it comes to 100 women that I could potentially look at and say, 'I want to date this girl,' I can choose from only 30 of them. Those are the girls, the one in three, that are bigger themselves." Carlos honed his sense of what he should be looking for. He's embarrassed that the calculation was so cold. It sounds mean to him now: "I tended to go after girls that were either less attractive, because

I thought I had a shot at it, or they somehow stood on the fringe." If he was isolated, he was going to look for someone who was on the outskirts with him. With girls who were normal weight, Carlos assumed he never had a shot. "I looked at them and had desire, but I just learned to not even consider them."

The strategy seemed to work. He needed to stay in the World of Warcraft, on Azeroth, until he could meet a woman willing to date him off-line.

* * *

KAYLEIGH had been to Azeroth—or rather she had sat around and watched her obese boyfriend as he ventured about the distant planet. She would bring Mountain Dew and potato chips to his house and sit and wait.

Kayleigh was only 4-foot-11, and when she reached 160 pounds, she looked even heavier. The high school she had attended in a small town in Illinois was not a particularly brutal place; she didn't feel ridiculed or rejected because of her weight, and besides, a good number of other students were heavy. But Kayleigh's younger sisters were thinner, taller, and had more fun, and it seemed to Kayleigh that boys flocked to them. "I wanted to be accepted, the way I saw other girls being accepted," she said.

How, then, to get the boys' attention? She would have to be an aggressive flirter. She sought out conversations with men, touching their shoulders when talking. "I would pursue that person, whether or not I was really sure I really liked them."

The strategy worked: She nabbed a boyfriend. He was, however, drastically overweight and a devout video gamer and online poker player, and that's how she found herself ferrying bags of potato chips and soda over to his house. "There was no activity outside of watching TV or playing video games," she says. "That was the majority of the relationship."

He continued to mistreat her, and she put up with it. "I always felt like I was never pretty enough or thin enough to find somebody else to move on and really be happy with another man." The couple eventually split up, and Kayleigh, who was attending a community college, fell into an endless series of sexual hookups. It wasn't a cheery acceptance of casual sex that motivated her sexual flings; her former boyfriend's antics had left her feeling worthless, and she sought out sexual relationships, not romantic ones, to numb her sense of inadequacy.

*   *   *

"HOOKING up" had become the norm for women and men in Kayleigh's generation. In their article, "Sexual Hookup Culture: A Review," Justin Garcia, PhD, a researcher at the Kinsey Institute at Indiana University in Bloomington, along with researchers from Binghamton University, chronicled how casual sex—brief and uncommitted sexual encounters—has gone from occasional to routine among young adults. A study published in 2010 found that 81 percent of undergraduate college students who filled out a survey said they had engaged in some form of hooking up, from oral sex to intercourse.

So were obese young adults hooking up, too? There were two competing theories about how heavy young adults would fare in the maul of hookup culture. The first predicted that heavier young adults would be more likely to "hook up" since they had less opportunity to do so within romantic relationships.[25] Sociologists and psychologists were concerned that overweight and obese teenagers—more likely to be novice daters—would be overwhelmed by adulthood. They worried that young, heavy white women, in particular, were less experienced in sexual negotiations, while others had displayed risky sexual behaviors. The second theory suggested that bias in attitudes of attractiveness and desirability would curb sexual activity compared to those with normal BMIs.[26] Researchers who study "mate preference" have seen little evidence that the stereotype of fat women—and to a lesser degree, fat men—as undesirable weakened as obesity became more common. Even as bigger bodies flooded the dating market, heavy women have remained just about everyone's last choice. A study of 22,000 users of an online dating service found that men preferred women with BMIs lower than their own, and understandably then, women with higher BMIs were less likely to receive "first-contact" e-mails. The more the women weighed, the fewer overtures they received.[27]

When Holly Rose Fee, a sociologist at Bowling Green State University, analyzed responses from nearly 14,000 young adults, she was surprised to find that *both* theories proved correct. In her 2013 findings, she reported overweight and "mildly" obese young adults (those with a BMI of 30 to 34.9) were 19 percent and 14 percent *more likely*, respectively, to report hooking up five or more times compared to their normal-weight peers. That contradicted the stigma of obesity argument that had predicted heavy women would be shut out of sexual activity.[28] But, young adults who were more severely obese (BMI 35 to 39.9) were shut out; they were much less likely to have on-off, nonrelationship sexual activity. "Normal-weight people probably have more bargaining power within their romantic relationships. They can pick or choose who they want their romantic partnership to be," Fee told me. "But these overweight and mildly overweight individuals, I would gather, have less power and less room to be choosy."

Fee also found some interesting differences between men and women and racial and ethnic groups. Although morbidly obese young adults (BMI of 40 or higher) hooked up less frequently, when they did, it was the women who were getting the action. Men who were as big as Carlos Romero and Rob Gaughan tended to get little sexual play. The differences among African American, Latino, and white severely obese young adults (BMI 35 to 39.9) were dramatic as well: Extremely obese black young adults were 66 percent more likely to hook up five times or more than whites, and Latinos, 175 percent more likely.[29]

At the same time, fat women are seen as easy targets for men seeking quick sex, and for some men, the hunt for bigger women—known as "hogging"—has become a sport. The baseball player Jose Canseco has described how he sought out fat women to break losing streaks. Another baseball player, Mark Grace, described how breaking out of a slump required finding the "fattest, gnarliest chick you can uncover."[30] In interviews with college-age men who admitted to "hogging," the sociologists

Ariane Prohaska, PhD, from the University of Alabama, and Jeannine
Gailey, PhD, from Texas Christian University, found that fat women were
seen as putting up little resistance to sexual advances.[31] One of the men
recounted how if men wanted "a quick sex fix," they would approach
"heavier set or . . . most people might consider your more ugly women to
satisfy their sexual needs instead of going after someone that would be
more attractive to you, because they know they can get a one-night stand
out of this girl instead of, you know, trying to chase someone you know
might already have a half dozen suitors." Hoggers, it appears, are not par-
ticulate.

* * *

THE cruelty of the dating market elicits different reactions. While Kayleigh may have decided to throw herself into the savage world of dating,
Sarah E., an aspiring opera singer in her early twenties, hid from it. Sarah
grew up north of Orlando and moved to Boston after college to earn an
advanced degree in opera performance. She sings in French, German,
Latin, Italian, and Russian, but her favorite songs to perform are Broadway
musical tunes. Her friends in high school and college had never really
teased her about her weight—she was short and squat—but she was convinced that other people treated her differently because of it.

In college and graduate school, Sarah was fatalistic about her weight.
She was eager to join a sorority but worried she was too heavy to be
accepted, so she decided not to pledge. She was a top musical performer, but
she sat out certain auditions: "I would go out looking for an audition dress,"
she said, "and I couldn't find anything that I felt I looked good in, so I just
didn't . . . do the audition." And when it came to dating, she kept her
thoughts to herself: "If I was interested in a guy, I would never, ever let him
know. I would never tell him because I didn't think I would be desirable."

If Sarah wasn't going to seek out a relationship, she would take whatever came her way. "If a guy asked me out on a date, I don't know if I ever
turned him down," she said. She didn't give much thought to whether she

was compatible with the men who pursued her. If a man showed interest in her, that was enough to arouse her attention. "A lot of it was just like, 'Oh, you're interested in me? What can I find redeeming about you?'"

When she did date, the relationships were miserable. Her boyfriends didn't comment on her weight, but that didn't seem to matter. Sarah worried that if she stood up for herself during an argument with a fickle boyfriend, she would lose him. She wondered, "Who else is gonna love me?" She had beaten herself into submission. When it came to sex, Sarah wanted to shrink away. "I never really wanted to be touched," she said of her college romances. She recoiled when a boyfriend wrapped his arms around her thick waist, and she never wanted him to see her naked. She would say, "Please don't touch me, don't look at me." When she went to the beach with friends, she never took off her T-shirt and shorts.

* * *

WOMEN tend to overestimate just how slender their bodies need to be in order to rate as attractive,[32] but the paranoia is understandable. Pamela Regan, PhD, a psychology professor at California State University, Los Angeles, wrote eloquently in her 1996 article "Sexual Outcasts: The Perceived Impact of Body Weight and Gender on Sexuality" about the self-fulfilling prophecy that entraps heavier people. A heavier person "prompted by his or her initial beliefs and expectancies, may come to elicit from the other person the very behaviors the individual expected the other to demonstrate."[33]

One of the most fascinating demonstrations of what psychologists call behavioral confirmation took place at the University of Minnesota in the mid-1990s.[34] Researchers led male college students one by one into a room and showed them photographs of women whom they were told they would soon talk to on the phone. Some of the women in the photographs were obese; the others were normal weight. Down the hall, a group of female students readied to talk to the men on the phone. What they didn't know was that the men had been shown photos that weren't of them.

Other experiments had found that men alter the way in which they speak to obese women. However, what was so surprising about this experiment was that when men believed, erroneously, that they were talking to obese women, the *women*—who were themselves not obese and who didn't know what picture their partner had viewed—became more antagonistic in their interactions than women whose partners believed they were normal weight. The women who were believed to be heavier—perhaps responding to the men's tone—became colder, surly, and unfriendly over the phone, according to the judges who evaluated the women's behavior and were blind to the conditions of the experiment. We would expect the stereotypes we hold of others to influence our own behavior, but what the experiment showed, says Dr. Regan, is that the "expectations held about obese individuals may actually affect their behavior in social situations, sexual situations, or both."[35]

Dr. Regan conducted her own experiment similar to the earlier Chris P. study. Instead, the participants were asked to imagine what the inner sexual desires might be of a normal-weight or obese "Jim" or "Julie." Similar to their views of Chris P., participants painted dismal sex lives for obese Julie and Jim. Obese Jim was viewed as unattractive, undesirable, and more than likely alone. Obese Julie's sex life was even worse: Not only was she considered less sexually attractive than her normal-weight counterpart, but the participants imagined she was most likely a virgin, unskilled in bed, frigid, difficult to arouse, and less desirous of sex. What interested Dr. Regan was how these beliefs about fundamental human desires—the perception that obese women yearn less for sex—might alter not only how obese women were treated socially and during sexual activity, but could change an obese woman's disposition and identity—that the *expectation* that she is somehow ungoverned by desire could alter the very characteristics and behaviors that define her personality. Dr. Regan writes:

> *For example, if an obese woman is presumed to be sexually unresponsive and undesirable, her partner may behave toward her in a sexually indifferent manner. Over a period of repeated interactions, the partner's*

behaviors may, in turn, induce her to gradually internalize sexual unresponsiveness and undesirability as a part of her self-concept, and to then behave in accordance with her self-image.[36]

* * *

BUT what if you could live in a world where no one knows you're obese? What if, instead, you're an ace fighter roaming around a lush and magical world in a massive online game with millions of other players?

When he was 22 and living in North Carolina, Carlos reveled in the anonymity of his heroic avatar on World of Warcraft. "Online, no one knew that I was 300 and something pounds," he said. "I was just really, really good at this thing, and garnered respect from people that way." Ill at ease in his portly body, Carlos found it easier to connect with people online than in person. "Even if someone, let's say, was into me or giving me cues or I thought there was a chance, I never had the guts to just put myself out there and say, 'Hey, do you want to get a cup of coffee?' or 'Could I have your number?'"

He began flirting with another World of Warcraft gamer, a woman who lived in Texas. Soon they were sharing photos and videos and live Web cam pictures of each other. His weight was no longer hidden—he was 340 pounds—but neither was hers. She professed to liking bigger guys. Soon after their online relationship began, she moved from Texas and into Carlos's house in North Carolina. "I was a terrible influence on her," Carlos remembered of the time they spent together. She adopted his sedentary life, and the two stayed indoors playing video games.

Carlos was not a practiced—or thirsty—lover. He first had sex when he was 16, and then not again until 6 years later when the Texas gamer moved in with him. "I had girlfriends. I just avoided intercourse," he said of that time. He laughs a bit, remembering, "I basically never took my clothes off." He had sexual stirrings—there was nothing medically wrong with him—but he was overcome with embarrassment, and his sexual reticence caused problems in his relationships. "Someone's trying to unzip your pants," said Carlos, "and you say, 'No.'" The women who had perhaps overcome their own embarrassment to reach out to him felt rejected, and then Carlos, in turn, felt bad for hurting their feelings.

The few times Carlos was sexually intimate, he found it maddening to stay in the moment. He disliked nearly every sexual position—he didn't like being on top of a woman or underneath her. He didn't like being looked at, and it felt like a struggle "to go for it," he said, since he could never be consumed by passion the way he thought he should.

It was a painful cycle: When he was in a relationship, he felt embarrassed and sexually incompetent; when he was out looking for a relationship, he felt restricted and rebuffed. "I was very angry at myself for my problems," he said, "so that translated into judging other people." If a woman passed him over, he would think to himself, "She's not interested in me, so screw her anyway." He dismissed those who dismissed him, and he imagined that he had more steel, more character, than people who were thinner. He knew what hardship felt like, he imagined, and that made him a more complex man. He turned rejection into an excuse for being haughty.

Now, at 29, Carlos lives in Seattle and mostly dates online. He's lost 180 pounds by changing his diet and exercising, but he's unsure just how much of his weight loss to include in his dating profile. "I don't think any woman is gonna want to be with a guy that says, 'I've lost 180 pounds,'" he said. He worries that romantic prospects would suspect his body would be permanently damaged, which he acknowledges it is. "You'd probably think, 'That dude has issues,' which clearly I do," he said, laughing sweetly.

Now that he isn't carrying around 180 extra pounds, now that his knees can bear his own weight, Carlos finds himself free to roam the real world. But although his body is much lighter, he's still self-critical. "When I look in the mirror, I see 437 pounds [his top weight], regardless of the fact that was 180 pounds ago. I still see every flaw."

Carlos's uncertainty over whether to acknowledge his obese past is not unfounded. In 2012, sociologist Holly Fee found that potential suitors were indeed reluctant to date formerly obese men and women.[37] One of the driving forces that led people to hesitate was fear that the romantic partner would regain the weight.

* * *

REMEMBER those gray female tree frogs that put potential mates through a fitness test with all that operatic singing? Those evolutionary enforcers who are listening to the lungs of potential suitors for evidence of virility and strength, who punish aspiring mates who are too heavy? Catherine Brinkman is like that. She unapologetically rejects fat men. "If you're fat," she says, "I'm not even going to look at you."

Catherine, who is in her early thirties, is ready to marry and have kids, and she wants the father of her future children to be a robust, able-bodied man. Catherine grew up near Silicon Valley; she swam in high school and in college. After graduation, she became a commodities broker and then launched an intense—and successful—career in politics as a fund-raiser and campaign manager. She ate her way through high-calorie work dinners and fueled late nights at the office with soft drinks and Snickers bars. She gained weight quickly, but her rapid career advancement inoculated her from feelings of inadequacy. "I call it Gwyneth Paltrow syndrome," she says. "I'm arrogant." She found that men, despite her weight, were drawn to her success.

She left politics for sales, where she's now a top performer, and during that career change, Catherine decided to lose weight. "I've learned to respect people more who are skinny," she says. "Those people who work out and watch what they eat. It sucks to have to work at this, but that's the way it is." She still craves red vines, gummy bears, and pizza pockets, and occasionally dreams of McDonald's cheeseburgers. Now that she's lost weight, Catherine is more aware of the contours of her body—she wants to tone her muscles—and she's revised her idea of the kind of man she wants to be with. "When you think of dating, do you want to be with someone who is at risk of dying? Raise kids with them? I think about that." She doesn't want to marry a man who, during a hike, would "keel over and have a heart attack," leaving her widowed with the kids.

* * *

A common refrain I heard in my interviews with people of size is: "There is nothing worse than a reformed fat person." They can sound like scolds. What is striking about Catherine—and other women and men like her—is that she emerged from a decade of dating in her twenties as a heavy young woman mostly unscathed. Her search for a fit partner isn't borne out of animus toward heavier men; she merely wants a husband who can sire healthy offspring and will have better odds of staying alive to help her raise them. For Catherine, the decision to exclude obese men from her pool of potential suitors is borne out of instinct and reason. One long-term study suggests that Catherine's mating strategy is a sober—and prescient—assessment.

Researchers in Denmark began tracking the health of 6,500 men when they were 22 years old and followed them until they reached their mid-fifties. Some were normal weight, others underweight or overweight, and the rest obese.[38] The results, published in April 2013 in the *British Medical Journal,* found that by the end of the follow-up period, nearly half of the men who were obese at age 22 had

* been diagnosed with diabetes or high blood pressure; and/or

* suffered a heart attack, stroke, or blood clots in their legs or lungs; and/or

* died.

Men like Carlos Romero or Rob Gaughan who began their twenties encased in fat—just as the romantic sifting, sorting, and pairing off was to begin—had a 50 percent risk of developing serious health problems by middle age. Those men who began their adult lives at a normal weight had a 20 percent risk.[39]

* * *

Rob Gaughan was trying to escape those odds. As he plunged into the dating pool at age 33, he was 98 pounds lighter, but still obese.

Tamara would become his first real girlfriend. When he asked her out that night after their AA meeting, she had said yes. Weeks after they went out to dinner, Rob gave Tamara a single rose for Valentine's Day (he had never before bought flowers for a date); a month later, they started having sex. Rob fell hard and fast. He found his love style, and it was *Mania*. Intense, insatiable, wildly romantic. What felt like new love was dizzying. "We were like the Kennedys," he told me, his booming voice rising. "We're both losing weight and getting sober." She wanted to hold hands at meetings, and he sent flowers to her at work every month. He once delivered a 4-foot-tall card to her doorstep in the middle of the night. But after a year of dating, Rob couldn't find his footing. "I felt ill-equipped," he said of the relationship. He didn't—or couldn't—figure out "what's her business and what's my business." He found himself constantly trying to please her and unable to say no. They broke up after a little more than a year.

Later that summer, when Rob was working on a construction project in Los Angeles, he met a tall, svelte blonde woman. They lived a few blocks from each other in Long Beach and started an intense romance. Rob—and his friends—maintain she was the most gorgeous woman he'd ever dated and that he was the most sexually attracted he'd ever been. But after dating for a year, his girlfriend seemed to be around less and less. Rob didn't catch on to his girlfriend's signals. He hoped for the best and stuck around until it was obvious that she was done with him.

Rob often called his best friend, Gabe, when he was going through the throes of first love. "The first relationship with Tamara was kind of like the high school relationship," Gabe told me. The next girlfriend was "like the senior year [of high school] or the first college girlfriend." There have been other relationships since and with each one, a swoon, a plunge, and a heartbreak. Rob maintains that he is only sexually attracted to women with athletic builds. He is the overweight man at the Computer Dance who is shooting for the "Attractive" date, and those expectations may be sabotaging his chance at a satisfying, long-term relationship. Gabe said that his friend has "a kind of disconnect for the attractiveness he's after. If people of similar attractiveness levels are attracted to each other, Rob has a pretty big disconnect of what he wants." His friend Kenny Lombino worries that Rob lags too far behind in his romantic life. "For a 38-year-old man, he has very limited experience. He's a sweetheart and so desperately wants love and to be in love."

Rob seems puzzled that he hasn't managed to catch up; that he has trouble seeing the red flags when a woman isn't right for him; that he is too eager to please and too quick to say yes. He is an excitable and extroverted person who, you get the sense, will never let life beat him down. But for now, he's working hard and trying to save up some money, with the hope that that might make him a more attractive catch. "A king builds a kingdom," he told me, sitting in the apartment he shares with a roommate, "before he finds a queen."

CHAPTER **THREE**

Marriage: In Thickness and in Health

Dana Englehardt stood at the end of her bed and slipped off her work clothes. She stood naked for a moment, turning her back to her husband, Larry. This moment of unveiling, when her day clothes dropped to the floor and before she could wrestle the thin, cotton nightgown over her head, always lasted too long; it was as if a cage dropped around her, a spotlight turned on, and there she stood in a predictable and daily display of shame, guilt, and dread.

The bedroom she shared with her husband was meant to be romantic: The yellow pastel paint softened in the moonlight; the windows opened to the upper branches of a giant Monterey cypress that shaded the backyard from the California sun; framed photos of the couple's wedding rested on the polished and uncluttered chest of drawers. On the wall hung a wooden jewelry organizer that displayed rows of glittery dangling earrings and necklaces. If Dana was going to draw attention, she wanted it to be from the neck up. What she didn't like, what she despised really, was her stomach, which looked bulbous even in her prettiest burgundy cowl-neck sweater and printed maxi skirt. At bedtime it reminded her of the entropy of her marriage. So she turned away from her husband's gaze, as if his eyes alone could make the rolls of her skin grow bigger and cut deeper, and scrambled into her nightie.

It was then that Dana could flop into bed. She propped her head on a pillow and let her legs stretch out. By this time of night, the pain in her knees was at its worst; bone scratched on bone and it was as if her skeleton, which was quite petite, had a personal complaint from holding up 265 pounds all day. Her body overheated easily, which caused more problems: Dana could only sleep with a light sheet and the windows open, and Larry was left to shiver.

Ensconced on her side of the bed, Dana leaned over and gave Larry a quick, perfunctory kiss. It was a coded message that Larry understood. The constraints Dana erected around herself, built by each episode of mer-ciless scrutiny—both public and private—and seeded in the soil of her personality, left no room for sexual self-abandon. She reached down to the small CPAP machine on the carpet next to the bed and turned it on. As the sleep apnea machine, which helped her breathe, began to whirl and pressurized air flowed into the plastic tube, she sat up and pulled a mask over her nose and mouth. With the wrought-iron bars of the bed and the straps around her head, the bedroom looked as if some kinky sex play was under way. But the donning of the CPAP mask was, Dana imagined, a sign to her husband that the day was over, and she was going to sleep.

Dana lay there in the dark, inches away from her husband, her mind disquieted. "Maybe I'm going to lose him if I continue this way," she thought. In the past, Larry had tried to make playful advances with his wife; he had curled into her, and when he touched her stomach, he would say how much he loved her body. Five years earlier, when they married, Dana was already a hefty woman at 200 pounds. Surely, he figured, she had to know he fell in love with her shapely size. Larry was a few extra pounds overweight, too, and his head shone in the places where his black hair used to be. Kindhearted and encouraging, an optimistic sort who had helped raise Dana's three children, Larry could not understand why his wife bristled when he touched her or why she would whisper, "Would you please not touch me there?" and then, after his repeated entreaties, quietly roll away from him and vanish. He was an uncomplicated man, and he came to resent the prison his wife had built for herself. Dana knew this, and yet, somehow she couldn't convey how these last 65 pounds that she'd gained had tipped her over the edge. Her existence felt materially different now; she felt like a monster. There were times when she forced herself to have sex with her husband, but she could never lose herself in the moment. Her mind refused to release her body, which as far as she could tell had no sexual urges of its own. As a result, she felt numb, cold, and humiliated. The intimacy was unconvincing.

Dana felt strongly that she was failing her husband—that she was unworthy and undeserving, and could ask nothing of Larry during daylight hours. She had been divorced once when she was just barely out of high school; she had lost a second husband to cancer. Now it seemed plausible that Larry would leave her, too.

Lying in her bedroom in the dark, the CPAP mask affixed to her face, Dana drifted off to sleep in a swirl of exhaustion, relief, and terror.

* * *

WHEN Dana Englehardt was a young girl in Belmont, California, in the 1960s, national surveys were beginning to detect a steady and unrelenting rise in the prevalence of obesity.[1] Rarely had a chronic condition such as obesity spread with the same speed and ferocity as a communicable disease, wrote researchers at the Centers for Disease Control and Prevention in the *Journal of the American Medical Association* in 1999.[2] By the end of the 20th century, a federal report found that some 300,000 deaths in the United States were associated with excessive weight and obesity.[3] By the time obesity was declared an epidemic in the United States in 2001 by Surgeon General Dr. David Satcher—when it had become, like postwar suburbs and the National Football League, something widespread and uniquely

American—an army of demographers and economists and cardiologists and earnest public health officers was busily sorting through the implications. The surgeon general warned that if left unabated, this new epidemic could cause as much preventable disease and death as cigarette smoking. He issued a "call to action" to all scientists.

The Obese American became a subject to study and dissect. Using computed tomography and magnetic resonance imaging, scientists could scan an obese person's body and build a cross-sectional model—a topographical hologram of accumulated body fat. What came into view was a constellation of metabolic disturbances; as fat pressed into the obese person's organs, blood pressure rose and low-density lipoprotein increased; blood glucose increased, contributing to the development of diabetes; cardiovascular disease took hold; internal organ cancers became more common. Even at the earliest signs of excess weight, the risk for diabetes began to tick upward. The search for a cause and a cure took on an increasing urgency. Obesity was a scourge that left soldiers unfit for battle, drained the nation's resources, and appeared to reverse a century of gains in life expectancy. It was becoming more than a condition that was associated with other diseases; it was becoming a disease itself.

Researchers wanted to know everything about the people whose bodies grew inexplicably big: What did they eat? When did they eat? Did they exercise? Were they genetically predisposed? Did their genes offer any clues? Those who gained or lost weight were weighed and measured; heavy people were reduced to a series of numbers: waist, height, weight.

Pharmaceutical companies at work on their own version of a cure for weight gain saw a tremendous business opportunity, but they needed to demonstrate that their antiobesity treatments did more than just help people lose weight. Prodded by a leading psychologist who argued that weight loss outcome studies should also evaluate body image, mood, and social relationships,[4] the industry might be able to show that even modest weight loss improved lives. A patient could feel "marked improvements in many areas of life, but actual changes to his/her BMI or cardiovascular risk are not apparent," wrote a group of researchers.[5] The promise that even a modest amount of weight loss could brighten a person's outlook might encourage less recidivism in weight loss programs—or better adherence to a regimen of antiobesity drugs that had never delivered the kind of dramatic results patients often hoped for, frequently causing them to abandon the prescriptions. Of course, the reverse could also be true: "While a pharmacological intervention's physiological efficacy can be measured through biomarkers, such as serum cholesterol and blood glucose, for example, the patient may not actually feel better as a result of treatment."

* * *

A person's weight was a knowable number, but on what basis should a person rate the experience of daily life? How do you define "quality of life"? How do you determine which life experiences are compromised by weight? And where along the body mass index do the negative effects begin? With scientists and scholars working at a frenzied pace to unravel the biological, genetic, social, and industrial origins of obesity, the notion of scholarly research focused on how obese people experienced life was considered trivial. The emotional trials of the obese—what it felt like to be fat every day—seemed to be treated as an inessential, even gratuitous course of inquiry. With the exception of some surgical interventions, "quality of life and the impact of obesity was rarely assessed in obesity research or practice," wrote two prominent psychologists.[6]

In 1995, after listening to the commonly expressed complaints of moderately to severely obese patients in intensive treatment for obesity, a group of clinicians, led by Ronnie Kolotkin, PhD, at Duke University Diet and Fitness Center in Durham, North Carolina, devised a series of scales to detect how a person experienced life at her weight. The Impact of Weight on Quality of Life questionnaire, known as the IWQOL, became the first instrument specifically designed to assess how obesity changed a person's life.[7] Other researchers had developed generic surveys such as the Sickness Impact Profile and Quality of Life Inventory that could evaluate general health, vitality, social and emotional problems, and mental health. The

SF–36, for example, is widely considered a gold standard measure for quality of life. It asks questions like "How do you physically feel? How do you emotionally feel?" But those broad questions were in some way independent from body weight, said David Sarwer, PhD, psychology professor and director of clinical services at the Center for Weight and Eating Disorders at the University of Pennsylvania in Philadelphia, and one of the nation's leading experts on obesity. "Ronnie's measure gets us more to 'How does your *weight* affect your ability to do these different things?'"

This specificity was important for large clinical trials for antiobesity drugs, as well. Scientists had concluded that instruments designed to gauge the impact of a specific disease such as obesity offered more accuracy and a degree of sensitivity. This meant that obesity needed its own measurement tool.

What was fascinating about the quality of life questionnaire was that it reflected the aspects of daily living that obese people *themselves* said were most affected by their weight and caused them the greatest concern. Used to being studied, prodded, and treated as specimens, the patients themselves saw the questions emerge from their own subjective experience; it was their own perspective, not what others perceived of their lives. The scales included common and obvious physical problems, like shortness of breath, difficulty getting up stairs, and swollen ankles; social difficulties such as feeling ridiculed and rejected by friends; a deflated self-esteem; and problems at work.

But something else arose as a central theme for many of the obese patients at Duke University's diet center (the average age in one of the study groups was about 48): problems with their sexual life. The Sexual Life scale would measure if they felt sexually attractive; if they felt little or no sexual desire; if they let anyone see them undress; if they had difficulty with sexual performance; if they avoided sexual encounters; and if they failed to enjoy sexual activity.

The prototypical fat person, after all, wasn't supposed to want sex. At least that's what social scientists had found were the prevailing beliefs about the obese at the same time the Duke team was finding out otherwise. In the Chris P. experiment discussed earlier, college-age students rated photographs of a man or woman named Chris P. as less erotic when bulked up to look obese than when the *same person* was presented at normal weight. As a measure of attitudes toward the obese, the experiment, along with other studies, suggested that at best, an obese person's physique dulled passionate desire; at worst, it snuffed it out altogether.

As new treatments for obesity began to fill up the drug pipeline, and speedier measurements of quality of life were needed for clinical trials, the Impact of Weight on Quality of Life questionnaire needed to be shortened. It was trimmed down from 74 items and eight scales to 31 items and five scales. Sexual Life made the cut. Enduring popular attitudes may have stripped overweight and obese people of their sexuality, but it was clearly an essential aspect of life, and if it was going to be trampled on, at least the scientists wanted to know by how much.

* * *

THE quiet surrender of his sexual life was not an option for Eric Leckbee. That was, in part, the reason why he and his wife were wobbling back and forth on a tandem bicycle near San Francisco's Fisherman's Wharf and trying not to plow into the throngs of tourists gathered at the cable car turnaround. They'd bought a coupon for a biking photo safari that would lead them along the city's northern border, across the fabled Golden Gate Bridge and into Sausalito. It would be a romantic adventure if the wind would quiet down and the sun would stop hiding behind the city's frigid fog.

The bike shop attendant had eyed them; he needed to get them outfitted with helmets for the ride. "I have a large skull," Eric's wife stated matter-of-factly to the attendant, "and I haven't had a haircut recently, just so you know." She could be wickedly funny, and when her humor ran dry, Eric took up the slack.

As the bike attendant handed the couple elastic bands to put around their pants, Eric declared his "nerd-dom" complete.

Outside, with their helmets on and pants properly tucked in, they would need to give the tandem bike a test ride. "Sir, can you step on first?" the attendant said to Eric. "Ma'am, you're going to get on second, and then you guys are going to take a test ride, okay?" The attendant counted down—"one, two, three"—and the couple swerved unsteadily, laughing at their clumsiness.

"That's actually kind of hard," Eric's wife said.

"It does feel like a relationship-building exercise," he responded, sounding surprised. The couple had been trying to find healthy activities to do together. The biking photo safari was a better bet than dancing, which his wife liked to do. Eric couldn't fathom moving his unruly body that way. "On top of not being a sportsy person, I can't dance either."

The couple had bought a low-tech disposable camera at a local drugstore. In their early forties and living on a middle-class income in a brutally expensive city, they had made a game out of thriftiness: At home, Eric's wife could be found revving up a sewing machine to make an A-line skirt; he could spend entire afternoons in a basement storage room sifting through his record collection. Together, they took great comfort in the makeshift backyard boardinghouse that they ran for feral cats in their gritty, southeastern neighborhood. Eric and his wife didn't want to become known as *cat people;* they were proudly childless and nerdy, and they bristled at such a categorization.

Before they headed out across the bridge, Eric leaned in close to his wife, brushing up against her with tender affection. She looked up with kind and generous eyes. He was at least a foot taller, with an envious pelt of brown hair and swarthy good looks.

"I've always wanted to ride a bike for two," Eric said eagerly. His shoulders tended to slump forward even when he was excited.

"That's sweet," she said, and leaned in for a kiss.

* * *

THE year before had been an especially rough period for Eric. His fluctuating weight had been a constant for nearly a decade, but this time he had bulked back up from 200 to 270 pounds. When he got this big, he couldn't help but think that being obese was a selfish thing; the wanton self-indulgence signaled, he believed, that he cared more about stuffing his belly and yielding to "that sudden rush you get from eating something tasty" than he did about his wife.

Eric was in his midtwenties when he met his wife at a San Francisco Bay Area company and they started dating. He had just returned from living in Prague and was full of captivating stories about his travels in Central Europe. He had always been tall and skinny, but in the pubs of what was then Czechoslovakia, Eric was content to bulk up on beer and sausage. The weight crept onto his body slowly and stealthily. "I've always had an aversion to looking at myself in mirrors. So I didn't really have that visual confirmation that I was gaining weight," he told me. His pants size, though, was a reliable—and ruthless—indicator of his expanding girth.

"I blackly remember the day that I first had to go to the Big and Tall—when I couldn't shop at a regular department store anymore because my pants size was too large. That's humiliating." Listening to music or sitting at his desk at work, where he managed software development, Eric could put his body out of his mind. But when he caught a glimpse of himself in a mirror or a storefront window, the reflection horrified him. "I would think of images of fat people I'd seen and think, 'Oh my God, that's me.'" Eric and his wife had married when they were both a bit heavy. Over the years, they each steadily gained weight—his weight gain was more severe than hers—until he couldn't deny that he'd crossed some invisible boundary: He felt compelled to admit that he was officially fat. It was a distinction that left him feeling unattractive and depressed. "Why would anyone want to be intimate with me?" he asked himself. "Why would anyone find me sexually attractive?" If he didn't like himself, how could anyone else?

When he felt down like this, Eric found it hard to fight the frequent urges to eat. He would stop at a fast-food restaurant, eat a hamburger, and then hide the wrappers from his wife. When she discovered his secret binges, the tectonics of their marriage shifted. "When I start hiding food, it causes trust issues," Eric said plaintively. "It causes the question of: What else are you hiding? I'm not being honest with her. I'm not being honest with myself."

On the surface, Eric was a temperate man, but underneath, his inner world was roiling. "When I hide the food, it isn't so much from her; it's almost more that I'm hiding it from myself. I don't want to see the evidence of my gluttony, of my failing, or what I feel like is failure." He was a considerate husband and felt burdened by the struggles he foisted on his wife. "When she finds evidence of my hiding food, that, of course, causes her to doubt me and my honesty within our relationship."

These episodes whittled away at the trust the couple had built up over more than a decade of marriage. As doubt crept into their daily lives, each withdrew; one stepped backward, then the other, until the emotional and sexual tethers that had once bound them together were stretched far apart.

"To be really, truly intimate with someone, sexually and emotionally, you have to be able to trust them," Eric said. "So she puts barriers up, and then I feel defensive, and I put barriers up. And then it causes more of a chasm to occur between us." That chasm—that emotional separation—made it difficult for Eric to enjoy the sexual intimacy that remained, and over time, he shied away from it more and more. His own self-contained civil war hadn't entirely crushed his desire for sex, but it had scared him into a corner.

*　*　*

In the pre–Industrial Revolution era, sex had been roughly viewed by scientists and physicians as a need for evacuation, not unlike the need to go to the bathroom. To the poets, sex might have been a vehicle for transcendence; to scientists, it was just another bodily function. The *impulse of detumescence* is how the influential German sexologist Albert Moll described the urge in 1897.[8] That crude construct was replaced by a more believable, if still unverifiable, theory that the impulse to have sex was an "instinct of reproduction." It wasn't until the early 20th century that sex was viewed as both a physical *and* psychological act.[9]

A man's girth was never considered a moderating factor, if it was considered at all. In the early years of sexual studies, it was syphilis—not obesity—that was widespread and widely feared.

The British human sexuality scholar Havelock Ellis wrote in the foreword to his fascinating book *Psychology of Sex* that "a man's sexual temperament is too intimate and essential a part of him to be viewed with indifference." Originally published in 1933, the book described how sexual intimacy was interwoven into the experience of being human. "Sex penetrates the whole person," Ellis wrote. "A man's sexual constitution is a part of his general constitution."

The measure of each man's—and each woman's—constitution can be quite different, though; the strength and appetite of sexual desire and the spectrum of satisfaction are entirely subjective. The sexual experience rests on the participant's rendering of that experience: the assessment of whether it is pleasurable or disappointing; whether it happens too often or not often enough; whether it leaves a lover feeling cherished or neglected. Like the assessment of pain, sexual intimacy—the intermingling of the psychological and the physical—is up to the judgment of each person involved. It can be held hostage by a person's mind, one that is profoundly dissatisfied with its owner's body.

* * *

A picture of yourself swims through your psyche; lurking, taunting, egging you on for a fight. The person in that picture can be quite ungovernable. The picture in our mind's eye can look like those maps of the world that are resized to represent a continent's population or Internet usage or age of death: Stomachs, breasts, arms, thighs, calves, chins are resized to comic proportions and streaked with stretch marks, pocked with cellulite, drooping with flabby fat and skin. Those images are often very different from the way other people see us. The people who love us—like Dana's husband, Larry—are usually more reliable mirrors, but we remain unconvinced.

Most Americans are unhappy with the way they look, and that

dissatisfaction is a major driver of the American economy, from fashion purchases to cosmetics to cosmetic surgery. But for people who become heavier, body image dissatisfaction can tip over into body image pathology, a destructive force that impairs how a person functions day to day. (This is also true, of course, for anorexics and bulimics.)

At her home in Belmont, California, Dana Englehardt had begun positioning the mirrors along the wall so she could see only her face and not the rest of her body. That was a common tactic that heavier women around the country reported. Dr. Sarwer, from the University of Pennsylvania, laid out the rationale he often heard from patients: "I am going to selectively look at myself . . . where I only see from my chin up, or even the upper part of my face. I'm almost in denial about how big my body is."

For people who are extremely uncomfortable with their body image, sexual intimacy undoubtedly suffers. "If your reaction to your body is affecting those more benign behaviors in that way," Dr. Sarwer continued, "then it makes sense that you are going to feel disconnected from your body when it comes to sexual behavior. . . . [F]or many patients there is a disconnect between the physical sensation of touch and then perceiving that as pleasure. . . . [If someone is] touching you gently, that should feel good. But there is also a cognition in the mind that says, 'This should feel good, but I am so embarrassed and ashamed of my own body that this doesn't feel so good.'"

* * *

ERIC wasn't sure how to describe his innate sexual constitution; he had a voracious appetite for food, but he didn't see sex as a daily, life-sustaining need. And yet he wasn't content to spend his adult married life emotionally and physically estranged from his wife. He didn't treat his sexual temperament with indifference. "I do think it's important," he told me. "I do feel that it's an expression of intimacy and of love and of closeness that I certainly need in my life." Even at the mercy of his battered self-image, and disgusted with the body that was the conduit for intimacy, Eric didn't want to imagine a life without sex. "I don't think that would be, for me, a healthy or enjoyable relationship. That would not be the type of partnership I would want for life."

His marriage got pretty rough for a while; the couple sought marriage counseling, and Eric, resistant at first, started seeing a therapist on his own. He needed to find out why he was so unhappy. In the way that he avoided mirrors and his own reflection, Eric felt like he was hiding from himself and from his wife. Intimacy was by far the most difficult topic in therapy; he didn't want to appear any more vulnerable and weak than he already was. His self-loathing was so great that surely, he imagined, his wife must loathe him, too. "And then once you start to lose that confidence, it's really hard to ask for sex," he said. "I felt it nearly impossible to approach my wife."

The self-imposed humiliation sent him spiraling: "Then I would think, 'God, you're a loser. You don't know how to hit on your wife—the one woman in the world who should be open to your sexual advances.' And yet, I would have that fear."

Rather than hovering enticingly nearby, sex was more likely to haunt the couple.

All of this crawled around in Eric's head, and he became quiet and distant. His wife would try to talk about their intimate life and even try to seduce him, but Eric didn't want to discuss it. "I would just say, 'I'm not in the mood.'" He seemed tired of being himself and tired of the shadow that followed him everywhere.

Eric didn't like it when he became dismissive and moody, but he wasn't sure what would make him feel better. He wasn't striving for some ideal image of the male body; he just didn't want to feel so crappy all the time. "I don't let the media influence my sense of self-worth or self-esteem," he said. "But then again, I'm 42. I'm not 21." He was under no illusion that he should have six-pack abs. "I don't really put that pressure upon myself. I want to feel good about myself . . . look good in my clothes."

Eric's personality had a dark streak, but it was never dangerous or malicious. He grew up in the port of Martinez, a working-class town that sits on a narrow stretch of the Carquinez Strait in San Francisco Bay. Eric's Mexican American father left the family when he was young, and Eric grew up with a younger brother and a parade of temperamental stepfathers. He was devoted to his self-described tribe of geeks who sparred over the board version of Dungeons and Dragons, but he was unwilling to share their impending fate when it came to girls. When he looked in the mirror, at age 14, with his glasses and long, greasy hair, he realized he needed to change his appearance. "As a guy geek, you notice girls, but you think, 'I look like shit.'" He had reached that moment, he thought, when he needed "to change or go full geek."

Eric got a job at Taco Bell to save up for contact lenses; he cut his hair and started wearing nicer clothes; he put away his Supertramp albums, and on the advice of an older girl, he began listening to the Sex Pistols and Dead Kennedys. During high school, Eric shaved steppes into his hair, pierced his ears, and took pride in the exotic T-shirts he ordered from England through paper editions of *Rolling Stone*. His teenage anger and irritability weren't atypical, but searching his past didn't seem to explain his relationship to food and the revulsion he felt toward his body.

* * *

BILL Hartman, a gregarious and sweet-natured clinical psychologist, was standing in a small kitchen at a medical office in San Francisco carefully placing jicama and carrot sticks in disposable plastic pill cups. In his hands, which were as big as paws, he grasped a bottle of salad dressing—a new low-fat, low-calorie blue cheese dressing that he was excited to introduce to his weight loss group that evening. Bill was tall and lean, with tanned skin etched with lines from all the hours he spent surfing along the northern California coast. His eyes lit up when he spoke. When poised to listen, he bent his tall frame forward in a gesture that conveyed concentration and enthusiasm; his smile was reassuring and kind. He was the perfect person to help raise battered and beleaguered spirits.

Bill's weight loss groups had met most weeks for decades, and Bill's hair had grayed as his charges lost weight, plateaued, and gained some or all of it back; fell in love, married, and divorced; and battled various afflictions, psychological and physical. Eric Leckbee and his wife had started going to Bill's weekly meetings nearly a decade ago, not long after one of their adventurous outings led them to a startling truth. They'd taken a ferry to Angel Island, the idyllic state park that sits in the middle of bustling San Francisco Bay. It was the first week that Segways were available to rent on the island, and Eric had always wanted to ride one. The personal scooters turned out to be a thrill to ride, and afterward, someone—he doesn't remember who exactly—snapped a photo. The spectacle of buffoonery—of two hefty grown-ups propped upright on Segways—had the effect of a humiliating injury. "We looked at ourselves, and it was just frightening," he said, recalling the image. Not only did Eric avoid mirrors, he rarely allowed anyone to take pictures of him. When he saw how big he'd gotten, he said, "Oh, my God, we [have] to do something about this."

The couple signed up for a supervised liquid fast that lasted 6 months, and then started attending Bill's group therapy sessions. They were expected to keep records of their physical activity and meals, and learn about reshaping their habits. Eric's wife maintained her weight loss, but he continued to fluctuate. "Fluctuating as I do is actually the norm," he said wryly of his tendency to lose, then regain weight.

Bill Hartman knew this about the people in his group. It was unlikely that he could nudge his patients to a healthy weight and get them to stay there; yet each week, for years and decades, he tried.

At the weight management meeting one winter evening, a group of men and women in their forties, fifties, and sixties sat around a plastic folding table. The majority of them were white, urban professionals who had varying degrees of success in managing their weight. There was a parade of diet soda cans on the table: Diet Barq's Root Beer, Diet Sunkist, and Sprite Zero. Bill passed around a tray with dice-size nibbles of a new lemon protein bar that his weight management clinic had developed, and the jicama and carrot sticks, each with a dollop of the new Bolthouse Farms blue cheese yogurt dressing. "It's hard to find a good blue cheese dressing," Bill said, not ironically, to the group. "They're really high-fat." The response to the dressing was tepid. "It was decent," said one man.

In weight loss groups, it's easy to spot the Professional Dieters. They can sound haughty at times, even though many of them, like Eric, swell and deflate regularly. They think of themselves as serious students engaged in serious study—not the fad chasers who take the pursuit of a healthy weight lightly. There was no aspect of Bill's patients' lives that didn't affect their long-term weight loss success—getting to a healthier weight was, in Bill's view, a psychological struggle—and as a result, he often asked about the stresses in people's lives. Of all victories, first and greatest is for a man to conquer himself, went the saying. Plato might as well have been writing about dieters.

Many of the people in Bill's group were married, and, like Eric, their inner conflicts spilled outward into their relationships with their husbands, wives, and children. Weight wasn't a novel or unique stress; instead, weight struggles seemed to exacerbate problems that already existed in their lives. Finances. Jobs. Children. Intimacy. For Eric and his wife, there were typical problems in their relationship, but his obesity and its concomitant forces made it worse. "Whatever else is going on with your life, your family, and then on top of that, you put obesity, and now you're feeling bad about yourself," Eric explained.

Instead of trying to tackle their problems together, Eric believed, obesity compounded their issues and deepened the chasm between them. "I think it kind of pushes both people into their own heads and into their own little world," he told me. "It breaks down the communication . . . because being heavy can be such a selfish thing." By this, he didn't mean that bigger people were morally deficient; he didn't see his obesity as some morality play. Unlike the attitudes that social scientists were continuing to register even among young schoolchildren—that obesity was synonymous with sloth—Eric described what seemed to be a common pattern for those engaged in their own battle: "It's just like, I don't care what other people think about me. I don't care what my partner thinks about me. I don't care, you know. All I care about right now is myself and the thing that I'm eating. I think that's how I mean it [that obesity is selfish]. And that scenario, if you engage in it enough, just kind of carries over into the rest of your life. You stop caring about how you look, you stop caring about how other people perceive you, and you just become very concerned with satisfying your immediate needs."

Although Eric tried to shield himself from the world around him, he was unable to wall off his wife from the consequences of his indulgences; within the ecosystem of marriage, any decision—"Honey, I brought home a pizza!"—could influence the other person. He felt bad that he was bringing his "bad behavior" into the house, he said, and making it that much harder for his wife to win her own battles. "That's the wrong kind of sharing. It's not the type of sharing that's going to breed trust or compassion or intimacy in any way."

Over the years, at the weight loss group, Bill had tried unsuccessfully to bring up sex. "Typical American reticence to talk about sexual taboos," Bill remarked. "The groups we run are not down and dirty." In one-on-one counseling sessions, though, patients often tell him that part of their motivation for weight loss, often through bariatric surgery, is establishing or improving their sex life. His single clients will often say they don't date because of their weight, or "I'm focusing on me." Many are women in their twenties or thirties who have never been romantically or sexually involved. "They didn't go to prom," Bill said. "They didn't date."

But it was clear that weight was taking a toll on the sexual lives of his married clients as well, and he had dedicated that night's session to the topic. The men in the group sat back silently in their chairs, reaching every few minutes for their cans of diet soda. The women were much more willing to share their experiences. One woman had been married for 4 decades, and although her husband had never made her feel undesirable, she had started Bill's weight loss program, in part, to improve her sex life. For many of these women, it was their husbands who wanted them to lose a modest amount of weight, if only because they would feel better about themselves; they would be happier, "more free," and perhaps then more likely to initiate sex. It was similar to being married to a spouse with chronic depression, remarked one woman. "This is what I bring to the relationship."

What if they could live in a world that didn't judge the obese so harshly? If they could do away with media images of gluttonous fat people and the condemnation hurled at them in their daily lives, could those changes in the cultural landscape ameliorate their sexual difficulties? One woman shook her head. "It's physically uncomfortable to be too big," she said. "It's a stress on the body parts. That's a personal and emotional and physical result of the weight. That has nothing to do with culture."

* * *

FOR Eric, the emotional whiplash continued. If the fluctuations didn't end—if healthy eating or exercise or weight goals could be met and then lost, spirits raised, then dashed—then how could he find some measure of calm?

Marital problems stemming from obesity and weight gain are more prevalent now among couples who seek counseling for relationship problems, although couples are often reluctant to bring up their partner's weight initially, according to marriage therapists. "Being overweight is a liability in marriage; of course it is, like not making enough money or being infertile," said one therapist who specializes in sexual intimacy counseling. "The concerns are . . . that there's a loss of attraction or that they're not having sex as frequently," said Eli Kassis, a licensed therapist in Vestal, New York. "Sex is probably one of the more frequent topics that get brought up. . . . People feel okay and comfortable talking about *that* more than they are okay with telling their partner that they're putting on weight, or that they don't look as good anymore."

Kassis encourages couples to be up-front about it—to acknowledge that one or both of their bodies has changed, and then to find a way, with his help, to talk openly about the problem without triggering the other's defenses. "I give them a series of questions that are kind of hard to ask your spouse, and I tell them . . . to try to come up with a way to say it, without making them defensive." For the last exercise, he asks the partner who is concerned about a spouse's weight gain to "tell your partner that [he's] getting fat." Kassis warns them every time that it's the ultimate test. When a couple has mastered that discussion without tripping into a fight or hurting a spouse's feelings, "then you've truly gotten it down."

Couples of all sizes often walk into therapy complaining that one partner wants to have sex more frequently than the other; "desire discrepancy" is a normal development in long-term relationships. However, when one or both members of a couple are overweight, therapists say the desire discrepancy can often be traced to mild to severe body image disturbances, and to one spouse's fear that her partner is no longer attracted to her. Even when a spouse like Dana's husband, Larry, wraps his arms tenderly and eagerly around his wife's waist, or Eric's wife reassures him of her interest, those encouragements are often not enough for overweight people to overcome the paralyzing fear of rejection or the isolation of self-loathing.

One of the tenets about body image is that "there can be such a disconnect between how a woman sees her own body and how other people see it," said obesity researcher Dr. David Sarwer. "She can almost be tone deaf to the messages of other people. It really doesn't matter if he . . . [tells] . . . her every morning that she is beautiful, and he treats her kindly and has never been demeaning or disrespectful in terms of comments to her. If, in her mind, she is concerned with her own body, she potentially has a difficult time relaxing and enjoying her own sexuality in that way, regardless of how complimentary or supportive he may be."

The image of how our body looks is fixed in our brain, and our zealous beliefs about what others *must* think of us are firmly held. "People can really get stuck," continued Dr. Sarwer, and "have a lack of flexibility in really being able to hear a comment from somebody else and let it sink in, and say, 'Okay, well, that is some objective feedback that maybe I am attractive to him. Maybe he *does* find me sexually arousing, and he *does* get turned on by the sight of my body.' But if in your own mind, you are thinking, 'Who would do this?' [Who would be attracted to me?], then all the compliments in the world aren't going to matter." The most powerful force is what people feel about themselves, said Alexandra Brewis Slade,

PhD, the director of the School of Human Evolution and Social Change and the director of Obesity Solutions at Arizona State University in Tempe. "Society is telling them in every which way [that] they are inadequate."

Correcting for sexual desire, in these cases at least, comes down to the hard work of repairing self-esteem and counseling the wounded spouses, like Eric and Dana, to learn to extend some generosity to themselves.

Dr. Sarwer remembers getting a phone call a few years ago from a woman whom he had evaluated for her bariatric surgery when she was in her late thirties. The two hadn't spoken since then, but she called to tell him that when she was in her twenties and early thirties, she didn't stand up for herself and would let men take advantage of her. "I didn't know how to ask for things that I wanted in a relationship, and I want to learn how to date," the woman told Dr. Sarwer. "So she came back in, and we worked on communication skills and dating skills and kind of role-played how she would act on a date." The woman ended up dating a man she met online. Dr. Sarwer picks up the story. "About a year later, around the holidays, I get this holiday card from her which is a picture of her and her boyfriend who's now her husband at their wedding on a beach in the Caribbean." It was one of the most rewarding cases of his career.

* * *

ERIC is a case study in just how difficult it is to set perturbed minds to rest. He's been an eager disciple; he's gone to marriage therapy as well as individual therapy to learn how to communicate his messy emotions and restore the trust in his relationship. He and his wife have enthusiastically pursued hobbies and outings, he's trying to focus on eating healthfully and exercising, and he has made it a practice to unhitch his sexual confidence from his weight.

"Now I'm more self-aware. Now I understand it. Now I'm able to look at it and go, 'My libido is really low right now because I've been eating too much and I'm feeling bad about myself.' I can express it to my wife and let her know I'm feeling this way."

For all the therapy, Eric said that his wife has played the most important role in helping him if not win the battle, at least see things more clearly. "I think it was really more my wife saying to me that, 'I love you and I'm attracted to you, regardless of your weight.' That was something I needed to hear and something I needed to believe. So, I don't think it was really the therapist or even the weight program; it was my partner letting me know that regardless of what I weighed." Eric laughs sweetly as his wife leans forward, as if she's taking a bow. "She's taking credit," he says, smiling. "Regardless of what I weigh, she will love me, be attracted to me, want to have sex with me, and enjoy having sex with me. And I think that was what helped me decouple my weight from my desire to have sex." He sounded triumphant for a moment. "Though I still struggle with it," he added. "I still struggle with it."

Eric doubts he'll ever be able to quiet the voices entirely. "I think it's there, and it will always be there. I think it's too deep-rooted and ingrained."

* * *

DANA Englehardt found it impossible to detach her weight from her desire to have sex with her husband, Larry; there was too much history wrapped up in her skin, fat, and bones. She wanted to make a break from her body; she wanted to cut away at it and drain the self-hatred out. She needed to go back to the beginning, when her body took shape, and understand how she came to view it with such vitriol.

In the early morning hours, Dana drove down the main street of Belmont, California, in an aging taupe-colored minivan to the hospital where she worked. As the cardiac catheterization lab's head prep nurse, she spent her day taking the medical histories of heart patients, drawing their blood, and getting their IVs started. Most of the patients she prepped were overweight and obese men, and she could often be found stooped over hospital beds, pushing their big bellies out of the way in order to shave the men's pubic hair. A long, thin tube would be threaded into a blood vessel through their groin; then a cardiologist would insert dye into the catheter, and the patient's coronary arteries, gummed up with plaque, would glow in the x-ray image.

Dana believed firmly that she would one day end up as a patient in her own lab and that her girlfriends at work would have to shave her and prep her for an angioplasty. Either her heart or her knees would give out, and she would have to quit work—then how would she get health insurance for her boys and Larry, who worked as a building contractor? No insurance company would cover her son Caleb, who had autism. Larry couldn't handle the mortgage alone; where would they live? Her mind often raced like this. The consequences of her own obesity were not hyperbolic distractions, but the rational adding up of a punishing mathematical equation. Her work as a nurse, which she had doggedly pursued against the odds, was yet another reminder of her own weakness.

When she wasn't swirling in scenarios of coming catastrophe, Dana ran the prep room with quiet confidence and efficiency. She had always been a hard worker; she started babysitting when she was 12, followed by an after-school job at a day care center. When she turned 16, as soon as she was allowed, she got a job at the mall. By her senior year in high school, she was working every day. Her ambition then was to become a roadie in a rock band. But fear kept her tethered to Belmont's sleepy streets. "I was never brave enough to move out of town" was how Dana remembered her decision to stay put.

Dana's father delivered bread, and her mother was an unsatisfied homemaker who had been born to Italian immigrants and raised in South San Francisco. Dana's Italian grandmother paid for music lessons and a modest Catholic school tuition; she made delicious homemade ravioli for Dana and her two brothers.

In the 1970s, Belmont and other towns on the San Francisco Peninsula had yet to be transformed into Silicon Valley; the homes were drab attempts at modernist architecture, with olive and mustard painted wood siding and chalet-style roofs. The local kids didn't strive to rise up and out.

No one had heard of an "epidemic" of obesity then. Vigilant actuaries at life insurance companies had figured out as early as the 1930s that excess weight was a pretty good predictor of early death. They used weight data to set premiums, and by the mid-twentieth century scientists were becoming ever more certain that the creeping tide of obesity had something to do with the increasing rate of cardiovascular disease.[10] However, in Dana's childhood, obesity was widely viewed as a psychiatric illness, and in towns like Belmont, plump kids were a rarity. Besides, there was a war in Vietnam to contend with and form an opinion about, and by sixth grade, Dana grew breasts and then the entire world, or at least the focus of the local boys, seemed to turn to them.

The only person who seemed to ignore Dana's new breasts was her mother. "My mom was in complete denial about puberty," Dana recalled. "I wasn't wearing a bra, and I was moving all over. I had armpit hair and felt embarrassed. Finally, my mom took me to get a bra and allowed me to shave." By then the pattern was ingrained; she had decided the best way to camouflage her breasts was to slump her shoulders forward. She stills stands this way today, almost 4 decades later.

In photos from her preteen years, Dana's silky blonde hair falls in a neat shoulder-length bob. When Dana looks at these photos now, she sees a healthy, normal-weight girl: There she is dressed up as a cheerleader for Halloween in a white turtleneck and miniskirt; in a photo from her eighth-grade graduation, she stands proudly in a pretty, above-the-knee floral dress and a string of pearls in front of a stone hearth. She said that her stomach would "pooch a little bit" and she envied the "skinny girls," but her body wasn't as fat as it is in the memories she has kept of that time. She was fleshy in the way that girls were fleshy in the 1970s, before the fashion turned to shoulder pads and fitness.

Dana didn't use her breasts to get boys the way she saw other girls doing. In eighth grade, she kissed a ninth-grader named Kevin, but they would have no future together; her parents had forbidden her to date, and the nuns at her Catholic school made any kind of intimacy sound shameful. She remembers receiving a book from her parents about female anatomy; her older brother had gotten *Everything You Always Wanted to Know about*

Sex (but Were Afraid to Ask). "I wanted to know, but I didn't want to do anything," recalled Dana.

According to the social exchange theorists, Dana entered the teenage dating market perfectly positioned; she had much to trade. By the mid-1970s, when she transferred to Carlmont High School, a public school in Belmont, the academic study of passionate love and sexual desire was still in its infancy. But to the social scientists beginning to decipher the dynamics of young courtship, Dana was a good candidate for success. In ninth grade, Dana thought she'd hit pay dirt at her new public high school; she was determined to find a boyfriend.

"He had to be a fox" was her guiding principle. "Looks were everything, and if he drove, that was even better."

The first fox had a beard. She wasn't ready for sex, and her opinion of penises was, she remembers, "Like ick, I'm not touching that. I didn't want to get pregnant and disappoint my dad." It wasn't until she walked in on her brother and his girlfriend that it even occurred to her that sex was something unmarried people could do. A few boyfriends later, when she was a junior in high school and 16 years old, Dana's curiosity about sex ripened. She and her boyfriend hatched a plan: "My neighbors hired me to water their plants, and they were away. So we went to their house." They snuck in through the garage and left all the lights off. "I remember being really nervous," Dana said. The intercourse part of the adventure was disappointing—she had wanted it to be like in the movies—and they broke up shortly after. "I was ashamed. You can't redo that again."

Adolescence is a series of moments, all building toward the establishment of the self: the little girl in a navy peacoat with a yellow patent leather purse standing next to her ravioli-making grandmother; the proud and smiling girl posing in a red communion robe, her shoulders beginning to cave forward, unsure how to face womanhood. At some undetectable point where all of these moments become part of a stream, which becomes part of a river that is then named and identified and put on the map, Dana became the person she would spend the next 2 decades fighting against—and ultimately, now in her fifties, trying to undo.

* * *

Looking back, you can spot when someone's life would turn out the way it did—when a boundless, unwritten future begins to look preordained. For Dana, that moment was in 1978, when she was a junior at Carlmont and she met a dreamy high school dropout named Doug. He was 2½ years older, and lean and strong, with brown hair that parted in the middle and flared out in layers of silky feathers. "I was so in love with this boy," Dana told me. "I thought he was really good-looking; he had his own apartment, and he liked hanging around my family." Doug's mom liked Dana, too, and she relished the acceptance.

By her senior year, Dana and Doug decided they wanted to get married, and they got engaged when she was 17. Dana had discovered polyester, and for her senior prom she wore a sky-blue, long-sleeved dress that plunged in the front and hugged her curves. Doug wore a black tuxedo with an oversize bow tie, a ruffled dress shirt, and a white carnation boutonniere. A year later, she wore the same dress for their honeymoon. Doug had been playful at the wedding, sliding a garter up past Dana's knee; in the photograph, he looks off to the side with a mischievous, bawdy grin. She sits on a rented ballroom chair festooned in white lace and a veil of tulle, flashing an unstoppable, toothy smile.

Once they were married, Dana saw quickly that her shyness left her vulnerable. "I didn't really know how to speak up for myself," she remembered. "It never really evolved from a teenage love affair." After 2 years, when she was 19 years old, Dana gave birth to her first son. Soon after, Doug lost his job, and he picked up some shifts at a grocery store. They worked opposite schedules, but Dana tried to make time to satisfy her husband sexually, believing that it was her "duty." Dana was 30 pounds overweight by then; she made frequent stops at Taco Bell. Her once oval face and thin nose, framed with feathered blonde hair, had broadened; her neck thickened and loosened into her shoulders; and when she sat, her arms had to make way for her breasts. When it came to her weight, she said, "I was very prickly. I'd clam up and start to cry." Dana had always been generous with others, but she had no empathy for herself. She walked around in a blanket of shame: "I thought I was really fat, that I wasn't worth people's time, that I'm a second-class citizen. Back then," she added, "there weren't many fat people."

Her mom was always after her to lose weight, and even paid for Dana to try Nutrisystem. It worked, but still Doug would harp on her. "Yeah, now she only looks 6 months pregnant," she remembers her husband saying. He was a smoker, living off cigarettes and coffee, and getting skinnier. "He hadn't chosen another one of my girlfriends," she said in trying to make sense of why she stayed with him. "He chose me."

Then, Doug stopped coming home after his shifts at the grocery store. The home phone would ring and the caller would hang up when Dana answered. She suspected he was seeing someone else, and when he did come home, he wouldn't look her in the eye. She told him, "If you want a divorce, you should just tell me." He left his wedding ring on the dresser with a note that said, "I'm out looking for an apartment."

Dana's parents felt bad for her; they helped her find a lawyer, who handled the divorce and child custody.

Timidity gave way to tenacity, and at age 22, with a certificate in dental assisting from a local college, Dana refused to fall any further. With Doug out of her life, she had to learn how to take care of herself and her young son; what life held for her came into a sharper focus. "It changed who I used to be. It used to be, 'Oh, he's so cute.' Now, I wanted to see how they treated their mother."

Her own sexual yearnings were not something that Dana spent much time considering. She had felt the rush of infatuation, to be sure, but the swoon seemed more in her head than somewhere farther down. She had peered at every inch of her body, taking great offense at its failings; she had offered herself up to boyfriends and a lousy ex-husband; she had felt the exhaustion of birthing a child.

But then she met a man at her church. He was 4 years older, and when they kissed, she wanted to keep going. "Before Bill, I hadn't felt sexual urges," she recalled, sitting under the shade of the tall cypress in her backyard. Bill was a virgin up until their wedding night—a courteous virgin with a scientific mind and a generous heart. With little money to spend on a honeymoon, the couple drove less than an hour away to the coastal town of Half Moon Bay to spend the night in a hotel. "He was nervous," Dana remembers. "We drank some champagne. We fumbled together that first night. He didn't know how long foreplay was supposed to go on."

That sex could be enjoyable surprised Dana; her mother had often said to her that men had it easy. *They have a built-in sex machine and a maid,* her mother would say. Dana had heard of "frigid women," and previously she had suspected she was one of them, whatever that meant. Having a tender and erotic sexual life with Bill felt like a discovery—like her life might not turn out as her mother had predicted. Bill was mildly over-weight when they married, and he and Dana gained weight together. He blamed her good cooking, but in truth she felt out of control around food; she couldn't stop reaching for something to eat. Bill knew that Dana was sensitive about her eating habits and her weight, and he encouraged her to get in shape. When it came to sex, Dana trusted her husband. She felt comfortable with him; they were both reserved but affectionate, and there was an ease and selflessness that comforted her. Every week, they found time to make love, but as Dana got bigger—she held the bulk of her weight in her belly—orgasms became more and more difficult. She couldn't move the way she wanted to.

A number of years later, when their youngest son was still an infant, Bill succumbed to cancer. Dana was by his side when he died.

* * *

DANA knew how she looked to people who passed her on the street: a haggard widow carrying a 6-month-old and dragging around her bulg-ing body. She couldn't imagine that anyone would ever find her attrac-tive again. Of course, she had looming practical problems that were obvious to everyone around her: raising three boys on her own, a house with a mortgage, and no college degree. But her mind often wandered to darker, more private fears—to a future in which she was alone and starved for physical affection.

When Bill died, the couple had just finished putting an addition on their home that sits along a busy street in Belmont. Larry's brother had gotten the construction job, and Larry worked on the project. Dana was home on maternity leave and found it easy to chat with Larry when he stopped by to do finish work on the house. She thought he'd make a good match for one of her girlfriends.

Dana's youngest, Caleb, was a year old when Dana called Larry to see if he was interested in working on some side jobs at her brother's new home in nearby La Honda. As a thank-you, Larry asked Dana out to dinner. After the dinner, he returned home and told his roommate, "I really had a great time with Dana. I think I might just ask her out."

They went out again the next week, and then again after that. "We just had a lot of fun together," said Larry, who is naturally outgoing and flirtatious. He was in his midforties and a lifelong bachelor when he met Dana; he had dated plenty, but Dana was the first person he wanted to get serious with.

Dana assumed Larry just felt sorry for her; after all, she had been widowed with an infant and was raising two older boys on her own. After the stress of losing Bill, she weighed under 200 pounds, which, in her view, was "not so bad." By then she'd made it a point in her life, after her disastrous love affair with Doug and the heartbreaking loss of Bill, not to make any special concessions about her weight for Larry. "I was a mature woman with three kids. I didn't want to goof around dating," she said. "I wanted to make sure he really wanted to go out with me and not some cute chickie." She remembers telling Larry that she didn't want to pretend that she was going to lose weight simply to have a relationship with him.

Larry had had enough of the "cute chickies," or at least the ones who picked at their food. He had dated mostly thin women up until then. "It was kind of nice to spend money on a woman who actually ate the meal," he said. "I never really looked at what she was eating. I was too busy talking, and I tend to do a lot of that. That's one of my downfalls." Luckily for Larry, Dana found his talkativeness endearing.

In the wedding photos, Larry wears a black tuxedo and brushes his cheek against Dana's tousled blonde hair; his eyes are closed and his mouth parted in a blissful smile. His hands are placed firmly—confidently—around Dana's wide waist. She looks at the camera, grasping a bouquet of ivory- and peach-colored roses, and offers a soft, calm smile. She is wearing a simple ivory crepe dress, and a crystal-encrusted jewel rests at the base of her neck. Larry loved buying jewelry for his new wife.

After the wedding, the pace of their lives stayed hectic, and Dana's weight crept back up. She and Larry now had three children to raise, including a young son who was showing signs of autism. Dana's job at the hospital cath lab meant she had to wake before dawn, and Larry did much of the cooking at night. Dana joked that her husband's favorite cuisine was "truck stop food."

Every time she crossed back over the 200-pound mark—she was only 5-foot-3—Dana would give up and her confidence would plunge. Larry remembered, "When we would go on our cruises, she was having a hard time keeping up with Caleb and me when we could go on shore leaves." On a trip to Barcelona, Larry thought his obese wife, with her aching, swollen knees, would surely expire climbing the steps of Antoni Gaudí's famous basilica, the Sagrada Família. "God bless her," Larry said. "She made it about a third of the way up, and then she quit." They both worried that Dana's knees would mean the end of their world travels.

His wife's sleep apnea had worsened, as well. "We would go to church, and she's falling asleep during the sermons." Larry chuckled. "That's understandable sometimes, but I mean literally when they're singing, she's falling asleep. Or we would just be driving to the church, and she'd go to sleep." Dana was exhausted all the time.

"If you put 140 pounds on your back and walk around all day and do all the things you normally do, you're going to be tired at night," said

Dana. "And you're grumpy. And I know it affected my family." Dana is still bothered by her youngest son's most vivid memories of her. Caleb said what he remembers most about his mother from that time is how she would often lose her temper.

Inside Dana's head, the running commentary never stopped. She would think, *You've gotta do something about your weight. You look terrible. You're unhealthy.* "It just goes through your head constantly, and you just get really sick of it." She had a hard time reaching over her belly in the garden and soon stopped helping outside; she stopped volunteering at her children's schools; she stopped going out as much with friends. She had become her most—and only—vocal critic. "I'm doing this to myself," she said. "Why can't I stop?"

Dana's weight gain didn't bother Larry. He had married her when she was heavy, and to him, the additional 60 pounds or so that she put on after the wedding had been a gradual expansion of an already big woman. He didn't spend time thinking about her weight. "Once I decided to put that out of my mind and allow the relationship to grow with the person I was falling in love with, her personality and how much fun we had together, it just really wasn't an issue."

Larry found losing weight easy. He was tall, at 6-foot-2, and his doctor had recently warned him that if he didn't lose a little bit of weight, he risked developing diabetes. It was the first time in his life that he'd ever tried to diet, and he lost 35 pounds without much thought.

As Dana's body ballooned, Larry continued to desire her. "I maintained the same level of interest," he said. "I was never uninterested." He found that he even liked to play with the rolls of fat on her stomach. "She would tell me not to do that, and so it would make me a little perturbed, but she's my wife. I'm not going to make a scene out of it, and if she doesn't want to, then it's something that I have to deal with, okay? I didn't realize that she was having problems because of her weight. I didn't realize there was a mental issue or whatever you want to say, an emotional issue."

Dana listened closely to Larry's version of the events. They had been sitting on the couch in their living room, telling me this story.

"I told you that I didn't," Dana said, turning to Larry. "Why I wasn't interested in sex."

"Yeah, I just . . . "

"And I told you not to touch my stomach fat, and you did anyway."

Dana laughed lightly. She couldn't fathom, really, why anyone would want to be with her, even though Larry was still clearly interested. When she looked in the mirror, she could only see a "monster." On the rare occasions when she forced herself to have sex, the mechanics of the act itself were awkward. "If you try to have sex with a beach ball between you, it's not easy. It's like when you're pregnant." Some bigger couples in highly functioning relationships might experiment to find more comfortable positions, but by then all Dana wanted to do was turn away from sex entirely. "I just kind of shut that part of me down."

On occasion, Larry tried to get intimate, but his wife's rejections made him feel vulnerable. "I still tried," he said. "But my feeling was, I didn't wait 'til I was 44 to get married to end something. When I said I loved her for better or worse, I mean, it sounds corny, but I meant for better or worse. And if she had a problem, she knows how to handle it. But I kind of thought it might be me."

The guilt was the worst part. Dana firmly believed she wasn't meeting her husband's needs. It seemed like she and Larry were more like roommates than husband and wife. They became physically—and emotionally—estranged. Dana didn't feel like she could talk to her husband about the disturbances in her inner world. "I knew that this was wrong," Dana said. "But I couldn't fix it on my own. I didn't seek help for that until much later."

Much of this went unsaid. Most nights, they would turn off the television around 9 o'clock and climb the stairs to their bedroom. Dana would pass by a mirror in the bathroom that was affixed to the wall just high enough so she could only see her tired eyes. She would slip off her clothes and scramble into her cotton nightgown in her daily ritual of embarrassment and shame, and then crawl into bed and put on her CPAP mask and roll over to her side of the bed, exhausted, relieved, and frightened.

* * *

DANA's health problems terrified her, and she feared she was becoming disabled. She worried that she would have to quit her job, go on disability, and lose her family's health insurance.

She also couldn't stop thinking that she was an "unlikable fat girl." Dana had obese friends who seemed less bothered by their bodies, but she couldn't seem to shake the self-imposed label. When she looks back now at pictures of her childhood, she sees a girl who was 10 pounds overweight. Over the years, no matter how overweight Dana was, she "always felt horrible, like it was an awful lot of weight, even when it was only 5 or 10 pounds."

With children of her own, Dana could begin to see how her own parents had shaped the way she saw her body. Beginning in high school, they weighed Dana and her brother every Saturday. As the week came to a close, the anxiety would set in. "I would get really anxious and worried. 'Did I eat too much?'" she remembers thinking.

Her parents were healthy and slim. Hardworking and economical, they wanted their children to make sound decisions. The weekly weigh-ins weren't meant to be punitive, she imagines, but her teenage self felt embarrassed and insecure. "As a teenager, I made some bad decisions, but was lucky enough to come out relatively unscathed," Dana wrote in a letter she penned to her deceased mother at her therapist's urging. "I know you and Dad probably agonized over my mistakes. Dad pointed out that all my friends were losers, and without pointing out that I was better than my behavior was, I could only surmise that I was a loser, too." Her parents hadn't been overly cruel; they wanted their daughter to make something of her life and, like most parents, weren't quite sure what levers to push. However, the pain that Dana felt from her mother's judgment hasn't eased; her willingness to trace her broken self-image is remarkable and courageous. There is a photo of Dana from the early 1980s in a strapless bathing suit; she is sitting on a plastic folding chair on a grassy field overlooking a lake, holding one of her young sons. In the letter to her mother, she remembers everything about that day. "When you told me that you cried about my appearance after the camping trip with the gang, I was stunned. It further blew my perception of myself. I was only 25 to 30 pounds over-weight, yet [I] felt like a circus freak."

She was grateful that her mother died before she reached her highest weight of 265 pounds. "My only atonement is that you never saw me when I was that big. That is such a sad statement," she wrote. She needed to tell her parents that their focus on her weight had led to lifelong problems, particularly her firm belief that she was never good enough and that she didn't deserve a good life. Dana is not a bitter and resentful woman. In fact, she is kind, warm, and welcoming. A smiling and eager parishioner at church, she is a hostess to raucous family dinners in her backyard with her brother and her father, who still lives a 5-minute drive away in the house where she faced off every week against a scale. Still, she doesn't sign the letter to her mother with any kind of closing. No "Love." No "Sincerely." Just "Dana."

* * *

EVERY day, Dana gathered evidence that the view she held of herself— that she was an unlovable fat girl—had to be right. When people looked at her swollen shape, Dana imagined they either felt pity or disgust. At the supermarket, she could see other customers looking straight through her as if she didn't exist. No one chatted with her in line or held doors open for her. She found it hard to wear clothes that didn't look shabby or dishev-eled; she could see that the world trusted those who looked well groomed.

Instead, it felt like the world just slapped her around. "Or maybe I just had a scowl on my face," Dana concedes.

At the hospital, on her feet much of the day, she perspired constantly, and she imagined her patients thought she was stricken with nerves and would surely fumble the delicate procedures entrusted to her. This was not just her imagination: Nurses who were overweight and obese reported in a study that they felt self-conscious about their size, and that patients had made rude comments about their weight. [11] (Nurses themselves are critical of obese patients. A review of the research in 2006 found that they often view obese adult patients as lazy, unable to control their urges, and non-compliant with medical advice. [12])

Dana imagined that everyone despised her.

As part of an exercise with a therapist years later, she wrote in a journal that she believed Larry had married her because he didn't want to be alone, and that she had provided the longtime bachelor with a ready-made family. "And after I read that, I thought, 'Well, wait a minute. Where did that come from?'" She'd had no suspicions about Larry's intentions when they started dating; she had been certain of their love. "It's just [that] my confidence got chipped down so far that it skewed my view of things," said Dana. Her obesity was threatening to undo her marriage.

If only she could rise up out of this body that was failing her, and walk away. She was beginning to think that her only option was bariatric surgery. Then, she was certain that the tensions with Larry would ease, desire would fill up her body, and she would want to be wanted.

* * *

Was there something about marriage itself that made some bigger people especially miserable? Why was it that some heavier people seemed to find refuge in marriage, while for others, wedlock magnified their problems with weight and sex?

Despite the fact that a majority of people in the United States have become overweight, the woman most desired in the marriage market remains slender and attractive; the ideal man is still trim and muscular. [13] Scientists poring over millions of online dating records and conducting experiments on weight preference in courtship continue to find that heavier people remain at a disadvantage when it comes to finding romantic love. [14] The desire for a thin date is so strong that in a ranking of six potential sexual partners—a healthy person, someone missing a left arm, a person in a wheelchair, a person with a history of suicide attempts, someone with a history of sexually transmitted disease, and someone who is 100 pounds overweight—hundreds of college students rate the obese sexual partner as their last choice. Young men are even more definitive than women about their rankings.[15] (In one odd twist, a pair of psychologists at University College of London found that men actually preferred photographs of fuller-shaped women when the men were hungry as compared to when their bellies were full.[16])

Healthy-weight men and women surely have an advantage in the marriage market and better odds of pairing off with a prized fiancée, but just wait until the wedding bells ring.

Social scientists and medical researchers have long regarded marriage as a positive health benefit: Married couples smoke less,[17] they live longer, and they have a lower risk of heart attack. (This does not appear to be the case for married black men and women, who fare the same whether they are living together or are legally married.[18])

The one thing marriage is not good for is girth. Thinner people might have an advantage in attracting a mate, but marriage, it seems, extracts a price. While brides in the United States tend to lose a modest amount of weight before their wedding days,[19] couples tracked over the course of their marriage gained more weight than those who remained unmarried.[20] People who are married, especially men, tend to be heavier than those who are not. (There are some fascinating differences in these patterns when researchers look more closely at race, ethnicity, and gender.[21] In one example, separation seems especially hard on black women: They are twice as likely to be overweight as married black women, a fact that scholars attribute to the instability of marriage and the burden of poverty in African American communities.)

Still, just about everyone in the United States eventually ties the knot: According to demographers, four out of five Americans will get hitched at some point in their lifetimes.[22] And that includes heftier people who had been left behind in the dating game.

Marriage researchers have long found evidence that body mass index is highly correlated between husbands and wives:[23] When researchers looked at snapshots of married people, spouses tended to be paired off with someone of a similar body size. But was that because people tended to choose romantic partners with similar body types and similar behaviors— in other words, they were both big from the beginning when they paired up[24]—or was it the case that by living together in the same household, they adopted the same habits and ate the same (perhaps less healthy) foods, and their bodies began to mirror one another? (Researchers call this spousal concordance, in which we fall in line with each other.)

It was difficult for researchers to untangle the effects of "assortative mating" and the "shared household environment"; they didn't fully understand the mechanism by which the development of obesity in one partner ended up increasing the chances that a spouse would also become obese. In one attempt to answer that question, a pair of researchers in the department of nutrition at the University of North Carolina at Chapel Hill followed a nationally representative, racially diverse sample of young men and women who were just transitioning from single and dating to marriage (and for some who were unlucky in love, from single and dating back to single).[25]

The results mirrored earlier findings: The longer a person lived with a romantic partner, the more likely they were to adopt behaviors that encourage obesity, and to become obese. For men, the effect was even greater: Longer live-in romances significantly increased the chances they would tip the scales into obesity. For women, it was the *transition* period into a romantic relationship that caused the most weight gain. (Pregnant women were excluded from the study.) The researchers surmised that women were impacted "through increased social obligations encouraging consumption of regular meals and larger portion sizes, resulting in increased energy intake." Married women had also been shown to get less physical exercise[26] and tended to worry less about maintaining their weight in order to attract a mate.[27] It was true that heavier people paired off with heavier people, but the UNC results suggested that it was the rite of marriage itself and setting up house that put young, otherwise healthy-weight couples onto the path toward weight gain.

* * *

A restaurant on a Saturday evening. Seattle. Boise. Houston. Kansas City. Scranton. Albany. It doesn't matter where. You look around and see dozens of young couples enjoying a romantic dinner. Their wedding rings are still shiny, memories of their ceremony and honeymoon still fresh. You notice some of the couples are a little heavy, others are quite overweight, and some are obese. Can you guess which of these couples is the most satisfied in their marriage?

The answer isn't as simple as "the couple that weighs the least."

The question has stumped social scientists, in part because the connection of body weight to romantic relationships looks like a mess of snarled tree branches: One branch is body image; another self-esteem; another the emotions of day-to-day insults that obese people tend to experience in public and in their jobs; still another the lower earnings that they, on average, tend to earn. There are profound social consequences to being obese that impact a relationship.[28]

Social scientists and economists have devised theoretical models that attempt to account for the human behaviors that arise when weight intersects with romance. The models are endless—the investment model, the shared risk model, the crisis model, the mating market model—and they make wildly divergent predictions. In addition, psychologists, sociologists, economists, and others have made great efforts to bring the "science" into the social sciences.

The models are fascinating, and they reveal a lot about the outlook of their authors. In the theoretical models that try to explain the relationship between marriage and body mass, there are two competing camps: the optimists versus the cynics. The health regulation model predicts that happy couples make for a happy and healthy home; that is, individuals who are satisfied in their relationship do things together that promote being healthy, and they are less likely to gain weight. So how does the model explain weight gain, particularly for couples in the first years of marriage? If the health regulation model is valid, weight gain should be a warning sign of distress: Strain in a marriage would disrupt healthy behaviors, and spouses who were dissatisfied would pack on the pounds. If that were true, the spread of obesity would signal profound and widespread discontent in American marriages.

Then there is the model that turns on a darker, more cunning human instinct: the mating market model. It rests on the notion that the reason we keep our weight down is to attract a mate. Once that goal is attained—and the legal papers signed and slices of wedding cake frozen—spouses are no longer motivated to ward off weight gain. As one woman in upstate New York said, "You've got your man; pass the pie, please."[29]

However, the underlying mechanism of the mating market model is always at work; an unhappy and hefty spouse who is considering leaving her marriage may decide to lose weight in anticipation of the need to attract a new lover. In that case, weight loss—rather than weight gain—would be a warning sign of marital distress.

So which model is right?

To answer that question, a group of inventive researchers recruited 169 newlywed couples without children and checked in with them every 6 months for 4 years. The couples reported their height and weight; they rated the stress level in their marriage; and they made a notation if they had thoughts of leaving their marriage, and if they had taken any steps toward separation and divorce.

In 2013, the authors reported their findings in the journal *Health Psychology*.[30] Those placing bets on the mating market model won: "When individuals or their spouses were more satisfied than usual, those individuals gained weight, and when they or their spouses were less satisfied than usual, they lost weight." This was after controlling for a number of stresses, like pregnancy and depression. "Consistent with the idea that spouses are more likely to lose or maintain weight when confronted by the prospect of needing to seek a new mate," the authors wrote, "these associations were mediated by changes in the degree to which spouses contemplated divorce."

This is perhaps a broader phenomenon, although the evidence is rudimentary: Married people in European countries with high divorce rates weigh less than those in countries with lower divorce rates.[31] Perhaps those hankering to lose weight are preparing themselves to reenter the marriage market.

* * *

IN the last year of what would be an 8-year marriage, Frances signed up for water aerobics classes with her friends and started to work out at the YMCA in her town in Washington State. She had married her husband a year after he talked her up at the local library where she was working as an assistant librarian. She was slightly bigger when they married, but not obese. After the wedding, she said, "The diet and the exercise went out the window again, and I ate anything and everything." While she was growing up in Michigan, then Alabama, her family had ridiculed her, saying she would never attract anyone because she was overweight. "Perhaps once I married," Frances said, "I felt as though the pressure was off me." She gradually gained weight over the course of her marriage, topping out at 297 pounds. Her husband, a hefty man with a cavalier attitude about diet and exercise, also gained weight, going from a 42-inch waist to a 60-inch waist. "We were both enablers," she said. "We would enforce for one another that 'we deserved a treat,' that we should enjoy ourselves. Food was most often that outlet."

Five years into the relationship, Frances was miserable; her husband had gained so much weight that he could no longer work, and money became an enormous stress. He batted away any suggestion that his morbid obesity was causing them problems. "When he broke the driver's seat in our car," Frances said, "he angrily shouted about how the Japanese made flimsy little cars that weren't meant for Americans, and so they should not be imported." Her husband developed edema in his legs and chronic respiratory problems. He slept, ate, and laid on the couch, watching television, and he showed no interest, Frances said, in being intimate with her, which was "a huge source of contention in our marriage."

Gradually, Frances believed that her marriage was something to endure. "I stayed because I felt that due to my weight, I would be unattractive to anyone else."

And then, before she left her husband, she inexplicably signed up for exercise classes, and she began to lose weight. In looking back at her marriage and at previous relationships, Frances, who is 32 years old, wonders if she somehow anticipated her return to the marriage market. "There's a pattern where I am slimmer when I am single, or perhaps when I subconsciously perceive that I might become single."

* * *

PRIOR research on newlyweds revealed that husbands or wives who lost weight were feeling less fulfilled and might be planning to exit a marriage, and couples who stayed together and gained weight reported less marital stress. But that analysis only proved the correlation between weight and satisfaction; it didn't answer the question: Among those couples spotted at a restaurant, which are the most satisfied in their marriages?

Excess weight clearly handicapped women, and to a lesser extent men, in the search for a spouse. But once married, was body mass index a reliable indicator of marital satisfaction? As more couples became overweight and obese in the late 1990s and 2000s, the question seemed especially relevant considering that marriage rates—the percentage of people tying the knot—were falling in the United States. In 2008, a group of economists said it was imperative to determine if there was "a link between the two trends."[32]

The evidence of any connection, however, was inconclusive. Different studies returned contradictory results: Thinner women and their husbands were happier in their relationships than larger women and their husbands;[33] heavy men were more contented in their relationships than smaller men;[34] or there was absolutely no connection between body mass index and marital satisfaction for men or women.[35]

Why were the findings so glaringly inconsistent?

It wasn't until 2011 that a pair of social psychologists in Knoxville,

Tennessee, figured out that they had been looking at the question the wrong way. What if it wasn't the weight of each spouse that mattered, but the difference between the two?

* * *

DINA Legg reached for the cell phone on her manicure table and swiped through a slideshow of intricately painted nails: a family of owls, a bat perched on a snarled tree limb, a shiny black Santa Claus belt encrusted in crystals. "That's my favorite," Dina said. Halloween was approaching, though, and Dina's client, a holiday enthusiast, decided she needed to get in the mood and opted for the bat in the spooky tree. Dina zoomed in on her phone and studied a photo of the scene; she could draw almost anything on a nail once she'd gotten a good look at it. Perhaps she would be an artist, she imagined, if she had more time.

Outside, the midmorning sun was warming up the asphalt along Main Street in Grasonville, a small, middle-class town overlooked by the tourists arriving at the Eastern Shore of Maryland on a nearby highway. The parking lot behind the salon was often one of the busiest places in town. Well-maintained SUVs came and went on the half hour; manicures and pedicures were a necessary luxury in otherwise modest lives.

Dina had gone out of her way to decorate the salon tastefully, with artful tile floors and desert-brown paint. Bottles of gold, fuchsia, and moss-green nail polish were neatly displayed on a black metal étagère near a pair of padded spa chairs with whirlpool footbaths. For her long work-day, Dina wore comfy black, capri-length stretch pants and a black nylon salon gown that rustled when she moved. Her eyelids were painted with electric blue eye shadow and her lashes long and thick with mascara. Under the sharp glare of a clip-on lamp, with her shiny black hair piled on the crown of her head, Dina worked quickly and skillfully in a flurry of cotton balls, emery boards, and nail clippers. Bits of dead skin fell steadily onto the floor. At times, she reached past a picture of her 4-year-old twins wearing wigs made of red yarn and took a sip of a chocolate protein shake.

Talk at the salon turned to decorations: One woman had plans to erect a fake graveyard with tombstones outside her house; another client bemoaned the high price of the pellets used to make fog: "I wanted to do a fog machine, but those things are so expensive," she said.

Dina was a master of salon talk; she moved easily between confession, comedy, and the story arcs of her favorite television shows. She had a strong Eastern Shore accent, a regional cadence that mowed over syllables with such speed and force that conversations could sound like the rattling off of prizes at an auction. Words were stripped down to their most essential syllables and then melded together. Bal-ti-more became *Bawlmore*. Longtime clients at the salon entrusted Dina with juicy and private details about themselves and their husbands and other people's husbands; she listened closely and seemed to intuit when a woman needed to vent, and when what she really wanted was counsel.

Her advice was often plainspoken and direct. Inside the confessional along Grasonville's Main Street, Dina sensed when it was her turn to jump in. She talked easily and openly about herself, turning preoccupations and small grievances into conversation; perhaps she had overreacted in disciplining the twins after a recent ruckus, she posed to one client; she told another of a worker on her husband's construction crew who had been slacking off; she planned to get a breast reduction after she lost weight, she said after taking another sip of her shake, but until then she'd rather look down at her boobs than her stomach. Her honesty wasn't self-disparaging or apologetic. She'd gone to dinner in Annapolis with her girlfriends, and "the outside seats are made for your size people," she said, gesturing to a petite client, "not my size people. I was like, 'Can we move inside?'"

Settled in a chair at her manicure table, Dina straddled her legs wide to make way for her impressive thighs. Her body often got in the way: She would absentmindedly reach down with her hands and heave her breasts up onto the table; when doing pedicures, she had to hunch over her protruding belly to scrub and buff her clients' callused feet. (Many of her clients were also big women, and Dina was used to the sight of skin sores caused by diabetes.)

Maneuvering her body around was an annoyance, and Dina didn't like how heavy she'd gotten over the last few years. "I've always been able to put my foot up here," she told me, unsuccessfully attempting to thrust her leg onto her manicure table, "and do my toenails, and it's hard for me right now because my stomach has gotten so much bigger, and my legs have gotten so much bigger." In her late thirties, Dina didn't have any pressing health problems, but climbing stairs left her winded. "This last 26 pounds has really done a number on me where I can't do things. I mean, I can, but it's a lot harder."

Dina was an unapologetic realist, and she didn't despise herself in the way some overweight and obese people did. The salon was lined with mirrors, and she hadn't thought to move them or steer clear to escape her reflection. "I see my fat ass all the time; that doesn't bother me. I know I'm fat. But I don't have that sense of, 'Ah, I don't want to look at myself' or 'Ah, I'm so disgusting,'" she said. "Even though I'm fat, I still have self-worth. You know what I mean? I know I'm a good person. I know I have a good personality. I think I'm cute."

Being a "fat girl" was a description, not a judgment.

* * *

DINA's family moved across the Chesapeake Bay to Maryland's Eastern Shore in time for her to start middle school. Her body got noticeably chunkier, and her breasts were much bigger than those of the other girls her age. She made friends easily. "I was always hanging out with the crowd and having a good time. My friends always accepted me for what I was, and never shut me out because I was fat," she recalls. She remembers only two times other kids mocked her size. Once, in middle school, in the dressing room getting ready for gym class, a friend noticed her thick legs and sneered, "It must take you 40 times around your legs to shave 'cause your legs are so big." (She never liked gym class.) Another time in high school, she remembers spiriting down the hallway with a group of friends, when one boy called out, "Oh, here she comes! Boom! Boom! Boom!" as if she was a giant stomping through the castle halls. "Those are the only two times when I thought, 'You frickin' assholes,'" she said, laughing. (She and the boy became friends as adults.) The barbs bounced off her for the most part, leaving no discernible festering resentment that followed into adulthood.

Dina's father was a corrections officer and her mother ran a day care; their days may have been spent ordering their charges around jails and play groups, but at home, they gushed with support and love. Dina's mother, who was also heavy, never carped about her daughter's weight. "She's like, an 'I am woman, hear me roar' type of woman, and that's come down to me. Even though I'm fat, whatever," says Dina in mock derision. "Like pah-shah, I can do whatever you can do."

Dina's devil-may-care attitude belies her chaste sexual history: She has slept with only two men—her first serious high school boyfriend, and the second, Gene, her high school sweetheart whom she met at age 16. The two dated on and off, and during their time apart, Dina got plenty of attention; she loved to dance and have fun. "I've always had guys in the bar scene say, 'Hey, let's go dance!'" Still, she pined for Gene. At one point back then, her mother pulled Gene over outside his family's liquor store and berated him: "You either love my daughter or leave her the fuck alone, 'cause I'm sick and tired of hearin' her cry over your sorry ass."

They got back on track, and one Valentine's Day, Dina was standing in the kitchen when Gene came in and handed her a sweetly wrapped heart-shaped box.

"He says, 'Happy Valentine's Day,'" Dina recounts, "and then walks away and goes into the bathroom.

"'Am I to open this?'

"'Yup.'

"Just bein' honest," she laughs. "He's in there, taking a shit. I open it. It's my engagement ring.

"I say, 'Does this mean we're getting married?'

"'Yup. Set a date.'"

Nine months later, when they had both turned 25, they wed.

* * *

GENE had a ruddy, round face with reddish eyebrows; he kept his mustache and beard neatly trimmed and his head shaved bald. With his broad shoulders, wide chest, and round belly, he looked like a perpetually sunburned lineman. They each built their own businesses—his in construction, and Dina's at the salon—and each partner's success earned respect and loyalty from the other.

He had a steady hunger for sex. Just a day after he came home from the hospital with a broken leg, he turned to his wife. "And he's like, 'Babe? Can we?'" Dina mimics her husband's bawdy request. "And I was like, 'Dude, really? You have six pins in your legs and a steel plate, and you wanna have sex? That may be the last thing on my mind.'"

A few years earlier, when Dina had lost some weight from a now-reversed lap band surgery, she welcomed his hands on her hips and butt while she was standing at the kitchen sink washing dishes. "When I lost the weight, I was like, 'Touch me wherever you want, 'cause I'm rockin' it,'" she said. But when she started to put the weight back on and her thighs and belly pushed outward, Dina became pricklier when Gene placed his hands on her stomach. During sex, she became more insecure and marked areas of her body as off-limits. The times when she was at her heaviest, she didn't like to be on top when they made love. "I don't like it at all," she said without any elaboration.

As hard as she worked each day at the salon, bent over buffing the calluses off ladies' feet, and then helping to manage her husband's construction business and tend to their two children, Dina was a conscientious and diligent wife: She didn't complain about her husband's sexual needs. "At the end of the day, I'm tired. I have two 4-year-olds. Trying to keep the house cleaned. I'm like, 'Okay, let's go,'" she would say mordantly. Her husband was a generous and conscientious lover, and Dina could get aroused and feel fulfilled during sex, but frankly, of late, she did it mostly out of obligation.

She had tried a few pills—a mixture of Viagra and testosterone—that she took for a few months as part of a study on sex drugs for women. Her girlfriend had told her about it, and she called right away to sign up. She had been considering talking to her gynecologist anyway about options for boosting her sex drive to keep up with Gene, and Dina, spontaneous and bold, was game for anything. (On the nape of her neck was a tattooed Chinese symbol, one of several she'd gotten on her girls' nights out, that means "to orgasm," and underneath was her husband's name in Chinese characters. She tells her prissier clients that the tattoo means "love.") For the sex study, she had to go into a local doctor's office a few times, watch a pornographic video, and respond to a computer screen with blinking colors. ("The video was soft. You see more on HBO," she said with riotous laughter.) When she came home with the medication, she cast a come-hither glance to her husband. "'Babe, I'm gonna take the pills tonight,' and he was like, 'Oh, hell yeah!'" She took the medication and promptly fell asleep. He said, "'Well, that worked well. So much for the sex study!'"

Gene couldn't understand why his wife got so moody about her weight. "My husband always tells me I'm sexy, even now," Dina said. "He's been very supportive with my weight. He thinks I'm dumb for feeling bad about myself. He's so confident with himself." Gene's own large girth hadn't ravaged his psyche; he faced off against other people's scathing attitudes about the obese with hostility. "'I'm fat,' he'd say. 'If you can't take it, don't look at me.'" Dina shared that sentiment, to be sure, and even though of late she "felt like shit," she wouldn't be brought down by it.

"I still think I'm worth something, and that follows through with my relationship with my husband. Although I don't want him to touch me in certain places, I'm still worthy of attention."

Disgust with one's body was a punishment unfairly administered by a punitive culture obsessed with thinness; it was the hand that squeezed the dignity and self-love out of people. But to Dina, who by the grace and luck of her upbringing and personality had evaded its grasp and given it the middle finger, that disgust could be motivation to get in better shape. She had contempt for her thickening body, but she loved the woman living inside of it.

* * *

WITH her husband shaking his head, Dina scheduled bariatric bypass surgery at a hospital an hour and a half away in Salisbury, Maryland. There was no way she could lose 100 pounds on her own, she concluded, and there was more she wanted out of life. "I don't want to be the fat mom," she said. "I don't want my kids to be embarrassed about me." In a year, they were going to Disney World, in Florida, and Dina wanted to do something that she never did: put on a bathing suit and splash around with her twins. "Plus, my sex life," she added. "Gene and I have all these fantasies, and I want to act out on them. I think that would be a lot of fun, but I'm not gonna do it at this weight. So, it would be fun to be more intimate with my husband in a fun, crazy way with him. And I'm healthy, but 10 years from now I might not be so healthy [if I'm] this big. Diabetes might start coming."

Years before the twins were born, she had decided to get a silicone band surgically inserted that would constrict her stomach and, the hope was, make her feel full more quickly. Back then, Gene couldn't understand her decision to pursue weight loss surgery. Dina remembers him saying, "I don't understand why you want to do that. I love you just how you are."

And then one day, before the lap band surgery, she woke up and found a letter that Gene had left for her. Her husband, a lovable and reserved man who shot pool with his buddies every Thursday and rode ATVs in the fields near their house, was not a letter writer. In the letter, he confessed to being scared: "I'm just afraid you're going to lose this weight and leave me," Dina remembers reading. "My husband is so confident, so when this came through, I'm like, 'Whoa! Where is this coming from? This isn't the husband that I know.'"

When she saw him next, she assured him, "Babe, I don't want to lose weight because I want to go bar hoppin'. That's not me! I want to feel better about myself." Her husband, it seemed, wasn't without insecurities; and now that she was headed back to the hospital, this time for a more drastic and invasive surgery that brought far greater chances of success, Dina worried that it might upset what was otherwise a really terrific marriage of equals. "I think if he was getting gastric bypass, and I'm this weight, I'd think, 'What's he gonna do with my fat ass if he's all skinny?'"

She tried to reassure him that she wanted the surgery to feel better about herself; she wasn't doing it to garner attention from other men. Weight was her own struggle; it wasn't a source of conflict in her relationship.

Still, the question hung over them: If her body was no longer as big as Gene's, would the rhythms of their marriage change? Was being heavy part of the reason that their marriage had been a success?

* * *

At the salon, Dina put the final top coat on her last client of the day. Nine hours had passed, and Dina looked wan from all that time spent hunched over, shaping and buffing and painting, like an obsessed miniature model maker. The speckles of glitter in her electric blue eye shadow had been swept by sweat into the soft creases around her eyes. She was tired and her legs were sore from sitting all day. She would have to leave first thing in the morning for the hospital in Salisbury; her gastric bypass surgery was scheduled to start at 10:30 a.m. Tonight, though, she would go home, pack her bag, and hug her children.

* * *

As Americans' waistlines have grown, so too has the focus on weight in the field of relationship research—the scholarly pursuit of how well we get along and why.

In 2011, Andrea Meltzer, then a doctoral student at the University of Tennessee in Knoxville, and James McNulty, PhD, at the time an associate professor of psychology at UT, and their colleagues pointed out that prior research into the consequences of weight in romantic relationships had looked only at the weight of one partner, and his assessment about the quality of daily life in holy matrimony. That makes sense, since weight is typically viewed individualistically—it's one of the characteristics that shape how we rate our day-to-day experience—but what about the weight of the spouse? Did a person's assessment of her marriage change, depending on how close or far apart she was in body mass index from her partner? What if, Meltzer and her colleagues suggested, where you stood in relation to your partner on the weight scale mattered more than where you stood on your own?

The basis for their approach reached back to an idea first advanced by two social exchange theorists in 1959. John Thibaut and Harold Kelley suggested in their book *The Social Psychology of Groups* that under what they called interdependence theory, partners would try to maximize the rewards each receives from the relationship and try to minimize any costs. Inside a marriage, then, a husband would be unsatisfied if he believed the qualities he brought to the relationship were more valuable than the qualities his wife brought in return. The same would hold for a wife. This logic could explain why some fat women reported higher levels of marital satisfaction in prior research. "They don't think of themselves as having to go back on the market," said Dr. Alexandra Brewis Slade, from Arizona State University. "People were less likely to try to get divorced. They weren't thinking about, 'Could I do better?' They were more satisfied with what they had." The message was, in simple terms, "I'm not trying to trade you up for someone else."

Meltzer and Dr. McNulty pointed out that this perhaps unconscious calculating of rewards and costs has been shown to manifest in relationship dynamics in other ways. In a fascinating experiment conducted in Los Angeles, researchers videotaped a diverse sample of white, Asian American, and Latino married couples discussing a variety of difficult subjects, including ongoing disagreements they had with each other and questions including "talk about something that you would like to change about yourself." Interestingly, the most popular topics discussed were getting into shape and losing weight.

Those couples who were judged to have expressed similar facial emotions during the conversation reported much more satisfaction in their marriages than those newlyweds who differed in their emotional response.[36]

And in perhaps what was a hint at the role that weight might play in relationship satisfaction, the more those newlyweds' personalities and emotional experiences converged—that is, the more they became alike in the
first 18 months of matrimony—the better they fared in their marriages.
"[T]hose who became less alike in personality and emotional experience
faced steep drops in marital satisfaction over the 1.5 years of marriage," the
authors wrote. This new line of research suggested that similarity was an
important ingredient in successful relationships.

Was this true for weight, as well?

Meltzer and Dr. McNulty turned again to newlyweds. Every 6 months
for 4 years, they asked 165 couples to complete questionnaires and answer
questions over the phone about how satisfied they were in their marriages.
The researchers calculated the relative body mass index of husband and wife
and mapped those results to the level of satisfaction each individual reported
privately. The first few years of marriage are an especially important time
to study; it's a critical period for marital development, and it's also a time
when people often gain weight.

It turned out that husbands were more satisfied at the beginning of
their marriages and over the course of the next 4 years to the extent that
their wives *had BMIs that were lower than their own*. Wives found that setup
the most satisfying, as well: They reported being happiest in their marriages when their husbands were bigger than they were. The reverse was
true as well: *Both* husbands and wives reported being unhappiest when
wives weighed more in comparison to their spouses.

That may seem obvious given the cultural preference for thin
women, but actually, it didn't matter if the wife was thin; she just needed
to *not be as big as her husband*. If you were an overweight woman, one of
the elements of marital success, it seemed, was that your husband had a
higher BMI.

After a feverish pursuit by social psychologists who couldn't quite pin
down the implications of weight in marital bliss, it seemed there was suddenly a way to reconcile the inconsistencies. While absolute levels of BMI
mattered in the marriage market (i.e., men in pursuit of romantic love and

sex preferred normal-weight women), once married, it was the distance between the spouses' BMIs that mattered more. This was true even after controlling for depression, level of education, and income. Each person comes into a relationship prioritizing certain rewards; previous studies had found that a partner's thinness was more important to men than to women. Thinness was something men valued; so, the authors wrote:

> *Accordingly, regardless of each partner's absolute level of BMI, men with partners who have BMIs that are lower than their own may be more satisfied with their relationships because they are over-benefited with respect to a resource that is particularly important to them, whereas men with partners who have BMIs that are higher than their own may be less satisfied with their relationships because they are under-benefited with respect to a resource that is particularly important to them.*

For women, marital satisfaction turned on their husband's experience: "Because partner BMI is relatively less important to women, relative BMI may affect them only through its effect on men," the authors wrote. "Women who have higher BMIs than their partners may become less satisfied with the relationship because their partners are less satisfied." Indeed, previous research had found that half of married overweight or obese women reported getting nasty comments or being put down about their weight by a spouse.[37]

Women didn't need to be thin to have long, happy marriages; they just needed to be thinner than their husbands. Indeed, women of any size could be happy in a romantic relationship, the authors wrote, "if they find the right partner."

The news seemed rather good for overweight or obese women who fretted about losing weight to maintain a happy life at home. But many wives have reason to be suspicious. Husbands might assure wives that they desire them no matter their size, but research has found that "heavier women were judged by their male partners as lower in attractiveness [and] vitality and as poorer matches to their partners' attractiveness ideals."[38] The insecurities that bigger women felt about their relationships were not unwarranted; they had every reason to believe they were being judged harshly.

* * *

CONFLICT in personal relationships is inevitable. Understanding each episode's genesis and the arc of the conflict and its consequences is essential to those trying to offer sound counsel to couples. The academic study of personal relationships can feel deliciously voyeuristic, especially when couples involved in these experiments are asked to keep detailed notes—some even videotaped—and have their blood pressure monitored during what most of us think of as deeply private arguments.

In trying to understand why marriages in which the wife is bigger than the husband are the most troubled, it would make sense to examine the aspects of relationships that might trigger fights over body weight: mealtimes and discussions about health and exercise. For overweight women (and some men, like Eric, as described earlier in this chapter), mealtime is fraught with anxiety. To please their male partners, overweight women have been found by one study to suppress emotions about weight. The tactic often backfires: Their male partners criticize them less, but the women report eating more on the days they stifle their true feelings.[39]

In another study—"You're Going to Eat <u>That</u>?"—dozens of couples were asked to keep a diary of their fights, from minor scuffles to major throw-downs.[40] They were to record when they ate together, and the tenor of comments about health or exercise (for example, my partner tried to make me feel guilty, pressured me to change, or ridiculed me and made me feel bad). They were asked to answer questions like, "To what extent do you try to change things about your partner that bother you (e.g., behaviors, attitudes, etc.)?" and "How often do you feel angry or resentful toward your partner?" and "To what extent do you communicate negative feelings toward your partner (e.g., anger, dissatisfaction, etc.)?"

The study found far more conflict reported by couples in which one partner was overweight and the other one wasn't. That was especially true when the woman was heavier. And there seemed to be a connection to mealtime: Mixed-weight couples who ate together more frequently reported flare-ups. "Not all conflict is bad conflict," Tricia Burke, PhD, one of the study's authors, told me. But the type of conflict that showed up with mixed-weight couples was particularly nasty: There were more daily arguments, and they lived in a kind of ambient discord of teasing, nagging, belittling, and judging.

* * *

WHEN Amy Love was dieting, she told her second husband, who has since passed away, that he needed to fix his own meals so she wouldn't be tempted. "He would make cocktails and lay out sliced cheese on the butcher block," she said, walking into the kitchen in her tidy Victorian house in San Francisco that she shares with a gray poodle named Scudo. She pointed to a doorway. "There's the stairwell up to the bedrooms, and there is the bathroom through the kitchen. I couldn't go to the bathroom without passing through the kitchen and seeing all the cheese." Her grandmother's nickname had been Mrs. Dumpling. Growing up in the Midwest, Amy was being treated for weight issues by the time she went to high school. "I like to say I weighed 150 pounds for 2 weeks in 1964. The doctors were giving out speed then." She had enlisted her first husband in her dieting quests, but after they divorced and she came to suspect it was because she was fat, she decided with her second husband to keep her efforts to herself. Still, there was that butcher block full of inviting cheese. "There's a level that you want to enlist your partner, but you can get unsexy when you become more like a coach or caretaker."

* * *

WHEN Sandi Deckinger thinks backs over her decades of marriage and her decades of dieting, both unsettled histories that at age 69 she is still sorting through, the times of peace came when she and her husband, Mike, had separate shelves in their refrigerator and freezer, and ate alone. "It was mostly because of the ice cream and cookies. When I opened the fridge, I didn't want to look at it." Her husband was tall and thin with a preference for double cheeseburgers, cake, and candy; she started her first diet at age 12, growing up in Newark, New Jersey, surrounded by her ample Russian relatives. Her husband was always after her to go to Weight Watchers, and that made dinnertime stressful. "I would get so nervous that he was watching every bite I would put in my mouth. So we decided I would eat alone and he would eat alone." The two kept separate schedules: His day started early in the morning, and she worked an evening shift as a nurse. Sandi remembers one particular fight: "During our last year before he died, one day I just blew up. I told him, 'Stop about the weight. It's making me more nervous, and when I get nervous, I eat more.' And he said [that he] wouldn't talk about it. And the tension level went down considerably." Still, she says her husband used her weight as an excuse for not being sexually involved with her.

* * *

WHY were these men being so critical? Dr. Burke and her colleagues wrote, "When a healthy-weight man is in a relationship with an over-weight woman, his unfulfilled desire for a thin partner might contribute to increased conflict in these relationships. Similarly, these overweight women might be aware that their partner would be more attracted to them if they were thinner. These women might feel insecure and/or critical about their bodies as a result, making them less likely to be affectionate and, ultimately, resulting in lower intimacy and greater conflict."

Sandi Deckinger was still trying to make sense of one of the most painful memories of her decades-long marriage: Her husband had discouraged her from going to his school reunion. He claimed he was being considerate, that she wouldn't know anyone there. And then, Sandi said, "it slipped out during an argument." They were fighting over something, she doesn't remember what. "I just blurted out that I thought he didn't want me to go to the reunion because I was too big, and he said, 'Yes.' I think it probably was in the back of my mind all the time. When he said, 'Yes,' I was very hurt."

Where is all this headed? Overweight women in mixed-weight relationships report frequent, harmful, and destructive conflict; that stress in turn can sink people's well-being and even exacerbate health problems. "If you compound the health consequences that people already experience from being overweight," said Dr. Burke, "then these couples are really at risk for health problems in the future: high blood pressure, increased heart rate, chronic hypertension, [gastrointestinal] problems, heart disease."

The wrong kind of sustained conflict can place a marriage at risk;[41] stress from that conflict can put a person's health at risk.

Marriage is hard enough: a constant balancing act of needs and wants, compromise and care. And while overweight couples can be as contented as their slimmer counterparts, there is no doubt that weight can add serious complications to marriages that are already dealing with a barrage of everyday demands, including children, careers, finances, and sex. An imbalance in any of those areas—a sense that one partner is giving less or gaining more than the other—can weaken those unions to the breaking point.

And that fragility can become all the more perilous when the body stops performing as it once did. Everyone ages, of course, and adapting to one's partner's aches and pains is a part—and sometimes a very sweet part—of growing old together. But sexual dysfunction is also part of the aging process—something taught to us nightly by television ads showing handsome older couples who are suddenly in the mood and eyeing each other with the help of a little blue pill. But that's just advertising. For millions of Americans, the problems of sexual dysfunction—often exacerbated by weight—are far more real than a television fantasy.

CHAPTER FOUR

Sex: The Birds and the Bees with Aching Knees

Of all the questions that have challenged scientists over the millennia—the nature of time, the genetic code, the common cold—there is one question that has consistently fascinated and vexed: What makes good sex . . . good sex?

Like economics and the social sciences, research into human sexuality is subject to fluctuations, mood swings, perceptions, and expectations.

How does one judge, say, the "normal range" for sexual frequency? Once a day, twice a month, thrice a year? "Normal" could depend on the couple, their work schedules, and their appetites. And what constitutes "satisfaction"? Some men might say ejaculation is the goal; many women, who are just beginning to warm up when their men are finished, would heartily disagree.

All of this has confounded efforts to address sexual problems, of which America has a few; in the general population, some surveys suggest that nearly half of women have at least one sexual complaint.

But understanding even the relationship between one's plumbing and one's pleasure can be tricky. Sex for men is more susceptible to health problems that can lower sexual drive and hamper performance. Women's bodies, meanwhile, are less vulnerable, but social and psychological factors can deprive many of happiness and satisfaction.

And while men's brains are hardwired to light up when they are aroused, women don't appear to have the same circuitry. Indeed, there can be a disconnect: A woman's private regions can be ready for sex—engorged with blood, flooded with lubrication—while her brain (and her heart) can be completely uninterested. Some attribute this to the need for women's bodies to be ready for childbirth, or more disturbingly, believe that this phenomenon arose as a protective measure during dark prehistoric times when sex likely involved more rape than romance.

There is also considerable disagreement over just what constitutes "female sexual dysfunction." Some argue that dysfunction can only be diagnosed if the woman herself is distressed, while others say it could be diagnosed by physical tests and other metrics (such as lack of arousal and desire, and difficulty with orgasm). But if there is no agreement about what is normal, then how do you measure dysfunction?

There is tremendous cultural and social resistance in the United States to categorizing sexual experiences. It is precisely because these judgments are rendered privately about intimate matters that there is much objection when people who are obese or overweight are deemed, as a group, sexually deficient. It's not that there isn't data to support that argument: Studies do show that overweight and obese people are more sexually dissatisfied than are normal-weight people. And heavy women are much more dissatisfied than heavy men.

"I don't think it's a debate," said Michael Eisenberg, MD, director of the male reproductive medicine and surgery program at Stanford University. "The data is very, very strong that obesity is definitely correlated with sexual dysfunction."[1]

Yet, in the public's imagination, the plight of the heavy person's sex life is considered self-evident and unexceptional, and entirely neglected; there is a presumption that people who are overweight or obese have terrible sex, or no sex at all. With two out of three Americans in that category, that is a far-reaching supposition, but the reality is far more interesting.

People who are overweight or obese arrive, often cautiously, into their adult sexual lives molded by the harsh judgments of their youth. Stephanie Nelson from Chapter 2 left Williams College a much more cynical "fat girl" than she was when she arrived as a freshman 4 years earlier. Those who become heavier later in life, like Eric Leckbee in the earlier chapter on marriage, are often taught their place, and the damage to self-esteem can be painfully fast.

Many obese people told me that they feel better knowing others are having problems, too; that a withering sexual intimacy isn't yet another thing—like the battle with weight—that others feel they could simply decide to overcome. And perhaps it's comforting, they say, to be seen as not simply a number on a scale, but rather as sexual beings who mourn the diminishment of their sexual selves and pray for the restoration of intimacy.

* * *

Scientists who study obesity's impact on sex generally break the field into two branches of research. The first is sexual dysfunction, in which medical researchers focus on the interplay between body fat and chronic conditions associated with obesity, like diabetes and high blood pressure, and the sex hormones and sex organs (erectile dysfunction, for example). Then there are the psychologists and therapists who focus on how obese and overweight people experience their sexual lives—that is, how they assess their sexual quality of life.

The two camps have different ways of working. Psychologists listen to the men and women describe their sexual dissatisfaction and help them bolster self-esteem and body image. Medical researchers use brain scans and bloodflow meters to figure out how sexual readiness fares in a body enveloped in fat.

The categories are not mutually exclusive, of course. Mild body image dissatisfaction can progress to clinical depression, leading to a chemical cascade that inhibits the release of hormones central to sexual pleasure. And ironically, the drugs prescribed to treat depression can lead to even more weight gain and decreased sex drive, thereby exacerbating the initial complaint.

*　*　*

EDWARD Karpman, MD, is a urologist at the bustling El Camino Urology Medical Group in Mountain View, California. The first time I met this smiling live wire of a man, all bustle and brio, he excused himself for a moment and sprang past me, flinging open his office door.

"Where's my penis model?" Dr. Karpman called out to the nurses. The women glanced at one another as if they were trying to remember where the stapler had gone. Then, someone found it: a hardened plastic mold of tubes and testes, which Dr. Karpman grabbed.

I had asked Dr. Karpman about a phenomenon that Eric Leckbee and other overweight men had described to me: As they gained weight, their penises appeared to shrink. This wasn't a matter of rounded bellies getting in the line of sight or wounded psyches distorting body image; the men's penises, when measured, were in fact not as long as they once were. They were being buried inside their bodies.

I had been skeptical about this, but urologists like Dr. Karpman confirmed it, complete with teaching me an unwritten rule about penis length.

"For every 50 pounds overweight you are," Dr. Karpman said, "you lose an inch of penis."

The mystery of the disappearing penis could be easily explained through a simple matter of anatomy. A man's penis is actually fixed to his abdominal wall, Dr. Karpman said, holding it in place. And the more a man's fattening belly grows outward, "the more it eats their penis."

"They get this little nubbin of a penis," Dr. Karpman said. And no one, he said, likes having a nubbin.

This anatomical relationship became obvious during penile implant surgery. "When I do penile implant surgery on obese patients, they might look like they have a 2-incher. But when we put in a penile implant, we actually have to go all the way to the base here, and we can measure the entire penis. And they actually have very good penile length, but it's just hidden behind all this fat."

All this made sense, looking at the penis model Dr. Karpman held firmly in his hands.

Taken to the extreme, severely obese men could develop something even more sinister sounding: buried penis syndrome. In this case, abdominal fat and skin, called a panniculus, drape out and over a man's pubic area, causing a host of problems. Bacteria and fungus can grow in the moist environment, which can lead to rashes, inflammation, and scarring.

In the worst cases, scar tissue on the shaft of the penis contracts, pulling the entire organ completely inside the body. Researchers have begun to suspect that the poor hygiene associated with a buried penis, among other mechanisms, increases the risk of penile cancer.[2]

The penis, it seems, is an organ under siege: The percentage of US adults considered morbidly obese—those with a body mass index over 40 and typically at least 100 pounds overweight—rose sharply during the past decade. In 2000, 3.9 percent of adults were morbidly obese. By 2010, 6.55 percent of adults were deemed severely obese.[3]

Urologists like Dr. Karpman warn that buried penis syndrome, once considered a rare genetic mishap in childhood or in a novel case of adult morbid obesity, could become more common.

"As obesity has become a national epidemic, the incidence of this phenomenon will inevitably increase,"[4] wrote a team of reconstructive plastic surgeons at Duke University Medical Center, which also had the unenviable job of exhuming buried penises and reconstructing them as best they could.

In 2012, a team of Canadian urologists concurred in a paper published in the *Canadian Urological Association Journal,* saying that "with the current global obesity epidemic, there will undoubtedly be more patients who present with a buried penis."[5]

And while the physical impacts of such an occurrence are obvious, the psychological consequences are even more profound.[6]

* * *

JEROME was determined to lose enough weight to join the marines. He had always been chubby and not much of an athlete growing up in Massachusetts; he always felt like the slowest player on the football field. The marines would whip him into shape, he imagined, and introduce him, a West African immigrant who'd grown up in the United States, to new people. He wanted desperately to break out of his shell. "The life I was living at that point wasn't the life I wanted," said Jerome.

In preparation for his boot camp weigh-in, he went without water, and when completely dehydrated, he squeaked by at 205 pounds. By the end of boot camp, 3 months later, he had lost another 30 pounds, a result of both the rigorous training and the constant bombardment of jibes and jabs delivered by fellow recruits and drill sergeants.

"In the military, especially the marines," said Jerome, "being overweight is really frowned upon."

In 2008, fresh out of high school and fresh out of boot camp, Jerome was deployed to Iraq. While stationed overseas, he started a long-distance relationship with a girlfriend back home who knew him as a lean and fit marine. But marine food is hardly low fat, and in the stress of a war zone, counting calories was the least of his concerns.

By the time his tour of duty in Iraq ended, Jerome had gained back 70 pounds and stretch marks began appearing on his stomach.

The binge continued when he got back to Massachusetts: He

indulged in fast food and beer and grew even heavier. And while his girl-friend was still in the picture, his penis, it seemed, was shrinking.

"Going from 175 pounds to 285 pounds in 3 years made me realize how much better my penis looked when I was thin," said Jerome, who knew his length, right down to the half inch. "As I gained body fat, I accumulated more fat around the base of my penis. This means less of my penis enters my partner during intercourse."

And that really kills the experience, he said bluntly. "Fat sex isn't fun," he said. "Being out of breath and sweating like you're on a run takes the sexiness out of sex."

Just 22 years old, at an age when most men are seemingly at the peak of their sexual powers, Jerome felt like anything but a stud. His self-confidence plunged, and he began losing his erection midway through sex more frequently—an epic confidence killer.

"Even when I was mentally turned on, my body wasn't reacting prop-erly," Jerome recalled. And even though his girlfriend had assured him—"I'll love you any way you are"—Jerome couldn't believe it. "[I] didn't think I could be a great partner if I couldn't please my woman physically and visually," he said.

He never saw a doctor about the erectile dysfunction; he assumed a doctor would simply tell him to lose weight. And he wanted to. Jerome hated how he looked, and he began to feel self-pity and self-doubt, two emotions he despised. The double standard he had set for his girlfriend bothered him, too.

"It was very hypocritical to expect my partner to have a great body, look beautiful, and have an hourglass figure, when I was shaped like a blob," he said.

All of which eventually put a heavy strain on him.

"At one point, I recall, we got into an argument—an almost break-up-for-good type of argument—and out of anger, she made a comment about how fat I was," he said. "It cut pretty deep, but it was true. I wasn't the much leaner man she had met 2 years before. And it wasn't fair to her for me to become obese and expect her to be okay with it."

＊ ＊ ＊

BIOCHEMISTRY is merciless.

That seemed to be what Dr. Karpman was saying, seated in front of an impressive library of books on anabolic steroids and photos of his attractive family. He was describing how testosterone levels in men begin to gradually decline starting around age 30. Men lose about 1 percent of testosterone a year, but obese men fare far worse; testosterone loss starts earlier in life and occurs more quickly. The loss effectively ages them.

"Men who are obese," Dr. Karpman said, "tend to have lower testosterone levels than the normal aging process that we see in our non-obese men."[7]

The association of low testosterone and obesity in men is well established, and the overwhelming evidence supports what researchers call a bidirectional relationship: As fat around the abdomen increases, testosterone decreases.[8]

And that dip in testosterone causes a dip somewhere else.

"I am seeing younger and younger men, men in their thirties, men in their forties, with real organic causes of erectile dysfunction," said Stanford's Dr. Eisenberg, echoing observations I heard from urologists and physicians at sexual health clinics.[9]

He continued, "In an obese man, function was okay when they were teenagers or in their twenties, but now things are not as good as they once were." A 30-year-old man with the penile function of a 50-year-old could face serious relationship problems, Dr. Eisenberg warned.

"Sexual function really impacts quality of life, relationship satisfaction, happiness," he said. "If you're taking that away from men at a younger and younger age, that certainly will have an impact."

＊ ＊ ＊

FAT ends up in different regions of the body for men and women. Men naturally gain weight around their bellies, a distribution pattern referred to as android, while women tend to store fat in the hips and thighs. Indeed, for a striking example of the power of one's gender when it comes to distribution of body fat, consider this: In female-to-male transsexuals treated with injections of testosterone, their body fat shifts within a few months from womanly—i.e., below the waist—to what is more typical of men—fat around the abdomen.[10]

And that is not a good thing. Belly fat is the most harmful kind of fat; the adipose tissue in the abdomen, known as visceral fat, secretes molecules that promote systemic and vascular inflammation, and contains enzymes that interfere with the body's natural rhythms. In short, belly fat doesn't just sit there like fat on the hips and thighs. Belly fat is *alive.*

Physicians had been perplexed by patients with significant excess fat who didn't exhibit metabolic abnormalities, while other patients with the same body mass index presented with an array of problems. For example, active sumo wrestlers, who are giants by most measures, tend to have very little visceral adiposity and maintain a normal sensitivity to insulin. But when these men retire, they gain greater amounts of belly fat and tend to become insulin resistant, a signature of diabetes, and develop high cholesterol.[11]

This curious distinction had piqued the interests of scientists around the world, and in the last quarter century, there has been a surge of research into the pathophysiology of visceral fat. The scientific literature amassed over that time, wrote two prominent Canadian researchers in 2013, had established "beyond any doubt that the proportion of abdominal adipose tissue is a key correlate and perhaps driver of the health risk associated with overweight and obesity."[12] An extraordinary collection of evidence pointed to what physicians like Dr. Karpman had observed in their exam rooms: Obesity is more dangerous in men because the visceral fat they tend to carry around their bellies significantly increases their risk of heart disease, stroke, and diabetes and can rob men of precious testosterone.[13]

For older men, lower levels of testosterone and the accompanying decrease in sexual interest is a natural progression, albeit one that many fight with increasingly popular "low-T" treatments. But what is it about men's big bellies that can lead to this biochemical downer happening earlier?

Among other wonders, abdominal fat contains an enzyme called aromatase that helps convert the male hormone testosterone into the female sex hormone estradiol. "The more fatty tissue you have, the more of that conversion that happens," Dr. Eisenberg explained.

That process has a cascading effect; in the hormone-manufacturing plant of the body, estrogen converted from testosterone travels up to the control center, the brain, with a message to shut down or curtail further production of testosterone. The mechanism has been well established: Obese men have been found to have elevated estrogen, which activates estrogen receptors in the hypothalamus that then trigger the inhibition of the hypothalamic-pituitary-gonadal axis.[14]

It is as if excess estrogen is short-circuiting a man's testosterone-accustomed system. (Similar signaling pathways also appear to suppress normal sperm production in obese men, which can lead to fertility problems.) And the reduction in testosterone is proportional to the amount of fat: The more abdominal fat that men gain, the more the estrogen-synthesizing enzyme goes to work. All of that can affect how well a man's penis functions.

* * *

DESPITE the seemingly simple stimulus (a pretty person, an erotic image, a passing breeze) it responds to, the actual command of the penis requires a number of sophisticated and complex systems working in concert: the nervous system, the circulatory system, the endocrine system, and a level of mental processing, as well. When any of these systems is impaired, a man can have trouble getting and maintaining an erection.

For men, sex occurs in four discrete stages, what the pioneering sex researchers William Masters and Virginia Johnson called the Human Sexual Response Cycle.

Excitement: A man becomes sexually excited, and his penis begins to become erect.

Plateau: The heart rate increases, the urethral sphincter contracts, and the muscles of the penis contract.

Orgasm: The moment of ejaculation.

Resolution: The body's muscles relax and blood pressure drops.

Testosterone plays a critical role for men in the first two stages: becoming sexually aroused and maintaining an erection. "You have a 65- or 70-year-old man who might be standing next to a very attractive woman and just thinking about sports, whereas in the same situation, a 20-year-old guy with normal testosterone is having sexual thoughts standing next to the same woman," Dr. Karpman said. "That's what happens to men as their testosterone levels go down. They just lose interest."

Sleeping problems—common for overweight people—can also have a debilitating effect on a man's penis. The condition of sleep apnea—when a person's oxygen levels drop below normal or the person stops breathing momentarily—can lead to arrhythmias, stroke, and hypertension. But the interrupted sleep and sleep deprivation also appear to decrease testosterone levels in men[15] and put them at an added risk for sexual dysfunction.[16]

The lower levels of testosterone in obese men have drawn the attention of pharmaceutical companies selling testosterone replacement therapies. Brochures for testosterone gels, for example, feature photographs of confident and fit men with strong jawlines and enviable pelts of hair, but the advertisements make clear that low testosterone is "common" among men with obesity.

The brochures typically include simple quizzes to pique a patient's interest: How is your sex drive? Energy level? Is it more difficult to enjoy life? Are you sad or grumpy? Are your erections less strong?

The answer to these questions for many overweight and obese men is an emphatic "Yes."

In recent years, the number of men given prescriptions for testosterone in the United States has exploded. A 2013 study found that the number of older and middle-aged men who had been prescribed testosterone had tripled since 2001. The treatments have been approved specifically for men with abnormally low levels of testosterone, a condition called hypogonadism, but the same study found that one out of four men prescribed the treatment had *not* had his blood tested, which is usually a requirement for such a diagnosis.

Some of the growth in testosterone prescriptions can be explained by aggressive direct-to-consumer marketing campaigns by pharmaceutical companies touting the benefits of testosterone replacement therapies—gels, injections, and subcutaneous pellets—to the nation's baby boomers looking to boost waning libidos. (These prescription figures, researchers say, exclude testosterone sold typically for cash at stand-alone low-T clinics or those purchased on the Internet.) Testosterone replacement therapy is also, interestingly enough, touted—correctly—as an effective way to reduce body fat and improve muscle mass. These effects have been demonstrated,[17] although the risks of long-term testosterone therapy are not well understood.

Interestingly, men in their forties represent the fastest-growing segment of recipients of testosterone prescriptions. While some of that interest can be attributed to heightened consumer awareness, sexual dysfunction—often obesity related—is presenting in younger and younger men. With one out of three adult men overweight or obese, makers of testosterone replacement therapies may owe much credit for their success to America's weight gain.

* * *

Low testosterone is hardly the only risk that obese men face. Diabetes, a condition often brought on by obesity and physical inactivity, has surged in the United States: From 1990 through 2010, the annual number of new cases of diagnosed diabetes almost tripled, according to the Centers for Disease Control and Prevention. In 2011, federal health officials estimated 26 million adults had diabetes.[18]

And the data on individual states is telling: Oklahoma witnessed a 226 percent increase; in Kentucky, the number of cases rose by 158 percent; Georgia: 145 percent; Alabama: 140 percent; Washington, DC: 135 percent. (Type 2 diabetes, which federal health officials say can be prevented through lifestyle changes, accounts for 90 to 95 percent of all diabetes cases in the United States.)

The combination of diabetes and obesity is especially troubling for men and their sexual lives. Diabetic men are twice as likely to have abnormally low levels of testosterone than men without diabetes,[19] and—perhaps not coincidentally—three times as likely to develop sexual problems as nondiabetic men of similar age.[20]

In addition, and perhaps more disturbingly, diabetes can take a permanent physical toll by damaging the tiny blood vessels that nourish the nerves, leading to nerve damage, a condition afflicting about half of all diabetics, according to the American Diabetes Association. It is not a pleasant sensation: People with diabetes describe feeling tingling, pain, or loss of sensation in their extremities, including their fingers and toes.

And, yes, in their penises: The penis is an extremity like any other, and its blood vessels and branchlike nerves, which play a crucial role in carrying out the commands of an aroused mind, can be damaged in the same way as a diabetic's hands and feet. (Researchers also suspect that nerves in the penis can be damaged independently by inflammatory chemicals released by fat cells.)

"That combination [of obesity and diabetes] is lethal," said John Foreyt, PhD, the director of the Behavioral Medicine Research Center at Baylor College of Medicine in Houston, who led one of the 16 research sites for Look AHEAD (Action for Health in Diabetes). This trial was the largest randomized study to evaluate the effect of lifestyle changes on overweight and obese men (and women) with type 2 diabetes, and the data is disquieting.

At the beginning of the trial, using a well-established questionnaire—the International Index of Erectile Function—heavy diabetic men reported less sexual desire, more problems getting an erection and having an orgasm, and less satisfying intercourse than similarly aged normal-weight men without diabetes. As for erectile dysfunction, half of heavy diabetic men had moderate or mild ED, and one in four had severe ED. Encouragingly, these men also reported being motivated to seek help: Among sexually active men in the Look AHEAD trial, 42.6 percent had sought help for their problem, and nearly 40 percent said they were using medications to treat erectile dysfunction.[21] (Interestingly, the rate of erectile dysfunction and the use of drugs known as phosphodiesterase-5 inhibitors, like Viagra, Levitra, and Cialis, that help the smooth muscles of the penis to relax and increase bloodflow, were similar across racial and ethnic groups. These drugs are effective in overweight and obese men, even if their penises have appeared to shrink.) All of this suggested that while overweight men are suffering, they don't intend to do it silently.

❋ ❋ ❋

So it seems that while surveys do detect lower levels of sexual satisfaction among overweight and obese men, the little blue pills and their ilk are likely ameliorating some of the symptoms. Beginning with the introduction of Viagra in 1998, pharmaceutical fixes have masked the detrimental sexual effects that have accompanied the rise of obesity, a trend that took firm hold just as these treatments became available. "The marketers have done a remarkable job saying, 'It's okay for guys to ask for help,'" said psychology professor David Sarwer, PhD, one of the nation's leading obesity researchers. At the end of an appointment, a heavy male patient might mention to his doctor that he saw an ad for Viagra. Rather than confronting the excessive weight that may be contributing to his sexual dissatisfaction with pesky lifestyle modifications, taking the little blue pill "is an easier first solution for guys," Dr. Sarwer told me. "As guys, we're just not trained and taught to communicate our feelings as part of our social norm. So, for guys who are struggling with sexual behavior, they just want to solve the problem. As opposed to doing exercise or reading a book about relationship development, I think most guys are going to say, 'Give me the pill.' "

Without these medical treatments for chronic sexual problems, quality of life surveys would likely pick up even more profound dissatisfaction from overweight and obese men. And the low-T phenomenon is just the latest variation on that theme. In 2006, the Endocrine Society, the medical group that sets clinical guidelines for endocrinologists, urologists, and others prescribing testosterone replacement therapy, began recommending that all men with type 2 diabetes be screened for low testosterone levels. Recent studies have suggested that physicians should screen all obese men for low testosterone, regardless of whether they have diabetes.[22]

Animal studies hint at the potential wide-ranging effects of obesity and low testosterone: At the annual Endocrine Society meeting in San Francisco in 2013, researchers from the Davis School of Gerontology, a laboratory at the University of Southern California, presented findings from an experiment in which male mice were fed high-fat diets to induce obesity and then separated into three different groups based on testosterone levels.[23] While their findings were accidental, they were also chilling.

In the experiment, the first group of mice had normal levels of testosterone; the second group was castrated so that they had low levels of testosterone; the third group faced a similar fate—castration—but had their testosterone levels boosted through a capsule implanted under their skin. The researchers at USC weren't interested in weight, per se. Instead, they had reason to believe that low testosterone was connected to Alzheimer's disease: In postmortem examinations of human brains, low testosterone appeared to be a risk factor for developing dementia in aging men.

As for the mice, they all became pudgy rodents on their high-fat diets. Blood tests showed they had high blood sugar levels and difficulty clearing glucose from their bloodstreams, which is evidence of diabetes. That was to be expected. But then when scientists looked at the varying levels of testosterone, things got more interesting: The obese mice with low levels of testosterone had even more body fat and worse control of their blood sugars. When the scientists examined the obese mice's brains, they found the brain tissue was significantly inflamed and less able to support nerve cell growth. But for those heavy mice with low testosterone, the damage was more severe.

"Our findings suggest that low testosterone and obesity interact to regulate inflammation of the nervous system," said Anusha Jayaraman, PhD, the study's lead investigator, "which may increase the risk of disorders such as type 2 diabetes and Alzheimer's disease."[24]

The next question is, how do they interact? Scientists at USC are still trying to understand the mechanism that links obesity to Alzheimer's disease, and the interplay among fat, brain inflammation, and testosterone.

* * *

In April 1998, Pfizer released its miracle drug Viagra, a phosphodiesterase type 5 inhibitor that increases bloodflow to the penis. Without a doubt, the little blue pill revolutionized sexual medicine. For the first time, urologists and other physicians had an effective oral therapy for men who were unable to achieve or sustain an erection sufficient for sexual intercourse. And boy, did they ever. "Doctors were giving it out like candy," Dr. Karpman remembers.

Curiously, though, many of the first patients who started taking Viagra for erectile dysfunction began showing up 3 to 5 years later in their doctors' offices with heart disease and in emergency rooms with heart attacks. But it wasn't Viagra that was causing heart troubles. By 2005, researchers had determined that erectile dysfunction was, in fact, a reliable warning sign of heart disease—"a sentinel symptom"—often preceding a heart attack or stroke by 5 years.[25]

"The penis is the dipstick of the body's health," said Harry Fisch, MD, director of the Male Reproductive Center at Columbia University Medical Center in New York, in an article in the *New York Times* in 2008. "If you're able to have sex and healthy erections, it's a good sign that your cardiovascular system is in good shape. If you can't, it's time to see your doctor."

Sure enough, there were other studies that also demonstrated just how accurate of a harbinger erectile dysfunction could be: In one study of diabetic men, ED proved to be the most efficient predictor of coronary artery disease.[26] In another study of more than 25,000 men, those with preexisting ED had a 75 percent increased risk of peripheral vascular disease.[27]

All of which may go back to anatomy. The arteries that supply blood to the penis are extraordinarily narrow; the diameter of the penile artery is about half the size of the main coronary artery that supplies blood to the heart. And according to an article in the *New York Times,* the same "factors that can clog up arteries and lead to heart attacks and strokes—smoking, elevated cholesterol, inflammation, and high blood pressure—also wreak havoc on the vessels that supply the penis."[28]

When a man is aroused, his brain releases a chemical that signals the blood vessels in the penis to dilate, allowing blood to rush in and an erection to take place. If those blood vessels are even slightly impaired, they can't dilate as well, making it difficult for a man to maintain a firm erection. "That process is just blunted with obesity," Dr. Eisenberg said in an interview at the clinic he directs at Stanford University.

Obese men have nearly all of these risk factors in spades. Obesity can raise the levels of "bad" cholesterol (triglycerides and LDL cholesterol) and lower levels of "good" cholesterol (HDL cholesterol), putting obese men (and women) at a tenfold higher risk for atherosclerosis, the dreaded buildup of fat on the walls of arteries. Cholesterol and other fatty materials cause the walls of the coronary artery to harden, and the clogged arteries make it more difficult for oxygen-rich blood to reach the heart. At the same time, built-up plaque can break off and block bloodflow through an artery, causing a heart attack or stroke.

The same process occurs in the narrow arteries in the penis. "Atherosclerosis is directly related to ED," Dr. Karpman said, "and this is why, compared to their non-obese counterparts, obese men will have a higher rate of erectile dysfunction if everything else is the same."

But even with a remission of erectile dysfunction, overweight and obese men sometimes have permanent vascular damage. "Once they develop those atherosclerotic plaques in the arteries, those aren't going to get any better," Dr. Karpman said. "The best thing you can hope for at that point is to stabilize them and prevent any more atherosclerosis from developing."

The most comprehensive review to date of sexual functioning and obesity, published in the journal *Obesity* in 2012, found that penis problems were almost indiscriminate in whom they affected: "Despite the heterogeneity of methods and the diverse geographical settings, all except one population-based study of men showed a higher occurrence of ED in obese men than healthy-weight men."[29]

There are nonpharmaceutical methods to treat overweight and obese men with sexual dysfunction. Those with low testosterone, depending on the severity of other medical conditions, can attempt to restore their testosterone levels by losing abdominal fat.[30] There are other benefits as well: Increasing physical exercise can also improve the functioning of the endothelial cells that line blood vessels and are critical for maintaining an erection.[31, 32]

But prescription medication promises a quicker fix, although it's not without controversy. Whether to treat overweight and obese men with testosterone therapy for decreased libido—not to mention Viagra, Levitra, and other PDE5 inhibitors—is a point of active debate among providers. Many primary care physicians and internists are skeptical of putting patients on medication before sincere efforts at weight loss are made.

At the same time, urologists, a fair number of whom are paid consultants or advisors to companies that make erectile dysfunction drugs, contend that a pharmacological fix is a more practical solution, given the dismal success rates among patients trying to lose weight. And while a number of studies have found that testosterone therapy can lead to increased muscle mass and decreased fat in overweight men, the ongoing treatment of hypogonadism with testosterone continues to raise questions.[33]

While that high-minded debate is going on, however, real men are trying to get on with their lives—and their sex lives. Greg Lucas is one of them, and his story—while far from definitive—is striking.

A senior program manager for an international software company in Dallas, Greg was 25—seemingly in the prime of life—but feeling unmotivated. He was having a hard time concentrating, and his interest in sex had waned. He was obese, and when he looked at a list of symptoms of low testosterone, he checked "Yes" for each one. His doctor gave him a blood test to check his testosterone levels—the standard medical measure of whether such a treatment is necessary—and they came back in the bottom 5 percent of normal. So Greg's doctor advised against giving him any treatment.

"It was something I brought up again over the next couple of years, but I always got the brush-off," Greg said about his discussions with his doctor. "I was like, 'You're not doing anything to address the symptoms. You can't just tap me on the head and tell me it's fine when I'm telling you it's not.'"

When his weight peaked at 350 pounds, Greg decided to go back to the gym, in line with his doctor's advice to lose weight. He met a coach there, and the two soon started talking about Greg's symptoms, which hadn't improved. The coach suggested he check out one of the low-T clinics that have proliferated in Texas and across the nation. Soon enough, Greg had gotten a blood test. And this time, there was cause for concern—and action. A blood test showed his testosterone level had fallen even farther.

The clinic recommended testosterone shots and urged him to get started right away. They also gave Greg an aromatase inhibitor, a drug that stops the synthesis of testosterone into estrogen.

Within a month, all of Greg's symptoms disappeared. "I felt better overall, higher energy, higher libido," he said. "I felt like I was the person I was supposed to be."

Within a year, Greg says he dropped 50 pounds of body fat and put on 20 pounds of muscle; he started training 4 to 5 days a week at the gym and began competing in the North American Strong Man Competition.

Not surprisingly, Greg has no intention of stopping testosterone treatment, despite the risks: Testosterone therapy can cause reduced sperm counts, acne, and thickening of the blood, and the longer-term risks are unknown. There is a spirited debate in the scientific literature over whether the therapy poses a risk in patients with a history of prostate cancer; there are still no long-term controlled studies evaluating prostate cancer risk.

Further, specialists who treat sexual dysfunction in men are more and more raising a red flag to obesity researchers and physicians who treat obese patients about low-T treatments. This concern is borne out in some studies, including one conducted by a group of men's health researchers at Bayer, the pharmaceutical giant based in Germany.

"The contribution of [testosterone therapy] to combating obesity in hypogonadal men remains largely unknown to medical professionals managing patients with obesity and metabolic syndrome," the group wrote, though it also noted that fears about prostate cancer were unsupported.

Still, Greg would rather take that gamble than return to the suffering he endured while he was obese. He rattles off a list of his physical problems that have since subsided: high blood pressure, glucose issues, and aching joints.

"I think it was risky for me to be an unmotivated and obese person," he says.

＊　＊　＊

In a shuttered cafeteria in a basement at a Catholic hospital in the San Francisco Bay Area, men and women from all over California and points beyond come together for a bariatric surgery support group meeting. The gathering is part revival and part barn raising.

Each meeting begins with the same ritual: The group's leader, an earnest and attentive nurse whom everyone calls Barb, calls on the men and women one by one to introduce themselves. Many of the people here at these monthly meetings are enormous and perch uncomfortably on the flimsy plastic cafeteria chairs. They spread their legs in wide Vs, arms folded on their bellies or braced against the table, and shift constantly, moving a leg out or pulling in a nearby chair to prop up an arm. The constant shifting stirs the stale air in the hospital cafeteria, which smells of instant mashed potatoes and cleaning solvent.

As Barb asks for volunteers, the lack of stillness infuses the room with a sense of anxiety, impatience, and hope.

"I'm Dave. I had my surgery in 2001. I lost 220 pounds," says one speaker.

"My name is Cheryl, and I had surgery on May 24 and I'm down 67 pounds," says another.

"My name is Linda. February. Down 120 pounds. Used to have five insulin injections a day, and that's all gone," says a third.

Everyone here has had bariatric surgery—some recently, some more than a decade ago—or is considering surgery. Some are also waiting for their health insurance companies to approve the procedure, which can run to $30,000.

Barb knows everyone's story by now; most people who come to the support group, in fact, can recite the details of their compatriots' journeys, though there is an undeniable gap between those who have had the surgery and those who are awaiting it.

The Befores look to the Afters with great affection and anticipation. As the Afters stand to tell their story—name, date of surgery, the pounds they've lost—someone keeps a running tally of the total weight loss in the room. Then Barb asks for a drumroll and walks over to a nearby table to check the number. She looks up to the expectant audience and shouts: "4,166 pounds!"

The cafeteria erupts in "oohs" and "aahs," and nearly everyone claps excitedly. Among those clapping is Ron Katz, a spry 60-year-old with chestnut hair, bushy brown eyebrows, and a buoyant smile. Ron is tall, but not quite lanky; he remains bell shaped around his belt line. Several years removed from bariatric surgery, he's taken on the role of advisor and champion to those nearing the same procedure, many with trepidation.

After one man mentions that his operation is approaching, Ron steps forward to assure him. "When I first came here, I was the heaviest guy in the room, and all these skinny people were telling me how it was going to be," he says.

Sitting nearby is Ron's wife, Karen. Her dark blonde hair is smoothed into a chin-length bob. She wears delicate gold-rimmed glasses and a bright pink cowl-necked sweater. "I'm Ron's support person," she announces to the room. Everyone claps as a few shout out, "Welcome!"

Ron is a Canadian who became fat the typical American way: adding a few pounds each year, decade after decade, which led to an unrelenting piling on of weight that went unnoticed until it was too late. By then, it felt inevitable—a fate to be endured.

All of which came as a surprise. Ron had spent his childhood as the "skinniest guy in class," a physique he kept through his college days, when he was wild enough to sneak into a Beatles concert disguised as a reporter. The charade went so far that Ron and his friends followed the reporters into a backstage pressroom. "We met John and Paul," he told me.

In 1974, though, the crazy days ended as Ron started medical school in Ontario. It was a hard year—his father died, at only 64—except that during a surgery elective at a local hospital, Ron met Karen, an emergency room physician. Karen was constantly behind in her record keeping, and in need of sustenance. Ron made it a habit to fetch her sandwiches. Soon, they started dating, and during a trip to China with a group of Canadian doctors, Ron proposed in Tiananmen Square. Mao Zedong died while they were there, and the Chinese people plunged into mourning. But there were two very happy Canadians in their midst.

The couple settled in Toronto. Ron, now in his early thirties, started an internship at a local hospital. While the work was fulfilling, it was hard to stay fit.

"I had no sleep," he said, "and no reliable nutrition."

Like many who struggle with their weight, Ron can pinpoint the exact moment his life—and his waistline—changed.

"I was in the cafeteria eating my meal, in my scrubs, wearing my pager, and they announced 'Code Blue,'" he said, referring to the alert for a patient in need of resuscitation. "I was starving, but off I went. Two hours later, I come back to the cafeteria and it's closed. It's almost midnight; no food. So I learned to eat faster. So, I'm on call on Friday, Saturday, Saturday night into Sunday, and Sunday night."

He started eating to stay awake. Then, when he and Karen began their own practice, the pace never slowed. He was often up all night admitting patients to the hospital and then had to be at the office the next morning by 9:00 a.m.

It wasn't binge-eating; it was just a steady intake.

"I wasn't the kind of guy who sat in front of the TV set and ate tubs of ice cream," he said. "I was really just mismanaging my diet." But the math was undeniable.

"I started gaining 5 to 10 pounds a year," he said. "When you're normal weight, and you gain 10 pounds a year, 10 years later, you're up to 100 pounds [overweight]."

His weight continued to creep up, from 225 to 250 to 275, to his peak at 285. Although he developed chronic back problems and stopped playing racquetball and tennis, he said he was largely in denial.

"I wasn't sitting around saying, 'People don't like me,'" Ron said. "As a physician, you're out in the world talking to people."

Indeed, at their bustling clinic, Ron had a number of patients who were obese, and he remembers counseling one obese man with the words, "You have the same right to enjoy this life as anyone else."

Still, friends told Ron they were worried about his health. He would thank them politely but quickly dismiss the concern. "I wasn't ready to do anything about it," he said.

But the evidence piled up: He couldn't sit in booths at restaurants and found himself bumping into people as he walked (he would often plot out how to navigate around the tables and chairs). He couldn't fit in the bathroom on plane trips. And then, finally, the ultimate in labeling: His wife applied for—and received—a handicapped tag for their car.

"This is my lot in life," he remembers thinking. "I think everyone who is overweight is in denial. They know they're big. They're not stupid, but they also feel that it's not that big a deal."

There was one realm in which that denial, though, carried a heavy emotional toll. Ron and Karen had built a respected and profitable business, but they faced insurmountable hurdles in building a family.

After a spate of treatments, Karen was unable to conceive, and the couple's sex life cooled considerably. At the same time, Ron was putting on weight. He developed diabetes and had to inject himself four times a day with insulin; his blood pressure shot up; he slept many nights propped up in a chair; and his appetite for sex diminished.

"When I got bigger, my desire went away," he said. He would try to force himself to maintain some semblance of his sexual self by masturbating, "but it just didn't matter to me or to Karen. I could orgasm, but I didn't bother."

The couple saw a sex therapist, but the sessions didn't seem to help. He didn't feel inadequate since his wife seemed uninterested in sex, too. But he didn't want to look closely at his own body, which felt sloppy and unmanageable. "You get into this mind-set that you're numb to the way you look," he said.

Looking back, Ron is in awe of his wife's kindness through all of this. "If I was grabbing some dessert, she would say, 'Wouldn't an apple be better?'" He didn't always listen to her, but he appreciated the loving support: "She didn't say, 'Hey you fat whatever. Get that out of your mouth! You already ate enough for a household of four.' That may have driven me into loathing and all the rest of it. But she never did that, even though she had to pay the price of taking care of a guy who was big."

Karen kept her thoughts to herself and dutifully took care of her husband, but she was not without an opinion on the matter of her husband's size and what she called his Buddha belly.

"It wasn't a slice of cheese; it was a hunk of cheese," she said of Ron's eating habits then. "It was not anything we could have a rational discussion about."

When friends visited, they would stay bundled up in coats since Ron, who was always hot and perspiring, needed the air conditioner on, even in the winter. They would go to parties, but often had to leave early since Ron tired easily. They couldn't explore very far on foot when they took their motor home on vacations.

"When we went out, it wasn't what I wanted to do: It was what we *could* do," said Karen. "And if we went home early, if I didn't get to take the extra 10 minutes to do what I wanted to do, I accepted that. And I guess from that point of view, I was pretty tolerant."

Karen didn't slam doors or get angry, but she worried about Ron's health. "It was like, 'What's gonna happen to him? Is he going to have a stroke? Am I going to be his nurse? Am I going to the nursing home every week?'"

Karen had become her husband's caretaker, and she viewed him as an "invalid." She used the word matter-of-factly, with no derision or resentment.

"It was like you have a very ill person that you're trying to make comfortable, and you're happy if you can get them out," she said.

Perhaps the perfect metaphor for Karen's support is this: As Ron ballooned, she carried a special, heavy-duty folding chair, the XX Daddy Chair, designed to support Ron's weight wherever they went—on cruises, at movie theaters and playhouses—and set it up for him, despite fear of running afoul of fire codes. She even lugged the chair to Broadway for a performance of the musical *Jersey Boys*.

"They really weren't thrilled that it wasn't a wheelchair," she said.

＊ ＊ ＊

PHYSICIANS, often squeamish about sexual health, have largely ignored the sexual lives of their bigger patients. As with the general public, the prevailing belief among primary care physicians and gynecologists—who might be a couple's first responder—was that obese people didn't have sex, and didn't want to. Physician surveys suggested doctors were reluctant to advise overweight patients to lose weight;[34] in one survey, more than half of the physicians viewed obese patients as awkward, unattractive, ugly, and noncompliant.[35]

The next generation of medical and mental health providers seems no more enlightened: Textbooks on human sexuality rarely mention obesity as a contributor to sexual problems.

Leah Millheiser, MD, director of the female sexual medicine program at Stanford University School of Medicine and clinical assistant professor in the department of obstetrics and gynecology, recounted a frequent and all-too-common conversation she had with colleagues:

"I don't ask them about their sex life," a colleague will say.

"Well, do you ask other people about their sex life?" Dr. Millheiser will respond.

"I do."

"Well, why don't you ask the obese patient about their sex life?"

"I'm embarrassed to ask. What if they are not having sex?"

"Well, do you know they are not having sex? Maybe they are; maybe they have an issue they need to discuss with you."

Dr. Millheiser said the mind-set among many physicians is that heavy patients have other priorities for the visit—"I'm more concerned with their general health and keeping them alive"—than worrying about their sexual health.

Dr. Karpman of the Mountain View clinic said he'd seen the same thing. "Most of the medical community looks at it as a peripheral issue," he said. "Sexual function, intimacy, is a perk and it's not essential. It's not vital. It's not going to kill them."

But Dr. Karpman said that was shortsighted and overlooked a powerful tool for coaxing people into improving their lifestyles: the potential for love and making love.

"The way I look at it is, you give a guy a good erection, and now he wants to have sex," Dr. Karpman said. "You give him desire and erection; now he wants to have sex. Then he looks at himself in the mirror: 'Now, I want to look good!' And that's his motivation to get in shape. What is your motivation to lose weight when you're 350 [pounds] and you have no libido and no erection?"

Of course, in the realm of obesity research, there are certainly matters that are more urgent than sexuality: With heart disease, stroke, debilitating diabetes, and certain cancers[36] on the rise, declining sexual health and physical intimacy has not been a top priority. But complaints about sexual difficulties and sexual dissatisfaction have long been common among obese patients, according to psychologists, sex therapists, and clinicians involved in weight loss programs around the country. However, even as obesity took hold in every state, there were a few efforts under way to look for patterns.

It wasn't until the early 2000s, in fact, that survey tools developed by researchers at Duke, and other questionnaires, were beginning to return the first data on how obesity was altering the sexual quality of life for heavier people in the United States.

There was a lag between reality and research: "Reduced sexual quality of life is a frequently reported yet rarely studied consequence," wrote clinical psychologist Ronnie Kolotkin in a 2006 paper published in the journal *Obesity*. "Only a few research studies have examined the relationship between obesity and sexual quality of life. In men, obesity has been associated with lower sexual satisfaction, increased erectile dysfunction, and penile vascular impairment. Less is known about obesity and sexual quality of life in women."[37]

The 2006 study involved giving more than 1,100 obese men and women a survey with questions that began with the phrase "Because of my weight . . . " and then asked each person to rate on a scale from "Never true" to "Always true" if they felt a lack of sexual enjoyment; if they lacked sexual desire; if they had difficulty with sexual performance; and if they ever avoided sex.

All of the survey respondents had a body mass index of 30 or more:

500 of them were participants in an intensive residential weight loss program; 372 were patients preparing for bariatric surgery; and 286 were obese people chosen at random as a control group. Most of the participants were white, and the mean age ranged from 41 for female gastric bypass patients to 51 for men in the residential weight loss program.[38]

The results reflected a punishing reality: One out of three obese women said that because of her weight, she "usually or always did not enjoy sexual activity, had little sexual desire, experienced difficulty with sexual performance, and avoided sexual encounters." And half of obese women said they experienced these kinds of problems at least some of the time.

For men, sexual problems hinged more on performance: One out of two men said he had problems performing during sex; 15 percent said they always or usually avoided sexual situations and didn't enjoy the sex they did have. Patients seeking bariatric surgery are typically more burdened by their weight, and that was reflected in the results: Male gastric bypass candidates had far higher rates of all types of sexual problems, from lack of desire to difficulty with intercourse.

And while some people are always going to be unhappy with their sex lives, the level of dissatisfaction among the obese study subjects was much higher than that of the general population in the United States. The authors pointed to a 1999 population study of American sexual dysfunction that showed 7 to 22 percent of women reporting little desire for sex, problems getting aroused, and some sexual pain. The numbers were roughly the same for men, with 5 to 21 percent reporting some erectile dysfunction, low desire, and premature ejaculation.[39]

And with Americans getting bigger, so, too, were the problems. With the prevalence of obesity increasing, the researchers suggested that sexual issues are likely affecting more people than previously recognized.

But it was more than just raw data; it was raw emotion, too. Battered by prejudice and often daily discrimination and suffering from painful body images, obese people are especially vulnerable, the study asserted. And that combination "may present social and psychological barriers to having sexual needs met," meaning that in addition to their bodies not cooperating, their heads and hearts were getting in the way, too. In conclusion, the authors urged medical providers to create a kinder, more welcoming environment in which patients could confide in them.

As the study of the sexual lives of heavy men and women picked up steam, the search for patterns in the group was complicated by differing definitions of sexual dysfunction and different assessment tools for men and women.

Kolotkin pioneered research into the internal lives of the obese with the design of the original Impact of Weight on Quality of Life questionnaire—or IWQOL—in the mid-1990s. The questionnaire was considered groundbreaking in that it endeavored to find out how overweight people were actually affected by their size.

In 2013, Dr. Kolotkin and her colleagues at the department of community and family medicine at Duke University School of Medicine in Durham, North Carolina, decided to review the literature on sexual functioning and obesity. By then, Dr. Kolotkin had administered her IWQOL questionnaire to more than 10,000 men and women, and had in fact discovered objective findings in what had been thought to be subjective experiences. After examining more than 100 other published studies, Dr. Kolotkin and her coauthors concluded that there is "a robust relationship between not only obesity and reduced sexual functioning, but also between weight loss and improved sexual functioning."

Further, big women—quite frankly—had it worse, Dr. Kolotkin and her colleagues concluded. "Women often talk about difficulties with enjoyment, low sexual desire, avoidance of sexual intimacy, as well as some difficulty with sexual performance."

* * *

When is a woman sexually aroused? This is a question medical researchers have been trying to answer for decades: Is it simply when blood can be measured engorging her vagina? Or is it when parts of her brain that play a role in sexual excitement light up on a brain scan? Does there need to be a physical record of sexual arousal for it to have actually happened, or can we simply take a woman's word on it?

It's not an easy puzzle to solve. Here's a classic example of an experiment to test female sexual arousal, this one from Stanford University: One by one, healthy young women were placed inside a magnetic resonance imaging machine, where they watched pornography—naked people doing naked things in all kinds of ways. Then they watched a video of trees. Just plain old trees. The researchers had placed a vaginal plethysmograph inside their vaginas; the instrument is a clear acrylic, tampon-shaped device that can measure changes in bloodflow to the vagina.

What the researchers found was a shock: When women who had clinically low libido watched scenes of couples having sex, they rated their own arousal on a questionnaire about the experience as very low. The brain scans confirmed this—the women's brains didn't respond to the pornography and they were not sexually turned on—but at the same time, the vaginal plethysmograph registered an increase in vaginal bloodflow. In other words, their vaginas were turned on, brains be damned.

And this is a large part of the dilemma in trying to help women, including overweight and obese women, who complain of sexual problems: the disconnect between vaginal arousal and what's called central arousal—a brain excited about sex and a mind that rates it pleasurable. The perception of what a woman is feeling—mentally, emotionally, sexually— is often much different than the actual, measurable changes going on in her bloodflow, heart rate, and level of lubrication.

This "desynchrony"—as it's unartfully known—doesn't exist in men. In laboratory experiments, men have been hooked up to penile plethysmographs—devices that fit snugly over the penis to gauge swelling— and brain scanning machines and asked to watch pornography. When these men rate their sexual experience, it almost always matches their erectile response.

There are a number of interesting theories about why a woman's vagina can appear sexually aroused, even when she says she's not. Anthropologists suspect that the vagina's ability to self-lubricate developed through evolution to protect the pelvic floor during childbirth and during rape, which, as mentioned earlier, may have been common during humankind's early days.

Indeed, for years, the concept of bloodflow—and particularly bloodflow into penises—dominated human sexuality. The traditional model described by Masters and Johnson delineated sex into a series of stages that followed the rise and fall of the penis: get excited, have an orgasm, and then everything resets back to normal.

And that was—mistakenly—applied to women. "Males tend to have a very linear course in the sexual act. They seek out desire, arousal, orgasm. That's an objective; it's a goal," said Scott Chudnoff, MD, director of gynecology at Montefiore Hospital in the Bronx and associate professor of obstetrics and gynecology at Albert Einstein College of Medicine in the Bronx.

With women, he said, sexuality today is understood as much more circular; desire need not precede arousal, nor does sex need to result in an orgasm for women to report feeling satisfied.

"It's not necessarily that she's per se seeking orgasm, as much as she might be looking for other types of physical contact," Dr. Chudnoff said. "She may not even be aroused or seeking arousal, but she has ulterior motives for her desire to be with her partner." She may simply want to feel closer to her partner, to please her partner, or to feel loved and appreciated. And while these emotions occur to men, a mind-body sexual drive—operating in sync—is almost always the norm.

Still, if you think that desynchrony is hard to believe, you're not alone. Since the mid-1970s, when research using vaginal plethysmography really took off, there have been complaints that perhaps the women just weren't recalling their experiences accurately. These self-report measures relied on women recalling how they felt, and perhaps the memories faded quickly after they'd been unhooked, as it were, from the machines.

So, in response to those criticisms, researchers tried to design devices—with varying degrees of success—that would allow women to rate their experience while they were exposed to erotic stimuli. Most involved pornography and elaborate joysticks that the women could "click" in the moment. (It didn't seem to matter whether the erotica was made by men or women.) Funnily enough, many versions of measuring involved flashing lights—and red lightbulbs seemed to be a popular, and ironic, indicator—and evolved with the time. Researchers at the Sexual Psychophysiology Laboratory at the University of Texas at Austin developed a nifty instrument called the arousometer, a computer mouse that allows women to click their level of sexual arousal in real time.

But most of these attempts to have women provide play-by-play commentary on their sexual arousal still haven't debunked the concept of desynchrony.

* * *

IN the case of heavy women, the vaginal sexual response is not as vulnerable to the vicissitudes of fat as are men's hormone levels or penile arteries. Still, gynecologists and others who study female sexuality say obese women have much to contend with during sex. Excess weight can lead to myriad gynecological problems.

For starters, the same belly fat that converts testosterone into estrogen in men sets into motion a similar process in women. And with the ovaries also in action, obese women can end up with something akin to an overdose of estrogen, leading to abnormal uterine bleeding, a condition known as endometrial hyperplasia.

"The more obese you are, the more estrogen your body is going to produce, and that in itself will stimulate the endometrial lining," said Dr. Millheiser, from Stanford. The result can be anything from spotting to very heavy, prolonged menstruation, irregular ovulation, and an oelevated risk of endometrial cancer, all of which can be dangerous and potentially devastating to a woman's general reproductive health.

These kinds of changes can occur even for moderately overweight women: Women with a body mass index over 25 are at greater risk for irregular menstrual cycles or cessation of menstruation altogether, which can impact fertility. "We tend to see the problems escalating as their weight goes up," said Dr. Millheiser.

But it's not just the uterus that can suffer. The vagina and clitoris are also vulnerable to physiological changes from excess weight. As in men, hyperlipidemia (high cholesterol) and diabetes can lead to vascular damage, thus decreasing bloodflow to the vagina and clitoris and impairing sensitive nerve endings, which can impede orgasm.

One of the more comprehensive studies came from Italy, where 90 women, ages 18 through 35, allowed their bodies to be fully inventoried, right down to their most sensitive spots.[40] The process was complex: Around the same time in their menstrual cycles, the women were put under ultrasonographic scans to map the size of their clitoris and color Doppler ultrasound machines that allowed researchers to see the arteries inside the clitoris. (The researchers even took precautions to "minimize the external effects on bloodflow" by putting all the women in a noiseless room with constant heat and light.) The women also had blood drawn to measure estrogen, testosterone, glucose, and other indicators.

The study also included a personal evaluation: They filled out a questionnaire on sexuality, body image, and depression, rating their sexual desire, frequency of orgasm, any pain, and their general sexual satisfaction. They rated how they felt about their sexual partner and the state of their relationship; they were asked about their ideal weight and how satisfied they were with their own body; and they answered an inventory of questions that can unmask depression.

Finally, based on body mass index, the women were divided into three categories: lean, overweight, and obese. And it was in that categorization that a revealing discovery was made about the difference between the sexual experiences of lean women and those of more formidable girth.

Based on images from the ultrasound, women across all categories had similarly sized clitorises. But the high-resolution machines that allowed researchers to see how well the clitoral artery was delivering blood also revealed that the obese women had the worst clitoral vascularization.

The Italian study stopped there, but the results pointed to this: Fatter women are at an increased risk of problems with blood flowing and delivering nutrients to their clitorises. Women's sexual health experts say that this finding syncs with a general understanding of vascular health; if plaque can build up in a heart, it can build up in the small blood vessels leading to the clitoris. Decreased bloodflow can mean decreased nerve conduction and lack of sensitivity, and those problems can add up to difficulty achieving orgasm.

"These are small vessels that can have a very large impact on their sexual functioning," Dr. Millheiser said.

And for women with diabetes, the problems can multiply. Diabetic women tend to report more problems with vaginal irritation and lubrication, perhaps because women with diabetes are more prone to fungal infections. Alison Huang, MD, assistant professor at the University of California, San Francisco, and a women's health researcher who coauthored one of the few studies to examine the effect of diabetes on sexual function in women, says that bloodflow is certainly an issue. But there are other problems, too.

According to a 2012 report by Dr. Huang and her colleagues at the Women's Health Clinical Research Center at UCSF, the women being treated with insulin were much more likely to report low overall sexual satisfaction—at 34.9 percent—than diabetic women not receiving insulin (26 percent). And what's more, insulin-treated women were more likely to report problems with lubrication and orgasm.[41]

A prior survey of nearly 2,000 middle-aged and older diabetics also found that women with diagnosed diabetes were less likely than other women and diabetic men to be sexually active.[42] And it wasn't just with another person: Women with diagnosed and undiagnosed diabetes were also nearly half as likely as other women to say they had masturbated, and more likely to be dropping out of sexual activity altogether compared to women of similar age. To the authors, the findings suggested "a reduction in sexual drive that was independent of partner status and of knowledge of the disease."

The reasons behind low sexual satisfaction among diabetic women aren't well understood. Certainly, problems with lubrication and orgasm could make sex painful or certainly unsatisfying. Or, as Dr. Huang suggests, it could be the daily burden of living with a chronic condition that requires measuring one's blood sugar throughout the day and taking medication, or even other chronic conditions.

And there are certain embarrassments that might simply make sex unpalatable. As weight increases, personal hygiene can become a problem. In interviews with heavy women around the country, many recounted in detail the difficulty of reaching around themselves to wash and the embarrassment they felt with sexual partners over personal cleanliness and the smell of urine, a result of weight-related incontinence.

"That's another big complaint from my patients," said Dr. Millheiser. "It is not just body image because of their weight, it is, 'I'm embarrassed because I smell.'"

And finally, for obese women, especially if they are with obese male partners, sex can be confounded by bad mechanics. Dr. Chudnoff says some of the patients in his gynecology practice in the Bronx explain that they feel like they're being "smothered" or they can't get close enough for satisfying sex.

"He may be a totally normal-sized male, but because of the fact that she has excessive rolls around the vulva area, there's barely any penetration that's taking place," said Dr. Chudnoff. "And she's like, 'He's just too small. I don't feel anything.'"

That was the case for Cindy, a 28-year-old Texas woman. She met her husband in college: She was a freshman and he was the friendly RA in her dorm who made her feel welcome. They were both big when they started dating—she was around 230 pounds and he was around 260—but they had an instant connection, in part because of their size, and in part because of shared struggles with their mood and anxiety.

"I feel better than I have in a very long time, but I now gain weight much more easily," said Cindy, who is on medication for depression. And that weight gain has begun causing problems during sex.

"My husband is heavy, too, and he is only of average size in the downstairs area." Both of those issues, she said, have "added to position difficulty. It has taken a huge toll in the bedroom."

Even when physical issues are taken out of the equation, there are emotional issues—triggered by the physical difficulty in performing even the smallest acts of affection—that can irreparably foul the mood for love, and, by extension, sex.

Tisha Combs is a 41-year-old Californian. A few years ago, she was living in Long Beach and started flirting online with a new love. They met a few weeks later and became inseparable. This new man, a computer technician, was fun and adventurous, and he loved to go out to eat. She had been married before, and after years of preparing meals for her ex-husband, a strict marine, the freedom to go to McDonald's for dinner was a relief.

"When we both went into it, we were both chunky people. I was probably 200 pounds, and he was probably around 220," Tisha said. "I'm not even sure what happened, but it just seemed like all we did was gain weight." It wasn't until she became pregnant with their son—and no one realized she was carrying—that Tisha started to see how big she had gotten.

Over the next few years, she and her new husband each gained more than 100 extra pounds. "As the pounds were coming on, my energy was going down," Tisha said. Her husband liked bigger women, but Tisha didn't feel good about herself. When he asked her to go out for a hike, she'd say, "We're 300 pounds. We have no business hiking."

He'd press her about going to the amusement park with the family. She'd say no, and the refusals always started a fight. "It was hard to actually say out loud, 'Okay, I don't want to go because I don't want to get stuck on a ride, and I don't want to get embarrassed,'" she said. "So it became a big issue for us."

Tisha had difficulty getting physically close to her husband, and she found even walking down the street holding hands awkward. "We're big, and we walk, you know, funny," she said. "Our arms are kind of swinging. He couldn't really hold my hand, and then we'd sweat, and our hands would get sweaty, and we couldn't hug each other very well. We carried our weight all in our stomach, so we kind of had to do a sideways hug."

And in the bedroom, the issues around their weight were only amplified.

"You couldn't really cuddle in bed because he's got so much heat emitting off of him," Tisha said. "And me, too."

Her lack of interest sent the couple spiraling away from each other, as actions—and emotional interpretations of those actions—ricocheted and resonated through their relationship. Her husband believed she had stopped loving him, and so in return, he stopped paying her compliments and showing her any love. And that made her less likely to want to have sex. Which made him less affectionate. And so on.

"He equates love with intimacy, so if I'm not intimate with him, then that must mean that I don't love him," she said. "And then it became this cycle."

Cindy, the 28-year-old Texan, seconded that. Her husband suffers from erectile dysfunction and withdraws emotionally, in part due to post-traumatic stress disorder. This leaves Cindy feeling unappreciated and unloved.

Their sex life "was already really crappy," Cindy said. "Now add my fat ass into the mix, and it really doesn't help. Our sex life is bad."

What Cindy and Tisha describe is all too common among overweight and obese women: a kind of sexual numbness that starts in the mind and then spreads into their bodies. Self-hatred can consume the sexuality of women of all sizes, but for those struggling with weight or experiencing weight-related conditions, like diabetes, and physical discomfort, such as joint pain, the experience is more acute.

The experience was familiar to Dr. Millheiser, a gynecologist from

Stanford University who often feels more like a psychologist or a marriage therapist when caring for her patients. Many physicians who practice female sexual medicine go on to get secondary degrees in sex therapy or marital therapy, and it's not uncommon for gynecologists to refer a patient for sex therapy, physical therapy, marriage counseling, and pain therapy.

"It's not just that someone is obese or overweight. It may be that they are in a dysfunctional relationship that's been long-standing," she told me at her office in Palo Alto. "With women, it's not just a bloodflow issue. You can increase a woman's bloodflow [with Viagra], she may have increased lubrication, but it is not going to change the fact that she is not attracted to her partner or she is not in the mood."

But Dr. Millheiser doesn't buy the idea that heavier people simply are doomed to have bad sex. "I don't think we should put everybody into a little box that says, 'You are obese, so you must have sexual dysfunction.'"

Indeed, for all of the physical and scientific challenges, there is hope on the horizon for many overweight women and men looking for a better sex life, whether through new surgical procedures, new pills, or new ways of motivating better eating, better lifestyle—and yes, better times in the bedroom. Several companies are chasing the magic bullet: a pill that would simultaneously spice up one's sex life and cause one to shed pounds. And more scientific study—even if it results in added willingness to address the sex lives of overweight and obese people—will no doubt reap benefits.

Finally, there is simple human resilience and the will to change, factors almost as mysterious as the scientific quest for the meaning of what makes good sex.

Take Tisha, for example, who finally had a eureka moment in the strangest of places: a parking lot. She had gone to the doctor and, to her surprise, he prescribed medication for high blood pressure. She took the prescription and wandered out of the office in something of a haze.

But what followed was a pure instant of clarity, she remembers.

"I sat in my car going, 'My God. I'm taking meds because I'm fat?

This is messed up.' I remember driving home, and it was late. And I picked up McDonald's for the kids," she recalls. She walked in with those familiar white paper bags full of salt and fat and grease, and plopped them down on the table, as she had done too many times before.

"And bing-bang-boom, they all sat in front of the TV eating their McDonald's," she said. "And I'm like, 'Alllll right. What am I doing to them now?' And that wasn't cool."

The very next day, Tisha made an appointment to have weight loss surgery.

CHAPTER FIVE

Pleasures: Sammee in Sin City

Las Vegas, Nevada

The stripper stage at Foxy's Las Vegas is surrounded by mirrors etched with cartoonish decals: In one, a figure poses in high heels, her toned legs in a seductive wide stance, one hip jutting backward. Her waist is pinched thin, and with her dainty elbows cocked, she holds two pistols at the ready. The swirling, pulsing bodies of the dancers reflected in the mirrors look nothing like the seductive, gun-slinging cartoons.

Spinning around a polished bronze pole in a whirl of lustrous black hair and loose flesh, a woman wearing a crystal necklace that spells out "Barbie" lands on the stage floor amid a bath of pulsing, candy-colored lights. The dancer kicks her thick legs—covered in lace-topped, thigh-high stockings—up in the air, her gestures precise and fluid, and spins onto her hands and knees. Barbie is here to gratify the sensual appetites of men and women drawn to bigger bodies, and with a sequin tube top pulled down over her belly, she lunges across the stage and sweeps her pendulous white breasts across the floor. As she crawls forward, she draws to her chest an admirer sitting on a bar stool—a thin, plain-looking young woman in a T-shirt and jeans who has been sipping bottled water.

On this wintry Sunday evening in January, Foxy's Las Vegas has been turned into "Thick Sundaes," an enclave for women whose bodies are ridiculed and reviled elsewhere in Sin City. The strip show features dancers and porn stars from the world of BBW (Big, Beautiful Women) and SSBBW (Supreme-Sized—or Super-Sized—Big, Beautiful Women); the performers had flown in from New York, California, Florida, Texas, and elsewhere to mingle in comfort with their fans and curious first-timers and put their bodies on defiant display. The events take place on Las Vegas's only down days, Sundays. Club operators are less reluctant then to rent out their venues to dolled-up obese strippers who more closely resemble in size the typical woman than do the silicone-enhanced dancers who swing around the pole at Foxy's most other nights.

* * *

THE dancers crawled on their hands and knees, scooping up stray dollar bills. In the back of the room, across from the stage, two women, both former cocktail waitresses and plump mothers of teenage girls, sat on stools with cocktails in hand, completely confounded by the sight of topless, obese bodies.

"I need to get a pole," said Jennifer, a black woman with chin-length, curly hair. "I need to start working out because I can't even get my ass up there," she said, her gaze turning to the dancer on the stripper stage. "And she's bigger than me."

"We've already decided we're going to start [practicing] on Tuesday," offered her friend, Laurie, a blonde white woman who claimed to have once met Larry Flynt, the publisher of *Hustler* magazine.

A neighbor, one of the show's organizers, had invited the women to Thick Sundaes. Neither of them knew much about the world of Big, Beautiful Women, and they had certainly never considered it a turn-on. "I don't mind saying my weight 'cuz it's just like my age," said Jennifer. "People don't think I look 40. I really don't look my weight. I really weigh a lot more than I look."

"How much do you weigh?" Laurie asked.

"Two hundred thirty."

"Well, at my scale at home, I'm 240."

"Is it," asked Jennifer, "at zero before you get on it?"

"Unfortunately, fucking yes."

* * *

FOXY'S was decorated with a red felt pool table and a bank of poker machines, and it was one of the few places still offering 99-cent shrimp cocktails in Las Vegas. Jennifer and Laurie had heard Foxy's was one of the worst strip clubs in town—a squat, gray concrete building that sat in an industrial area just east of the Las Vegas Freeway. Laurie worked as a cashier at the Hard Rock Hotel and Casino, a richly decorated playland with a glittering circular bar and topless pool parties that peddled the fantasy of the self-indulgent Vegas rock star, where the men were hard-bodied and rich, and the women, taut and full-bosomed. That fantasy, it seemed to Laurie, could not withstand the cruelty of her own growing waistline. "Well, I used to do cocktails for 14 years," Laurie said. "Once I got bigger, I had to stop and become a cashier. They take you from day shift to graveyard, where you're making 100-some dollars a day. They cut your hours. I mean, doesn't somebody like healthy girls who eat all of their food?"

Some of Laurie's old customers from her cocktail waitressing days still called her up when they visited, and she would go out with them. But she was losing money and trying to raise her teenage daughter on a cashier's lowly income.

"In Vegas," offered Jennifer, "being overweight is against the law."

* * *

ALONG the Las Vegas Strip, stooped and speechless Filipino men handed out cards for "Girls, Girls, Girls." Street corner vending machines that in other cities contained the local news advertised the escort services of toned women with comically enlarged breasts. Trucks pulled up on traffic medians hauled billboards with photos of panting women that seemed to lunge at drivers passing by.

Las Vegas was rough on women of size who wanted to work as cocktail waitresses, card dealers, hostesses, and dancers at marquee casinos and resorts, but it also offered singular opportunities. The city's reputation for satisfying any erotic practice meant that some very heavy women were prized by men known as Feeders. They sought bizarre sex play like "feed 'em and fuck 'em" fantasies: At privately arranged parties or through a discreet concierge, call girls weighing 300 pounds or more could be brought in to have sexual intercourse while being fed cake, doughnuts, and any number of treats.

That kind of sex work was beyond the moral bounds for Sammee Matthews, the mother of two girls, and soon-to-be grandmother, and the SSBBW adult entertainer who'd started the Thick Sundae parties in July 2012. Sammee's body had consumed her. Flesh poured over her arms and elbows; her breasts and stomach lurched forward; her thighs pressed outward. When she walked, Sammee toddled side to side on the outsides of her heels, wincing often at the pain in her knees. She popped ibuprofen throughout the day to tame the swelling in her joints. Her figure only narrowed at the extremities: Her fingers were long and bony and elegant, like a concert pianist's; her wrists, delicate and graceful.

In her early life, before she turned the camera on herself, Sammee had once operated a phone sex line out of her Las Vegas house to pay her bills. She advertised herself on a phone sex Web site as "Marissa," with a picture of a blue-eyed, bottle-red-haired, 125-pound seductress. Over lunch at Tony Roma's, Sammee recalled the wretched memory of her telephonic persona: "She could be whatever you wanted her to be for 15 minutes. You could shit all over my face in your fantasy, and I would say," Sammee leaned in and spoke in Marissa's soft, rich, kneading voice, "Thank you. Give me more, please."

At the time, it seemed to Sammee a necessary and cruel way to make a living. She had been working toward a nursing degree and taking some shifts as a secretary at a local hospital. She weighed 450 pounds then and had difficulty tying her shoes and zipping up her pants. Her morning routine entailed slipping on her house shoes, pulling her bobbed hair into a pony-tail, putting on a flannel shirt and eyeglasses, and making "about a bazillion cups of coffee." At first, she was stumped by some of the men's requests and found herself researching the details of their fantasies on the Internet: men who fetishized being bathed, diapered, and nursed like babies; men who wanted her to pretend she was dead, or some kind of animal.

Sammee's voice turned dark: "I resented it. I resented myself. I *RE-SENT-ED* sex," she added, spacing the syllables with unmistakable disgust. She feared her own imagination was being warped, and the humiliation led her to new lows. "I'm telling you to get off shitting on me, and I'm eating a Ding Dong."

In her own sexual life, Sammee was appalled by porn. She was married then to a poker-playing construction worker with a taste for hard-core pornography, and as she thought back to that moment, she said, "I didn't understand what this person on the screen had to offer him. I'm a physical person. I'm 60 feet away from you. What's wrong?"

* * *

THE memory of how Sammee ended up naked, holding a birthday cake on a gag gift bag, is imprecise. She remembers that someone got in touch with her over MySpace and asked her to do a "plumpers" photo shoot. Up until then, Sammee knew little of the BBW community. She had been chunky ever since she was a child. A Polaroid photo shows a young Sammee gripping a fishing pole and holding out her catch—a wisp of a fish the size of a maple leaf. She is maybe 7 or 8 years old, with feathered, tawny hair, standing on the rocky shore of a lake in a short-sleeve printed shirt and burgundy polyester pants pulling against her wide thighs. Her father is standing next to her in dark sunglasses, worn blue jeans, and a white T-shirt stretched over his bulging belly. He is looking down at Sammee as she smiles into the camera. It had been a few years by then since he had told her she was his princess and that he had a magic wand and convinced her to have oral sex with him.

The photo shoot seemed like a playful way to make good money off her bulbous body, and Sammee was flattered, after portraying "Marissa" to her phone sex customers, to be on camera as herself. At the shoot, she was asked to take off her clothes and hold a birthday cake. She expected to earn $1,000, but in the end she received $100, and in signing some legal papers inadvertently gave the photographers the rights to use the photos in any way they wanted, in perpetuity. For years, the novelty gift store Spencer's, a nationwide chain with hundreds of stores that sell everything from lava lamps to the Fatty Patty Inflatable Love Doll, has sold, Sammee said, novelty gift bags with her naked, cake-wielding frame. "I'm naked, and I'm holding a birthday cake," she said flatly. "What is so funny about that?"

Morbidly obese people are commonly perceived as sloppy, lazy behemoths. Sammee, however, was on the move. Industrious, ambitious, and uncowed by her bad fortune, Sammee told herself she deserved more. At home, she started playing around with a camera and learned to shoot pictures of herself that she hoped to sell online. Sammee understood that she needed to branch out and sought out photographers in online chat rooms and meet-ups: How should she use the camera to compliment her bigger size? How should she position her scars from an automobile accident and her stretch marks that came from bearing two children?

Soon, she was going to meet and greets, BBW-themed club nights, and BBW fan festivals; she launched her own Web site, and photos of her started appearing on SSBBW and BBW adult sites: Sammee kneeling on an upholstered chair, peering over her shoulder in a daffodil-colored satin slip; Sammee, her swirl of frosted brown hair pinned back in a barrette, lying on a bed, touching another supreme-size woman's knee. Like other "girls" with adult sites, Sammee cultivated her fan base, turning to Facebook and Twitter to build her brand.

Still, it seemed that many of the men drawn to this peculiar niche of adult entertainment were titillated only by the enormity of the women's bodies, gawking at them as some freakish novelty. The attraction seemed boorish, sinister, and objectifying. Sammee wanted big women to be seen as sexy, as erotic and pretty in their own right.

She surmised that there was a growing market of customers for more pedestrian but big-bodied erotic pleasures. While Sin City still continued to peddle the fantasy of svelte, bosomy women, the tourists, bachelor and bachelorette partiers, and conventioneers who visited Las Vegas were themselves getting heavier. Mainstream porn stars still strived to resemble human Barbies, but YouPorn and other user-generated Web sites revealed what seemed to be a growing appetite for wider-girthed, pan-ethnic erotica. Surely, Sammee surmised, some of these people would pay for a big girls' striptease? If it worked, she imagined she could expand to sell lingerie and shoes that didn't pinch the plumper feet of plus-size women.

With a business partner whom she had met at a Las Vegas BBW meet and greet, Sammee hosted the first Thick Sundaes event in July 2012 at Foxy's. She would go on to promote Thick Sundaes as "Las Vegas's ONLY Amateur BBW/SSBBW/PSBBW (Porn Star BBW) Event."

* * *

AND that was how Regina Nunes, a California housewife who enjoyed a daily diet of plus-size porn and was also the mother of three young children, came to hold April Flores's breasts in her hands.

Many of the patrons at Foxy's had come to see April perform her first live stage show. A plus-size Jessica Rabbit, April Flores had creamy Latin skin and wavy, shoulder-length scarlet tresses. She had starred in the BBW erotic films *Behind the Red Door* and *Dangerous Curves,* among others. Her porn name was Fatty D (Fabulous All The Time, Y'All), and she had big ambitions.

"Can I touch you?" Regina asked April. This curvaceous form that she'd known only as a pixilated character was now standing in front of her in the violet neon lights next to Foxy's stripper stage. April raised her arms, and Regina, a short, stout woman with sparkling, wishful eyes, marveled at the flesh she held in her hands. "Can my husband touch you?"

April turned to Regina's husband, Peter, a former navy sailor who had been a virgin in his midtwenties when he and Regina married. Nervously, he stroked April's breasts.

April had status among the Thick Sundaes crowd. She was one of the few BBW performers who had consistently gotten work in the mainstream porn industry: She had posed for the cover of *Bizarre* magazine and had been featured in *Australian Penthouse,* discussing the growing popularity of plus-size porn stars. *AVN* magazine, the trade journal for the adult video industry, had nominated her in 2011 as the Crossover Star of the Year and coined the phrase "the April Flores Effect," based on the belief that the Mexican-Ecuadoran beauty was making her way into the mainstream with explicit pornography and erotic performance art, and other BBW performers would follow.

At Foxy's, the crowd filled in with tattooed women in bustiers and men in fitted sport coats. Lionel Stewart, who went by the name "Static," collected money at the door and, when needed, wiped down the bronze stripper pole. This was the first time Sammee Matthews, the evening's organizer, had put him on payroll for a Thick Sundaes event, and it was his job to encourage patrons to line up for lap dances. (The dancers kept the proceeds, and Sammee wanted the women to make good money to ensure they showed up for future events.) At 25, Lionel was "out" to his friends about his preference for bigger women. "Whenever there's a group of girls, and there's a big girl, they're like, 'There you go, Lionel!'"

The days when bigger women were insecure and easy were over, said Lionel. "They're starting to come out," he surmised. "Events like this, it lets you know they're coming out. And they got attitude just like anybody else. You gotta work to get a big girl. Just like you gotta work for any woman."

The clipped, breathy R&B singer Jeremih came over the club's sound system as April Flores took the stage for the first time in knee-high red stockings, platform heels, and a turquoise mesh leotard.

April moved slowly across the narrow stage, flooded in soft light. The stools that ringed the platform filled up with a line of bigger women, some weighing a modest 200 pounds, others extremely obese at 400 pounds or more. Sammee, who had been preoccupied much of the night, lumbered onto a stool. Regina, who had taken her own seat at the front, yelled to her husband, "Give! Me! Money!" as if she were a schoolgirl at a carnival game. Another woman cried out over and over, "Oh, my goodness!"

Unlike traditional strip clubs where the dancers were reduced to component parts—headless, servile breasts—and the action—on the pole, in the booths, in the VIP rooms—was to gratify the wanton needs of male patrons, the Thick Sundae enthusiasts sought something else: They were groupies, like Regina, who hoped through some willed transference that they could imprint April Flores's big-girl confidence onto their big-girl bodies. It was as if they wished their own shame and self-punishment could be washed away by the power of witnessing April pull down the straps of her turquoise leotard and let her stomach unfurl.

Through adoration, they would come to see themselves as good enough.

* * *

REGINA and Peter had driven 8 hours with their three young children from California's Central Valley to Las Vegas for this chance at salvation. They were a conventional, middle-class suburban family who lived on a cul-de-sac of sterile beige homes. Peter worked as a security manager for a local utility company; Regina stayed home with their baby and carted her two older kids to elementary school and Boy Scouts, and pestered them about their homework. Like many parents juggling small children, Regina could efficiently sweep up her whimpering baby even as she explained in great detail, as one might a china plate collection, the boxes of Japanese anime dolls that lined her dining room.

Home life was a geekier, kinkier version of *The Feminine Mystique:* a BBW-loving, tattooed housewife who saw her role as caring for and feeding her family; who valued her femininity; and who aimed to excite her husband by learning new makeup techniques, squeezing into custom-made satin bustiers, and learning to dance like the heavy strippers she so admired. Her favorite photograph of them as a couple was a re-creation of the iconic 1945 *Life* magazine shot of the Victory over Japan Day in Times Square. At a local photography studio, Peter had dressed up to look like an American sailor back from war, and he clutched Regina—who wore a white, flouncy nurse's dress—around the waist and bent her backward in a forceful kiss. The framed black-and-white photo shows Regina kicking up her heel in a flirtatious sweep.

Regina had always been prudish about porn: She distrusted her ex-husband's penchant for it, and on several occasions became irate when she found adult videos and photos on Peter's laptop. She felt betrayed by the attraction.

It had been just before she gave birth to their youngest child when Regina caught her husband watching porn. Peter was a virgin when he married Regina, but before their wedding, when he was in the navy, he lived for months on end at sea. His computer had been used as a communal library for pornographic videos.

When Regina found her husband's X-rated videos, he denied that they were his, but the whole episode sent her reeling. She despised the notion that Peter became aroused by slender women with buoyant silicone breasts when her own breasts sagged from the wear of childbirth and her stomach rippled and rolled. She wondered if she was good enough. It seemed an essential question, and she lived in terrible insecurity. "What's wrong with *me?*" she thought.

In daily domestic life, Regina wasn't embarrassed to be naked in front of her husband. Although Peter had been a sailor, Regina was the family captain: She kept the family moving in swift, efficient fashion; she often finished Peter's sentences when he paused; he seemed practiced in yielding to her with a toothy smile, his pronounced overbite signaling retreat.

Regina didn't like her husband turning to pornography on his own, but she was game to widen their sexual boundaries. Desire rose up in her body frequently—it had ever since she was a girl—and she felt entitled to sexual pleasure. It was a physical yearning that she either tended to herself or turned to Peter to satisfy. Her growing weight had done nothing to dull her bodily urges; it was when she suspected Peter was comparing her to other women that Regina's assuredness evaporated.

The first time she saw April Flores was on an adult Web site: It was a short video clip of April with a man that she remembers was named Mr. Pete. She and Peter, together on the computer, followed April's trail across the Internet and found the *Bizarre* magazine photo spread. Peter started to stir.

"Does that," Regina asked her husband, "turn you on?"

He answered with a grunt.

"Do *I* do it for you?"

And he answered yes.

The logic was unassailable. "If he's looking at bigger women," Regina figured, "then obviously I got something he likes."

The two started watching X-rated videos of April together, and when April sent out messages to her fans on Facebook that she was going to do a live Webcam show, Regina and Peter paid to watch.

The boundaries of their sexual play widened. It wasn't that the couple, the parents of three children, tried the kinkier arts. It was that as Regina's confidence in her own body grew, she became more daring. She had come to mimic—at least at times—the precocious, scarlet-haired idol that she adored.

The discovery of an idol soon led to merchandise.

In their suburban home, down the hall from the baby's nursery and the kids' rooms, posters of April went up on the walls. In between a flat-screen television perched on a wooden dresser and a *Lord of the Rings* poster, April gazed out from a large glass frame. She wore large pink satin panties that cut across her thick, sturdy thighs, and, with the crooks of her arms, she gathered in her breasts like unruly basketballs. (Gravity had the same effect on April's breasts as it did on Regina's when left to hang down.) Red heart-shaped stickers covered her nipples. With her candy red hair, she was a plump vision in rouge. The poster was signed, "LOVE FOREVER, April Flores." She had added a smiley face. There were smaller promotional posters and prints for April's movies—*Voluptuous Biker Babes* and *Kiss*

Attack (A New Chapter in the Vampire Myth)—and an autographed headshot of April.

Regina often watched April's videos and used the April Flores Pussy Stroker masturbation toy when Peter was at work and the baby was napping. However, she didn't want her husband lusting after April Flores on his own. At home, before the trip to Las Vegas to watch her idol perform at Foxy's, Regina noticed a 1-inch by 1-inch image on Peter's laptop. He had been designing a takeoff on Dungeons and Dragons for his friends, and had created a small avatar of April with her mouth open and her tongue reaching out as if to lick something. Regina confronted him.

"What is that?"

"I did this the other day."

"Where's the file?"

He had deleted it.

Her husband was being cagey, Regina thought. "Why didn't you say, 'Hey, I have this on my computer?'"

It came off as if her husband was hiding something; it wasn't exactly a breach of trust, but it was too close to her past experiences. "He knows I've been hurt in the past by guys looking at porn, and then lying about it and then saying, oh, they didn't do it."

They agreed to only watch porn together. "That way," said Peter, "there's no miscommunication."

* * *

It was hard to remain dour with topless women wandering about. "We're drinkin' and we're thinkin'," said Jennifer. The sight of rippling stomachs, sagging breasts, and cellulite sexed up on stage had stirred in the two former cocktail waitresses questions about not just how Vegas viewed them, but how they viewed themselves. "We've been thinking all night since we've been sitting here, for like 3 hours, going, 'What is wrong with us?'" said Jennifer.

The women seemed surprised that men could find these fleshy bodies titillating. In their own sexual moments, with uncertain intimacy, the women felt embarrassed by their size and preferred to cover up.

"I can't have sex without my T-shirt on," said Laurie. "Without a *long* T-shirt." It was a burdensome awakening to have on a Sunday evening at a BBW strip club in Las Vegas. "I don't know why."

"My man was always like, 'Let's go in front of the mirror,'" said Jennifer. "'Let's do this.' And I'd feel like things are hanging out and my body was sagging," she said plainly and without pity. "I feel self-conscious. I feel I can't have a good time because I'm focusing on that. I'm not focusing on what we're doing. And he's having a good time. He wants the lights on." Jennifer seemed to grasp where this was headed. "Watching these girls, and watching these guys pay for lap dances, I'm like, 'Well, okay, she has *way* more stuff hanging out.' This is definitely a self-confidence booster." And then she wondered if it might be rude to draw her newfound self-love from the fact that she wasn't quite as heavy as the strippers on the stage.

* * *

APRIL'S performance at Foxy's was demure compared to the raw, raunchy dances of many of the other BBW and SSBBW dancers like "Golden XXX Creamy" and "Milky Diva," who lifted and hurled their extravagantly large breasts up over their shoulders and shook the clumps of lumpy cellulite that protruded from their backsides and thighs in what seemed more like a circus act than a striptease. April was less explicit and more evocative.

Regina looked up, beaming, and April seemed to revel in Regina's attention without becoming undone by it.

Aspiring BBW performers understood that interacting with their fans was a strategic necessity. In between stage performances, April displayed the patience and discipline needed to grow into a star.

"I hope I don't make you feel uncomfortable when I mention this," said Regina, whose lips were painted a creamy red similar to her idol's.

"We watch a lot of your movies. And I usually jerk him off with your toy."
She gestured toward Peter.

"Ahh, nice." April seemed genuinely pleased.

"And I'm like, 'You're getting April!'" Regina chortled. "That's as close as you're going to get."

Regina was ebullient as she thanked April for the live Webcam show they had all shared a few months back. Now, she had too much she wanted to tell her, and it all came blurting out: how she was only 32 years old and her hair was graying, a curse for the women in her family, and she had dyed some streaks red, and she just couldn't understand how April kept up her neon red hair.

"Shortly after the Webcam, we were watching *April Flores World*," Regina tattled on. "And I think [you mentioned] Glory Story was one of your favorite vibrators."

April laughed.

"I've been wanting one, but I heard they're really powerful."

"They *are*," said April. "Did you get one?"

"No, I wanted one."

"I challenge any woman to last more than 2 minutes. That shit is strong."

"I'm afraid I'm going to break it."

"It'll break you," said April and mimicked a stuttering mechanical vibrator.

* * *

SAMMEE Matthews also liked a good vibrator and joked about buying stock in Duracell. A vibrator didn't reject you; it didn't complain about being crushed; it didn't make you feel bad; and then you could turn it off and put it away in a drawer. The only good things that had come out of her romantic relationships were her two girls. There had been a long line of stealing, cheating boyfriends who took what they wanted and expected Sammee to let them take more.

Her first love had been a 16-year-old sophomore named Ryan, whom she met at a Sears in Las Vegas. She was 13 and already well developed, with large breasts and ample curves. Her parents had divorced, and her father, now out of the house, had stopped pressing Sammee for oral sex. She had become uncontrollable, she imagined, since she no longer believed in fairy tales or in princesses or in his magic wand, and she suspected her dad was afraid she would tell. She didn't.

She was out shopping for a formal dress for a dance, and Ryan was renting a tuxedo; she mouthed him her name while her mom was at the checkout register, and he mouthed his name back. Sammee's mother didn't want her dating but liked Ryan, and Sammee assured her that his grandfather was home when the two would visit.

There was only a halfhearted seduction. One day at his house after school, Ryan asked her to take a shower and then, feeling warm and sleepy, she laid down on the bed and he had intercourse with her. She remembers only that she fell asleep.

The memory of losing her virginity was not noteworthy, and she recalled it with indifference. It was while exhuming the moments when she let herself be used in other ways, repeatedly, with a sad and ferocious predictability across the decades, that an emotional crater yawned open. Her grade-school sweetheart had taken her lunch money, or perhaps she had given it to him freely. Decades later, in her early forties, one of her boyfriends believed he was entitled to half of the proceeds from her adult Web site, even though, as she held up the check, the monthly amount was a paltry $84. In every relationship, she had put up with or endured or welcomed sexual indiscretions, and still, despite her pliancy, she was always left behind.

She envied the normalcy and tenderness and romance of the intimate relationships some of the other women at Thick Sundaes seemed to have, and she confessed that she wanted a well-ordered domestic life: A husband, a house, a dog, a car, and a vacation topped her list.

But nothing was well ordered. She had hosted a swingers' party at her home, where she was pushed out of the bedroom only to sit on the couch watching the Cooking Channel. "And then he can't understand why I don't want to participate," she said of her boyfriend. "Really? Where was I at? You were getting yours. I was getting a recipe."

Sammee was rarely promiscuous, but with a trusted partner, the boundary lines between normal and transgressive had faded away. She had pushed herself into consensual, savage sex play: An argument over whether she was a "size queen"—a person who preferred extremely large penises— ended with her partner inserting a baseball bat into her vagina.

Whether these impulses arose from physical desire or flights of daring had ceased to become knowable.

* * *

SAMMEE plodded along in her aging sedan, in a city of perpetually turned-on bodies that looked nothing like her own. The gold-flecked powder on her face sparkled in the Las Vegas sun, and a delicate gold necklace rested on her sternum. Her sky-blue eyes were tastefully made up with eyeliner and glamorous eyelash extensions. A car of young men passing on her left gawked, gasped, squealed, and blasted the horn. And then they yelled "Fuck You!" to Sammee, who was only trying to drive to Tony Roma's for lunch.

"What?" Sammee roared back, as if she had made some unintended traffic error, but her eyes flickered out the window and the insult was unmistakable.

Sammee had lost weight at different times over the years, but things always went haywire when she did: Her menstrual cycle was disrupted; the skin under her arms sagged; and the smell of her bowel movements became foul. Once, when she had lost 26 pounds, some of the fat around her feet dissipated. "You have all this fat that protects you and you don't know nothin' about what's going on underneath," she told me. Her feet narrowed and ached terribly. A doctor told her she had lost "the fat bridge," and that she was now walking on the bones of her feet, which had extreme bone spurs. It hardly seemed worth the added suffering.

Sammee was reluctant to admit the major dysfunction that weight had caused in her life for fear it would discredit her as an SSBBW promoter and would cost her the modest earnings from her Web site, where people paid to see her buttocks, which measured an enviable 90 inches across. The free market didn't exactly reward the wounded.

There was still a code of *omertà* about the troubles bigger women endured, and publicly admitting weakness and suffering could only invite the very ridicule that Thick Sundaes and the BBW comradeship meant to keep out.

The fact was, Sammee was in pain every day. The winter was the worst, even in Las Vegas, where the cold wind seemed to sting her throbbing knees and bulging varicose veins. She needed both her knees replaced, and her stomach muscles were slowly tearing apart. Sitting on ill-proportioned chairs, Sammee looked uncomfortable; she shifted and winced, unable to stay in one position for too long. Like other big women, Sammee worried about her body odor. She was clean, of course; she showered and scrubbed, and often told other big women about the wonders of the long-handled scrub brush. But the excessive sweat between her skin rolls was an unavoidable by-product of flesh and fat.

The "girls" at her shows didn't talk much about their health problems, but in private they confided in Sammee their worries about diabetes, cancer, and other ailments. What would it be like when she was in her sixties or seventies? She had developed bronchitis not long ago, and with her stress incontinence, Sammee had needed to wear adult diapers, which she couldn't bend down to put on properly. If she fell, who would pick her up?

To the generals in the war against the war on fat people, such talk was heresy. Size acceptance activists trying to undo the shame and stigma rejected the word *obesity* as a medical term that implied poor health and pathologized otherwise healthy people. People could be healthy at any size, if only Americans weren't so cruel about it.

Sammee didn't like the term *obese* either, or *fat*, especially when the word was used by men who had a penchant for big women, and she waged her own kind of ground war. At a casual dinner party one night, as waiters walked from table to table with spit-roasted slabs of meat on long skewers, Sammee began to steam as she listened to one of the guests.

"Every other word for emphasis was 'the *fat* girl. The *fat*, the *fat*, the *fat*,'" she said. She interrupted the conversation.

"Excuse me, what is your name again?"

And he said his name.

"Do you have to continually use the emphasis on FAT? Every time you speak about a woman of size?"

And he said, "Well, how else would I address it?"

"How about *blossomed*? How about the *thicker person*? How about her *NAME*?" Like a preacher on the threshold of a sermon's climax, the prosody of Sammee's voice changed.

"I said, 'We live with this every day. We get up with it. We walk with it. We talk with it.'" Sammee starting clapping her hands in a rhythmic rage.

"'We wash it, we maintain, EVERY. SINGLE. DAY. OF. OUR. LIVES. Why, for the last hour and a half, have I had to be reminded I have a fat ass?'"

The man said nothing, and he changed the subject.

* * *

THICK Sundaes was a refuge from those daily humiliations—for Sammee, for the professional and amateur women who danced onstage, and for the heavier women who felt like freaks at other clubs in Las Vegas. "She knows at least for the time she's at the event, she's not going to be degraded," said Sammee of her typical patron. "She's not going to be talked to like she's shit. She's not going to be looked at like she's a punching bag anymore."

* * *

SAMMEE's past had not claimed her. She had talked to her father on the phone shortly before he dropped dead. It was around Halloween, and she told him about her daughters' costumes. Her father had heart complications, diabetes, and other ailments that she couldn't remember, and she suspected he knew they wouldn't talk again. "He told me, 'I love you, Sammee.'

"And I said, 'I'm sure.'"

"I really do. I want you to know I'm sorry I ruined your life."

"I said, 'What are you talking about?'" They had never discussed his abuse.

"He said, 'You know exactly what I'm talking about, and I wish I never had hurt you.'"

He went on: "If I don't talk to you before the holidays, know that I love you and you're going to be okay." Sammee then playfully told him to go to hell, that he was too mean to go to Hades, and surely he wouldn't get into heaven because his ass was too fat. He died a few days later. Her mother, from whom Sammee was estranged, died on Super Bowl Sunday just a few months after the first Thick Sundaes party.

It seemed miraculous that a woman so grievously injured by a molesting father, so choked by circumstance, could summon the entrepreneurial spirit to create a Vegas strip show for big women. Still, there were limits to her sense of possibility: She had created a refuge for others, a haven of fantasy between the mirrored and decaled walls of Foxy's Las Vegas. But inside the dimensions of that aging, neon-lit strip club, Sammee saw too what she was doomed to live without. She wanted the admiration heaped on April Flores; she wanted to perform the same tricks as the more able-bodied women; she wanted to dance and swing around the stripper pole. "I wanted to be looked at," she said in a sad, broken voice, "and have someone in awe of me."

Thick Sundaes was a benevolent crusade, but it was never entirely altruistic.

* * *

SHE had to hold on to her girth. That was clear. Without her 90-inch ass span, Sammee would cease to be extraordinary. There were rules for such things: Only women who wore size 1X to 3X could qualify as BBW; women who wore size 4X through 8X and above earned the title SSBBW.

Big Girl porn could be punishing. Like jockeys who starve, sweat, and purge themselves to race weight, bigger women who wanted to play the game had to stay big.

Adherents and admirers of BBW and SSBBW could be cruel to those who lost weight. "If I lose more than 50 pounds, I'm not considered an SSBBW anymore," said Sammee, who had long ago capitulated to life's arithmetic. "If I lose a couple of sizes in my breasts because I lost weight, oh, man, then the world is going to cave in. I've just become your average lady."

BBW and SSBBW performers seemed to live and die by their lavishly large, proudly unadulterated breasts.

The BBW performer Julia Sands, who started exotic dancing to pay for graduate school, weighed 300 pounds when her father's sister died of cancer. Her aunt's death, Julia said, had been hastened by diabetes. "Before she passed away, she told me, 'Whatever you do, just take care of your health. Don't let diabetes attack you like it did me.' And I really took that to heart." As Julia lost weight, some of her fans didn't like her smaller—albeit still BBW—size. She tried to reassure her fans, many of whom tuned in for live Webcam performances, that there would still be plenty of her to see. Julie tweeted, "Omg today I weight [sic] myself & I am 198lbs Today #LoseIt I feel so good about myself plus I still wear a G-cup bra."[1]

Other "girls" had a harder time: One of Sammee's out-of-town performers from the East Coast had gastric lap band surgery—her weight had been causing health problems—and as she lost weight touring at different BBW events, her skin began to sag and layer into folds on her body. Sammee remembered a Thick Sundaes event in Las Vegas the year before: The crowd didn't embrace the flapping, sagging woman the way they embraced the fleshy BBWs with plump skin.

For most performers, these gigs didn't pay their bills. Many of the women, like Sammee, had day jobs and walked a tightrope between maintaining the size requirements of BBW and SSBBW and being ambulatory enough to earn a steady paycheck and keep their health insurance coverage. Sammee worked for a company that helped poor and disabled Nevadans secure public benefits, and she couldn't do her job from a wheelchair or a scooter.

*　*　*

REGINA got what she wanted. By 2:00 in the morning, she had a delicious memory of a lap dance from April and a souvenir to take home—a signed April Flores sex toy. The toys were cheaper on eBay, but Regina figured it was better to get it straight from the source.

Peter had been a little uptight during one of the lap dances, Regina explained. "But me? I was all grinding up against her. Touching her, and she was grinding up against me. Pulling my hair, like *Oh, God. Amazing.*"

The night had changed everything. Regina knew it. The picture of herself in her mind's eye had shifted. "I boosted my confidence, like 50 percent more," she concluded. "I just know that I need to learn to love my body and be like those women." Later, she would go home to California, put on lingerie, and pose like April in front of the full-length mirror.

She was part of the BBW tribe now: the women and men who emerged periodically from their everyday lives to this safe harbor off the Las Vegas Strip to be embraced and celebrated and titillated. Regina just needed to remember that they were out there, and that this wasn't all a fantasy.

*　*　*

AT some point, at the end of the evening, the performers would have scooped up any stray dollar bills lying around the stripper stage; someone would turn off the club's soft violet lights. April would go back to the Golden Nugget Hotel with her husband and remove her lipstick, her eyelashes, her makeup, and crawl into bed. Regina and Peter would return to their time-share at a Mayan-themed resort where their three kids slept under the watchful eye of a babysitter; and Sammee would go home to her North Vegas apartment and hope that her daughter was fast asleep.

CHAPTER **SIX**

Futures: Weight Loss

Dana Englehardt awoke from bariatric surgery with her innards transformed. She was praying the same might soon be said of her marriage.

The week before, Dana's health insurance company informed her that it wouldn't, after all, cover the $35,000 procedure, and the news hit the family like a tragedy. Still, Dana's husband, Larry—watching his wife, so heavy, sore-kneed, and seemingly broken—said they would press ahead anyway; they could get a loan against the house and figure out the rest later. Dana was overcome with gratitude for her husband.

During the surgery, John Rabkin, MD, a renowned bariatric specialist in San Francisco, had reconfigured Dana's intestines and cut out part of her stomach, making it a miniature version of its former self. In a world well stocked with medical wonders, the surgical process is still stunning to witness. While the actual science has taken decades to perfect, the simple idea behind the surgery is this: reroute the small intestine to limit the absorption of food, and restrict the amount of food intake by shrinking the stomach.

But first you have to get into the belly. With tiny cameras mounted on the end of a probe, the surgeon enters the patient's abdomen by punching through a series of small holes, watching the progress on a series of high-definition screens mounted in the operating room, which more resembles a television control room—or NASA HQ—than a surgical suite.

As the probe cuts through the outer layer of the skin, the camera displays a thrilling plunge inside the body: passing through the spongy pink dermis and firmer layers of muscle until the probe springs through the other side and into the cavernous abdomen, thick with the bulbous, moist meanderings of the intestines. And, of course, in the case of bariatric patients, fat—mounds and mounds of it, everywhere the camera looks. Clotted and creamy yellow, the fat tissue has grown onto the sides of the abdominal walls, attaching itself to the stomach and other organs like mold.

Once inside, the surgeon begins bushwhacking through to the organs, tugging on the fat with what looks like a miniature tweezers and is called a trochar. The fat gives way easily, stretching its branchlike fibers. It is simultaneously fascinating and grotesque, seeing organs in their native environments, which are nowhere as clean or well defined as the models one might see in a doctor's office or an anatomy book. And it's even more unsettling to watch these operations, which are, at their core, invasions of a person's most private imaginable space.

Not that the surgeon lingers; the procedure is speedy and unstinting. Fat is cut away—snip, snip, snip—to give access to the organs that must be rearranged and cauterized. That includes the stomach, which is cut into two pieces: one that will stay and continue its work of digesting, and one that will be removed.

Smoke—actual smoke, dark and drifting—rises with each burning stitch, floating away from the spotlight and into the dark, moist cavity. When it's all over, the surgeon clamps the resected bit of stomach in the trochar and then the camera reverses out of the cave, speeding backward through the subcutaneous tissue and red muscle and pink dermis, until the tip of the cut-away stomach peeks out from the pencil-size hole in the belly. The high-resolution screens turn blank, and the room's focus turns to the bloody pulp stuck part in and part out of the belly.

In this moment, the surgeon abandons precision for brute force, grabbing hold of the slippery section of stomach and pulling until it literally pops out of the small hole. The surgeon tosses it into a tray, and it's heavier and larger than one might imagine—a foot long perhaps—and still warm to the touch.

* * *

UNHEARD of a half century ago, bariatric surgery is changing the shape of modern America.

What started as a curious side effect of a procedure first developed in the 1960s—when physicians noticed patients undergoing partial stomach removal for ulcers were losing serious amounts of weight—is now viewed as the most effective way to induce significant weight loss. Over the last decade, the number of Americans undergoing bariatric surgery has risen sharply; in 2009, some 220,000 procedures were performed in the United States. That surge has corresponded with the development of minimally invasive laparoscopic techniques, coupled with the growth in obesity and extreme obesity in particular.

Unlike programs that combine exercise and dieting, which lead to slow and often unsuccessful attempts at weight loss, bariatric surgery is transformative: Most patients experience half of their total weight loss during the first 6 months after surgery, and the remainder within 2 years. That makes bariatric surgery patients a fascinating group to follow: There is a before and an after, alongside dramatic physical and psychological changes that can be measured and studied.

Insurance companies and public health officials have taken note. Bariatric surgery is generally considered the most commonly covered obesity treatment, and a majority of large employers, and almost every state Medicaid program and Medicare, cover the procedure, although most patients are under the age of 55. The results don't come cheap: As Dana's family discovered, an hour-long procedure can cost tens of thousands of dollars, and even when covered by insurance, co-payments can run as high as $7,500. (And that doesn't include the cosmetic skin removal—more on this later—which is often necessary for patients suddenly draped with skin that literally no longer fits them.) Insurance companies also typically require that patients first try other weight loss methods and undergo a psychological evaluation before going into surgery.

Still, only a fraction of men and women heavy enough to qualify for bariatric surgery actually get it done, and surgeons and some advocates say the need is urgent and overwhelming. Indeed, most experts fear that if current obesity trends hold, life expectancy in the richest nation in the world will fall.

"I think we're at a real crossroads when it comes to obesity," John Morton, MD, director of bariatric surgery at Stanford University and chair of the National Committee on Metabolic and Bariatric Surgery for the bariatric surgeons' association, told me at his clinic in Palo Alto, California. "I think we've finally gotten real good awareness around the issue. We've got some resonance around prevention. Our next step, just like any other disease, is now treatment."

Dr. Morton likened the current state of obesity medicine to the state of heart disease in the 1970s, when few treatments were available. "In fact," he said, "surgery was probably the only treatment available. But from surgery, we had a platform for change and understanding around the disease."

Scott Kahan, MD, director of the STOP Obesity Alliance, and a faculty member at the George Washington University School of Medicine, concurred. "Bariatric surgery is a radical treatment when you look at it anatomically," he said, "but no more radical than other areas, like coronary artery bypass surgery."

Not that it is for everyone: While heavy people with a BMI of 30 who have obesity-related health problems can qualify for bariatric surgery, it is recommended primarily for the most obese patients, a group that is the fastest-growing segment of the population, researchers say. A RAND study published in 2013 found that between 2000 and 2010, 15.5 million adult Americans—or 6.6 percent of the population—had a BMI over 40.[1] (For those not well versed in BMI charts, that means a weight of about 250 pounds for a woman standing 5-foot-6 or about 300 pounds for a 6-foot-tall man.)

"Almost everyone is gaining weight in our country," Dr. Kahan said.

And in some places, people are gaining weight faster than in others. In the Deep South, for instance, where obesity rates are some of the highest in the nation and the prevalence of extreme obesity is alarmingly high, physicians view bariatric surgery as the best—and first—line of attack for addressing multiple chronic conditions.

"In Mississippi, we have a lot of patients with BMIs over 50, and people are lined up at the door right now with BMIs over 70," Erin Cummins, MD, director of the bariatric program at Central Mississippi Medical Center, told me before scrubbing in for surgery one morning in Jackson.

The patients she operates on typically take 8 to 10 medications a day before the surgery—and fewer after. "They can narrow that down to maybe two or three, which is gonna save money in the long term," she said with a distinctive southern drawl. "And it's gonna extend their life."

To be sure, many complications of obesity, like sleep apnea and high blood pressure, are reversed by bariatric surgery. Multiple studies have found that 80 to 85 percent of diabetics, for example, can stop medication in the first year. When asked about the parts of their life impacted by their health, bariatric patients report significant improvements, especially within the first 2 years,[2] though it is not clear yet how lasting those changes will be, or if—as is hoped—they can last over a lifetime.

These physical successes have encouraged obesity researchers to turn their attention to the effects of weight loss on the inner lives—and intimate experiences—of those who are severely obese. Men and women who seek surgery are more likely to suffer from mental disorders, symptoms of depression, and lower self-esteem. These conditions can feed—and be fed by—negative body image,[3] that image of ourselves in our mind and our attitude about it. And whether it is accomplished through behavioral changes, antiobesity drugs, or surgery, weight loss does bolster body image and leads to marked improvement in how attractive a person feels, as well as a lessening of shame.[4,5] ("Because of my weight, I am ashamed of my body" reads one of the questions posed to patients in psychological exams.)

These changes in outlook can be detected even in the earliest weeks following surgery, before the body begins to shed pounds—something psychologists suspect is tied to "patients taking an active role in changing their lives, together with their hope and optimism, leading to psychological improvements, even while they are still overweight."[6] (A very limited number of small clinical studies on adolescent bariatric surgery patients have also signaled similar outcomes, including a substantial reduction in symptoms of depression and better self-esteem among teenagers within the first 2 years.[7])

Still, for all of those positives, bariatric surgery is not a silver bullet, nor is the optimism around the procedure universally felt. For example, men seem to have a more positive, lasting psychological change after surgery. Comparing preoperative mental health scores to post-op results, men's mental health scores continued to rise; women, however, reported better mental health up to 5 months after the surgery, but almost 2 years later, their mental health scores had dropped back down and were no longer significantly changed.[8] The results, the obesity researchers wrote, "might underscore the emotional toll that obesity takes on some women." All of which is even more significant when you consider that 90 percent of bariatric surgery patients are women.

Curiously, those who lost significant weight reported that the negative effects of body image on their quality of life had lessened, but they still remained deeply dissatisfied with their body shape. That is, body image seemed to take less of a toll on their emotional state, their relationships, eating and exercise, sexual experiences, and life at home and at work, but they still reported high levels of distress about the weight and shape of their body. "In some respects, the lack of consistent changes across the body image measures was surprising," the researchers wrote, but they noted another team had found similar discrepancies. Perhaps, they speculated, the measurement tool, the Body Shape Questionnaire, which was originally developed to evaluate eating disorders, was a poor fit for obese patients. Or, those patients who had lost the most weight undoubtedly faced loose and hanging skin, an unwelcome by-product that required expensive plastic surgery to fix that was rarely covered by insurance. "Although this relationship has received relatively little empirical attention, it could help explain why larger weight losses were not directly associated with additional improvement in weight and shape concerns within the first 2 years of bariatric surgery."

For all of those caveats, however, what does seem to improve after weight loss—whether through bariatric surgery or nonsurgical means—is sex. Perhaps not surprisingly, those who lose weight report feeling more sexually attractive, more sexually aroused, and face fewer difficulties performing. They are less apt to avoid sexual situations and more willing to be seen getting undressed. They enjoy sex more and have sex more often. What's more, regaining small amounts of weight doesn't seem to take away these newfound results.[9]

There are also the sheer visual pleasures: Eric Leckbee from Chapter 3 is a prime case. A self-effacing software developer with a wry sense of humor, Eric had always experienced weight fluctuations, but when his weight dipped down, he felt more confident. The thrill of his weight loss was followed by bursts of sexual interest, something he talked about with other men in his weight loss groups. "We're like, 'Wow! We're having more sex with our partners,'" Eric said. "That's great!"

There was also the novelty that his penis had seemed to grow.

"When you start losing weight, it looks bigger. You feel better about yourself, and you want to use it more often," Eric told me. "It's funny because you know in your mind that it's utterly illogical; it hasn't changed. It's the same as it ever was. It's all a matter of perspective and proportion. Does. Not. Matter. Your emotions take over, you feel better about yourself, you feel a lot better about him down there, and it really boosts your self-esteem."

And while in the past there has been a paucity of research on sexual functioning after weight loss surgery, in particular, that is beginning to change. One early study took place in 1996, when a research team at the University of South Florida led by Mario Camps, MD,[10] asked more than two dozen bariatric patients, and many of their sexual partners, about their sex lives. Before the operation, 64 percent of the patients said they enjoyed sex. But after the operation, half of those patients—and, more tellingly, 78 percent of their partners—said they enjoyed sex even more. Two out of five patients and partners felt their orgasms had improved. And perhaps most striking was this: Before the surgery, 27 percent of patients felt they were attractive. And after? Eighty percent thought so.

Dale Bond, PhD, assistant professor of psychiatry and human behavior at Brown University in Providence, Rhode Island, who studies bariatric surgery patients, has found more recently—in 2011—that women report a remarkable resolution of problems with sexual desire, arousal, orgasm, sexual satisfaction, and sexual pain.[11] Six months after women undergo surgery, there is a dramatic reversal of sexual dysfunction, and patients' complaints about sex are about the same as in a normal, healthy population.

This is surprising, given that most female bariatric patients lose a significant amount of weight, yet still remain obese after the procedure. But even some weight loss seems to lessen insecurities and loosen inhibitions: Before surgery, for example, 50 percent of bariatric patients said they undressed in the dark; after surgery, 25 percent did.

Although some researchers have raised the possibility that changes in reproductive hormones after weight loss could contribute to the easing of sexual dysfunction and distress, psychologists suspect that it has to do with women feeling better about themselves, particularly in the first 6 months, when patients experience rapid weight loss and often draw praise from friends and family.

Nonsurgical weight loss has been shown to have beneficial results as well: In December 2012, at the European Society for Sexual Medicine conference in Amsterdam, Italian researchers presented evidence that severely obese women who lowered their body mass index through an 8-week residential weight loss program showed a range of sexual improvements, including more frequent sex, greater sexual desire, and even better vaginal lubrication.[12] And while women undergoing bariatric surgery might experience some erosion in mental health and emotional scores, they appear to be better off than obese patients who forgo surgery, reporting improvements in their health and the aspects of their lives touched by weight.[13]

Bill Hartman, PhD, a psychologist with the Weight Management Program at California Pacific Medical Center in San Francisco, tells his patients that even a modest amount of weight loss improves body image, self-esteem, binge eating, and depression. And, conversely, when patients regain weight, dissatisfaction comes rushing back in.

The studies continue: David Sarwer, PhD, the pioneering psychologist at the University of Pennsylvania in Philadelphia, is tracking changes in bariatric patients across the country for 4 years. He's looking for changes in sexual behavior, romantic relationships, and sex hormones, and comparing the intimate lives of bariatric patients with those of similarly obese people who didn't undergo surgery. So far, the study echoes past research: The heaviest patients at the beginning of the study, before their operations, report the greatest levels of sexual dysfunction, and there is an association between the severity of the obesity and the impairment in sex hormones—primarily testosterone and estrogen—and decreased sexual behavior. The question Dr. Sarwer and his colleagues want to answer is: What's driving the dysfunction? Is it hormones? Depression and self-esteem? Or some combination of the two?

Whatever the conclusions Dr. Sarwer and his team draw, anecdotal evidence—at the very least—seems to suggest that when weight drops, one's sense of one's own attractiveness and the often concomitant urge to have sex increase.

And many times, that takes some getting used to.

＊　＊　＊

WHILE Dana's body was still big in the days after surgery, her new stomach was anything but. All told, her tiny, now-truncated tummy could hold only 3 ounces of food. "When I came home from the hospital, I could eat maybe half an egg at a time," she told me during one of our many interviews at her well-kept home in Belmont, California.

And it wasn't just solids: If she drank too much water too quickly, it shot back up in a violent rejection. But the surgery also quickly began to work: With her intestines reconfigured to absorb fewer calories, Dana lost a pound a day for the first month.

Still, she viewed her weight loss with wonder and caution, and every morning she would step on the scale and hold her breath, certain that the weight loss would stop. And at first, hardly anyone noticed the change.

"Even the first 50 pounds, people didn't even notice," Dana recalls. "Even 70 pounds, people didn't notice."

It wasn't until she hit 100 pounds—often a benchmark for the obese—that heads started to turn and compliments began to flow. Her work wardrobe was one of the earliest indicators: At the hospital where she prepped patients for surgery in the cardiac catheterization lab, Dana was continually handing in her scrubs for a smaller size.

But there were changes at home, as well. At night, as she and her husband Larry sat on the couch, Dana sensed that he was staring at her, and not the television. The reason, they would soon discover, was simple: He came to believe he was looking at a stranger.

For decades, Dana's face was a round mound, propped up on a thick neck that blended in with her jaw; her nose was bulbous and her eyes, even with makeup, were deep set behind plump cheeks. As she lost weight, though, Dana's features emerged. The bones in her face were surprisingly delicate. There was more room for her smile.

And while her childhood friends and her family might have remembered Dana when her jawline was still visible, her husband had only known her as a big woman.

Finally Dana broke the ice. "I said, 'Okay, what? Why are you staring at me?'" Dana recalls. "And he said, 'I just don't recognize you anymore.'"

Larry, too, remembers the moment when his wife asked him why he was staring at her.

"Right next to the TV is a picture we had taken as a family about 3 months after the surgery. And in it, she's a heavy woman," Larry said. "I tend to watch TV and see that picture. And then all of a sudden, I just turn to the side, and it's, 'Wow! It's a different person. You're the same person inside, but you look different.'"

These reactions from loved ones, friends, even minor acquaintances are often freighted with negative emotions for those losing the weight. In fact, some formerly heavy people cringe when friends or acquaintances delight in their newfound faces. "You've always had such a pretty face," someone might say, which is meant as a compliment but can be a cruel reminder of the slights and snubs that they have endured daily for years. "I am the same person now as I was then" is what many overweight people told me in interviews.

That said, there also is something quite amazing about watching a face emerge from the folds—the rediscovery of a visage that is both more defined and more identifiable. If a face is what makes a person unique, with features granting it individuality, those features do come into sharper focus when not swollen and shrouded. At a bariatric surgery weight loss meeting, one woman, who herself had lost more than 200 pounds, recounted seeing the contours of her sister's face emerge after surgery.

"When she lost the weight, I just cried because I hadn't seen that face in years," she said to the group.

It wasn't just Dana's face that was changing, however. Without all that fat to plump up her skin, Dana deflated. The skin that had once stretched to accommodate her ample frame dangled off her stomach and hung loosely down the back of her legs; her breasts swung like pendulums. She had heard horror stories from other patients about stretched-out skin—how it could torpedo all the good feelings that came with weight loss—something echoed by Mickey McCabe, a licensed clinical social worker in Binghamton, New York, who performs psychological evaluations for bariatric surgery patients.

McCabe, an expert in all things addictive (food, alcohol, gambling), said that loose skin can be a source of real concern, as well as bring on borderline depression. "The weight will start coming off real fast, and all of a sudden they'll realize, 'Well, yeah, I'll look great when I have clothes on, but I look *horrible* when I don't have clothes on, because now all the loose skin is there,'" she said.

And hanging skin can be a major turnoff in the bedroom. "The husband might say, 'You look so hot,'" McCabe recalled her clients saying. "Then they go to bed to have sex, and all of a sudden the husband realizes how uncomfortable it is because of all the loose skin." (There are other unsavory aspects to living with altered intestines; truly horrific gas can dampen intimacy and interrupt sex in the moment.)

Dana had always planned to get plastic surgery to tighten everything up, but this, too, came with potential pitfalls. Nearly 2 weeks after her tummy tuck, she woke up with purple legs. From her experience in the cath lab, Dana knew immediately that she had a serious blood clot. She spent the ensuing weeks in the intensive care unit.

Through all of these changes and challenges, though, there was one thing on Dana's mind: the potential pleasure that could come from her "new body," as she called it. With most of the complications of plastic surgery behind her, Dana was anxious to reclaim her sex life. "I knew I had a totally dysfunctional marriage, and a lot of that was my fault," she said. "I thought if I lost the weight, everything else would fall into place."

After all, Dana did feel better: She had more energy and interest in life, and she was delighted to again feel the stirrings of sexual desire. And she fully expected Larry to pounce.

"I was thinking he was going to go, 'WAHOO! Let's go!'" Dana said.

But that wasn't the case for Dana, nor for other postoperative couples. Many, in fact, struggle after bariatric surgery to rediscover, and redefine, their sexual and emotional connections.

"One of the things that we will often talk about with our patients who are in committed relationships is the [effect] of weight loss on the dynamics of the romantic relationship," said Dr. Sarwer.

In Dana and Larry's case, Dana felt it was partially her fault. "I think that he went so long with me being uninterested, that when I was interested again . . . " she said, sitting next to Larry during an interview we did at their home. She paused and looked at him. "I don't know if you had trouble believing that I was interested again, but it took a while for you to come around."

Larry agreed. "It took a while for me to realize what the signs were," he said.

At one point before the surgery, the couple had gone 6 months without having sex. "And I was almost climbing the walls, okay?" Larry said. "But you get to the point where you've been denied, and so you just turn the other cheek. You just turn away, okay? I don't want to go to bed mad. But I would go to bed very disappointed."

So, now that his wife was offering him kisses—and more—Larry didn't know what to make of it.

"I asked him why he wasn't interested anymore," Dana said. "I thought, 'Well, maybe he liked me bigger.'"

Larry interjected: "I didn't know that you were interested anymore. And so I had to basically learn, and I'm still learning, when she's interested and when she's not."

The wounds had gone deep for both of them. Dana was emerging from years spent buried under layers of fat and pain, but Larry was himself digging out of years of rejection, both overt and implied.

"It sounds weird," Larry said, "but it's hard when you're so used to being denied, and that's a part of rejection. And I don't like rejection. So in order to not lose my cool or not get perturbed about rejection, you don't let yourself reach the point where you will be rejected."

There were other problems as the couple tried to restart a sex life that had long been winterized.

"When I wanted to resume our sex life, he thought I was looking for him to perform," Dana said. "He was afraid he wouldn't meet my expectations. Then he couldn't get an erection. That made it worse."

At one point, she suggested her husband try Viagra. He refused, and the couple went to counseling, which led to a big blowup. Larry was afraid that if he wasn't good enough, Dana would go looking for someone else.

And with good reason: When his wife was at her heaviest, Larry had let himself go. He ate what he wanted, when he wanted. Dana's weight loss, however, had suddenly made him look less well kept. The shame and humiliation were now Larry's to endure.

"A woman said to Larry," Dana recalls, "'Is she the trophy wife?'"

Dana had to reassure her husband that she wasn't going to leave him. But the combination of awkwardness, impotence, and an emotional disconnect soon crept toward the ultimate fear of many couples: infidelity. Dana admits that she had started having fantasies about other men, and while she never acted on her mind's wanderings, she decided to see a therapist on her own.

"I was imagining myself anywhere but in my life," she said.

                              * * *

If a relationship is a sensitive ecosystem with each person representing an essential, and somewhat predictable, variable, then weight loss—especially sudden weight loss—can lead to troubling imbalances.

Indeed, while it may not be healthy, obesity in a family can actually be a weirdly reliable constant that—when removed—can destabilize that dynamic.[14] Some sociologists have suggested that a family member's obesity serves a purpose within the family system—a thought echoed in a 2000 paper stating that "being overweight may be the result of a struggle for control in the family (who can tell whom what to eat), a matter of family loyalty (family pattern of obesity), or a way to manage intimacy (avoiding sexual intercourse or extramarital affairs)."[15] In this view, obesity becomes a family matter: "The obesity and eating behaviors can become central to the family or marital relationship in the same way that alcoholism can become the defining characteristic of a family or marriage." And if that changes—much like a spouse getting sober when the other partner continues to drink—the result can be dramatic, and sometimes fatal, to a relationship.

The problem is common enough that psychologists raise it during the evaluations all bariatric patients must undergo before getting surgery, often cautioning that while weight will disappear, the troubles that existed in a relationship when one or both spouses were overweight or obese will still be there after surgery.

"People often have fantasies about what life will be like after they lose weight," Ronnie Kolotkin, PhD, the North Carolina psychologist who helped design a seminal quality of life survey for the obese, told me. "Part of the fantasy is that everything in their life will change and every-thing will improve. But if there were sexual tensions and marital distress before the weight loss, that's not going to go away."

And for women, whom society judges more harshly based on their looks, the change from heavy to suddenly smaller can set off a cascade of emotions and actions. Women who've lost weight can stop—or at least reduce—the number of nagging medications; they can rid themselves of diabetes, hyperlipidemia, and other conditions. But adapting to a new body can be challenging to the mind.

"A lot of the mental wiring is still there," Leah S. Millheiser, MD, a gynecologist at Stanford University, told me. "They still think the same way."

Dr. Millheiser recalled a heavy patient who trimmed down, but was still haunted by years of negative thinking. "She said, 'I can't get rid of the fact that I had poor self-esteem my entire life, and just losing weight is not going to deal with that.'"

Physicians and weight loss experts all made this point: Weight loss is no panacea for deeply held beliefs. "You have to fix what is on the inside, and I think that is a big part of the treatment of sexual dysfunction in women who are obese or who have lost the weight," Dr. Millheiser said. "What caused the problem?"

Sometimes, too, there is another side effect: pure and simple lust.

Once buried within layers of their body, women who spent years—even decades—emotionally numb, who overate or were addicted to food, all of a sudden awaken inside a body that for many feels vivacious, sexy, and alive. And they are often ready to sexually act out.

These were frequent concerns of Dr. Kolotkin's patients: "Now that

I have so much attention, it's terrifying for me. I don't know how to make good decisions. Do I sleep with everyone? I never had much choice before, and I don't know how to handle it.'"

Most experts in the field have stories of once-weighty women gone wild: mothers strutting around in their teenage daughters' clothes; newly emboldened wives threatening divorce; and single women, once shunned, becoming very promiscuous.

"It's like they don't know how to talk about all of these feelings that have been locked in their bodies for so long, and they are 'symptom switching,'" said Heidi Schelling, PhD, a clinical social worker and therapist in Fresno, California. "They go from emotional overeating to sexually acting out, or acting out with alcohol or gambling, or anorexia."

Therapists who run weight loss groups have a name for the period after a previously obese woman loses weight; they call it the whore phase: when women can't wait to draw attention from men.

"They are the ladies in the room who are in the short skirts and adolescent haircuts, and they are a terror," said one person who runs a support group and didn't want to disparage women she has taken great pains to care for. Women who missed dating in their teens and twenties can be too eager to jump into dating and sex; they can be too easily trusting of new sex partners, and can face higher rates of sexually transmitted diseases and unintended pregnancy.

There are also practical concerns—and potential pitfalls. Barbara Metcalf, a registered nurse who ran weight loss support groups in cities around California for men and women for 15 years, said that in the weeks and months after surgery, patients need someone to care for them at home and help them adhere to the dietary requirements.

Spouses can be enormously helpful and effective as emotional cheerleaders postsurgery.[16] But it can also go the other way, particularly if it becomes evident that a spouse can't—or won't—provide support.

"Some men like their women fat because they stay at home. But guess what?" Metcalf told me. "She feels free. A weak marriage typically won't survive that."

And, as in any marriage or serious relationship, the issue of sex is usually never far from the surface, Dr. Sarwer said, particularly when obese women suddenly shed those pounds.

"Intuitively, we would think that as she's losing the weight, she's going to feel better about herself. Her quality of life, her body, and her self-esteem are going to improve," he said during an interview at his clinic in Philadelphia. "And because of the improvements in her appearance and her self-esteem, she may be more interested in sexual behavior. We'd think her husband may look at her and say, 'Wow, my wife looks fantastic. I'm more interested in engaging in more sexual behavior with her.'"

But as Larry and Dana proved, while the interest may be there, the execution may be lacking—particularly when years of desire have been repressed or shunted aside. After all, husbands and wives typically form agreements—usually unspoken—about the amount of sex in their relationship. Some couples might have sex once a week—the average for middle-aged married couples[17]—while others may have sex or some sort of sexual behavior a few times a year. Typically, when the couple is in agreement, the marriage in no way suffers.

"But when a partner loses weight with bariatric surgery, it can throw that dynamic off," Dr. Sarwer said. "So even though the wife has had surgery and is very comfortable with the current rate of sexual behavior, she may not be interested in her husband's advances. At the same time, as the husband is seeing his wife lose weight and get more compliments from other people, he may feel very threatened by her weight loss and extra attention. He may become more jealous and possessive, which can really cause a rift in the marriage."

And that rift can become a permanent divide: A fair number of women end up getting divorced after surgery, according to Dr. Sarwer.

"What they'll tell us is [they are] feeling better emotionally after they lost the weight, and the improvements in their self-esteem helped them get out of a really bad relationship. So it wasn't so much that the surgery destroyed a good relationship; rather, it empowered these women to take better care of themselves and to get out of an unhealthy relationship."

Women return to support groups or individual counseling and say to Dr. Sarwer and his staff, "I settled with my first husband because I didn't think that I could find somebody who would treat me the way I deserved to be treated. But now that I feel better about myself, I'm going to find that person."

Those tensions started to percolate in Tisha Combs's marriage after she decided to have bariatric surgery. Shortly after she was back on her feet, it became clear that her new lifestyle—one that didn't involve the McDonald's drive-thru and a constant river of food and soda—was going to be a problem for her husband. He remained obese, and the couple, who shared a home in Los Angeles, no longer shared the same tastes.

"He would come home from work, and I would say, 'I'm making this food,'" she said. "And he'd say, 'Well, that's not what I want.'"

Nor did he want to go for a bike ride or a walk with her, complaining, as she once did, that he didn't have the energy. Tisha suspects that her weight loss made her husband, who was from an extensive Cuban family who loved to feast and had never had any other serious relationships, feel vulnerable.

"To have me lose weight and then have the attention and confidence that I was getting—that was always kind of there, but it was just hidden— I don't think he felt comfortable in that at all," she said.

And he never did get used to her regained self-assurance. Tisha says she and her husband drifted apart, separated, and eventually divorced. And while she still thinks about him—and flirts with the idea of getting back together—it's hard to imagine being attracted to a man who is severely overweight. For her, it signals that he doesn't care enough about himself.

"I didn't need someone with a six-pack, but I didn't need someone who can eat a double chili cheeseburger and deluxe chili cheese fries and the biggest Coke that you've ever seen on God's creation, and then lay on the couch for 2 hours because he's so stuffed, he's sick to his stomach," Tisha said. "He was abusing his body that way. It was sad."

When both partners are overweight or obese, the spouse who wants to lose weight is often viewed suspiciously, said Mickey McCabe, the

Binghamton therapist. "If it's the wife who wants to lose the weight, the overweight husband is saying to her, 'Oh, you just want to lose weight so you can look better. You're gonna look hot, and the next thing you know, I have to worry about you leaving me,'" she added.

That echoed what I heard from weight loss professionals and from the couples themselves. Psychologists find that, not surprisingly, husbands don't like when their wives become attractive to other men and garner attention in new ways.[18] Husbands and wives perceive a new temptation to flirt or have sex outside their relationship; they become suspicious about infidelity.

The decision to lose weight, especially through surgery with its strict postoperative meal protocols and dramatic results, can be threatening. The spouse who doesn't want to lose weight "cannot tolerate the thought," McCabe said, that his soon-to-be smaller spouse will look better. Often he tries to sabotage any weight loss by assuring his spouse that he loves her just as she is.[19] "'Really? You love me just the way I am, even though I'm unhealthy, and you're saying this is okay?'" McCabe said, recalling the conversations her clients have with each other.

Of course, for those obese people who have severe diabetes, heart disease, or other conditions that could diminish with weight loss, a partner's insistence not to lose weight can seem almost sinister.

"Which in turn," McCabe said, "can end up with a breakup in a relationship or marriage."

The evidence that weight loss can lead to marital problems by changing the ways husbands and wives interact with each other is not new; marriage researchers in the 1980s wrote about the trend.[20] And in the early 1990s, patients undergoing treatment for obesity were found to have more marital breakups and family dysfunction than control groups.[21] But the rising popularity of bariatric surgery over the last decade has brought a greater focus on the disruptive power of weight loss.

Barbara Metcalf said that she has witnessed hundreds of couples experience the aftereffects of weight loss. "Morbidly obese people are very skeptical. They've been mistreated too many times by their partners, by everybody—parents and other kids." The reactions range from emotional wounds to outright hostility. "There are some anger issues, trust; all those emotions come to a head during the process," Metcalf said.

All of which, she said, can be daunting to the newly diminutive.

"We have a saying: A good marriage will be better after this," she said. "But a bad marriage will probably end."

* * *

WEIGHT loss after surgery can reveal deep and unsuspected rifts for some women. But men aren't immune. Ron Katz, MD, a physician in northern California, said that his bariatric surgery had, in fact, led to an unexpected restoration of his sexual self, so much so that he felt as if he were buzzing with surges of hormones. "When I lost 200 pounds," Ron said, "I was really feeling the force of testosterone. My erections lasted. I was interested in sex."

But over the decades of their marriage, Ron and his wife, Karen, had come to a comfortable, if unspoken, agreement about sex: She liked hugging and touching, but no more, and certainly not intercourse. His own interest in sex had also faded away as he got bigger. And so they spent years contented—quite happy, in fact—in a sexless equilibrium.

When Ron emerged from sexual dormancy, however, his wife's interest in sex didn't shift, and he was unsure how—or whether—to go about asking for a change to the rules of their marriage. Ron feels blessed to have a wife who saw him through his time as "an invalid"—i.e., too fat to move or live normally. And he still wants to live out their lives together. But—and this is not a negligible issue—he told me that he feels "reborn" and more sexual.

He moves easier and looks younger, and it seems that the world recognizes his existence in a way it never did before. Small things, such as people making idle conversation with him at the grocery store, for example, took Ron by surprise. "I thought, 'Why are people talking to me?'"

In his movie club, a group of friends who get together to discuss selected films, some of the ladies changed their behavior toward him.

"They wanted to kiss me on the lips," he said with an innocent laugh.

In the medical practice that he owned with his wife, Ron often counseled patients on weight loss, and he remembers a married patient who felt so good about himself after weight loss that he told Ron he wondered, "Is this really the right woman for me?"

Ron suspects that had he lost weight in his thirties, his renewed enthusiasm for sex would have caused problems. "It would have been a major confrontation," Ron said. "But I'm in my sixties." The couple has been married for 35 years, and Ron says he's never given his wife a reason to doubt him. He doesn't intend to now. Still, the attention is flattering, and he seems excited, if uncertain, about the possibility that his sexual life could come back into existence.

For now, he's content to masturbate.

* * *

To celebrate her 50th birthday, Dana donned a body-hugging blue floral dress and threw a party in the backyard. Larry had been cooking for 3 days straight, and now their family and friends sat around fold-out tables set up on the outside patio, eating his legendary enchilada casserole, Thai barbecue chicken legs, and lasagna. Larry and Dana had hired a bartender to lug a margarita machine into the yard, and the machine roared intermittently. The whirling appliance never dimmed, and the volume of the party rose with each drink.

Amidst the party, there were some guests, women mostly, who sat perched on plastic folding chairs without plates of food in front of them, sipping motley shakes. They were patients who'd recently had bariatric surgery—friends of Dana's from the weight loss support group she attended religiously since her own surgery—and their intestines and stomachs were no match for Larry's casserole.

Well into the afternoon, Dana slid open the glass door, her petite frame and shapely legs outlined in sunlight, and stepped into the kitchen.

She was giggly from the tequila, and blushing. One of her guy friends had just said she looked "pretty good" in her dress, and if Larry ever fell off a ladder—Larry was a contractor, after all—she should call him.

Despite her shapely figure and the sexual urges now coursing through her body, Dana had remained suspicious of how she looked to the world. She was shocked when strangers held doors open for her, shoppers smiled in the aisles, and shopgirls eagerly asked what she was hunting for in clothing stores.

All of which took a while to get used to.

"I still kind of saw myself as an unlikable fat girl," Dana said. "When I looked in the mirror, I knew in my head I'm not fat anymore, but I still kind of felt like the undesirable fat girl."

But like the tiny pinprick scars on her belly—remnants of the laparoscopic entryways—those insecurities have started to fade. And nicer, newer memories are taking their place: When Dana thought back to that delightful flirtation at her 50th birthday party, for example, she blushed.

"I felt like a lot of people would look at me and feel sorry for me, or just kind of be disgusted," she told me one afternoon at her house. "But now I can just not worry about how I look. I can relax and not feel that I have to be invisible so people don't notice me."

She liked feeling sexy and attractive to other people. Her friend's flirtation had been a nice reminder, Dana said, that she was pleasing to look at.

Larry didn't seem to mind the harmless flirting, and after the initial shock of having a "hot wife," Larry himself had learned to read his wife's come-hither signals again. Of all the changes that occurred after the surgery, Larry seemed most thrilled that his wife desired him again.

"She is now interested in having a sexual relationship," Larry told me. "And that's fantastic." When he and Dana crawled into bed together, she no longer pulled back from his wandering hands. And night by night, she and Larry began to reconstitute their marital intimacy. She didn't worry as much when Larry looked at her; she felt energetic and, most important, present: "I can just kind of lose myself in the moment and not be thinking, 'Oh God, he's touching my belly fat again.'"

Years earlier, she had told herself that sex wasn't an important part of her life. Looking back now, she saw something different: "I think people tell themselves that as a defense mechanism." Now, she imagined, her sexual urges were even stronger than her husband's, and she sometimes struggled to read *his* readiness for sex.

Still, nothing's perfect, the couple admits. The sex wasn't any better, they both agreed; they just had more of it.

"It's just more often, and that's what's better," Larry said. "The love has always been there, and it's just . . . "

Larry paused for a moment and looked at Dana.

"It's back," he said.

Author's Note

When I first started thinking about intimacy and weight—and wondering how the changing shape of Americans might be altering human rituals like courtship and dating and social institutions like marriage—I'd been reporting on health for a number of years. The reporting I did, primarily for NPR News, took an expansive view of health: Health was physical and psychological, of course, and it was a result of the messy mix of genes, behavior, and the environments where we live, work, and play.

When it came to covering obesity, though, I was dissatisfied by the limits of the work: how children and adults were reduced to a series of numbers—waist circumference, weight, and body mass index—and how those numbers were then used to chart the unrelenting spread of obesity that had taken hold of our nation. The public discussions and pervasive private beliefs about obesity, in my view, were contradictory and simplistic: Fat people were either gluttonous failures or victims of genetics and circumstance; they should either cower in shame or revolt against society's condemnation with a healthy dose of optimism and superhuman resilience.

Obesity was seldom depicted with nuance and candor, almost never when it came to dating and marriage—and sex. My curiosity about weight and sex wasn't prurient nor did it center on the mechanical (although I often did hear that question from slender people while reporting this book:

"How *do* they do it?"). To me, that was the least interesting question. Indeed, in reporting this book, during hundreds of hours of interviews, rarely did mechanics come up. (The exception to this was during discussions with urologists who have, in no small way, been on the frontlines of obesity's toll on sexual functioning for years.) The questions I wanted to answer were much more difficult to discern and, in my view, more vital: How has the rapid and extraordinary change in Americans' bodies shaped intimate human relationships and sexual desire? Has the emergence of the sexual self in adolescence—important milestones on the way to adulthood—been altered by obesity? Does it matter if the majority of teens around you are also overweight? Was the weight handicap in the dating and marriage markets lessening as more 20- and 30-somethings grew bigger? If the status of heavy women was diminished, how did this alter power dynamics in marriage? How did couple dynamics shift when weight appeared or disappeared? Was weight an increasing factor in divorce rates? Was it driving more people to watch plus-size pornography? Why exactly did abdominal fat cause the penis to falter? Could Viagra be masking widespread, obesity-related sexual dysfunction in men?

I am not a big person. I was often asked at the many weight loss classes and bariatric surgery support groups I attended during my reporting, and by the trusting and courageous people who patiently answered my questions: "Why do you want to know about fat people and sex?" To which I said, "Overweight and obese people are viewed as a medical problem, an economic drag, a threat to military readiness even. But amid the all-hands-on-deck response to the obesity crisis, shouldn't we ask how weight is affecting emotional and physical lives, the very essence of what makes us human? I was amazed at the number of heavy people who did indeed want to talk about their intimate lives; men and women who, once they started talking, would look up and say, "This feels like therapy." I tried to be a good listener, and, in a way, I came to believe that not being big meant I didn't bring my own injuries to their stories.

That didn't mean I came without my own biases: I do believe the human body—and human beings—suffer under too much weight. I don't think people need to be slender to feel sexy and in love, and I'm buoyed by the modest changes in popular culture that are beginning to make way for larger shapes. I also don't think ridding television, magazines, and movies of whippet-thin celebrities will do much to relieve heavy people from the profound challenges they face. The wounds are much deeper.

In a nation with some 150 million overweight and obese people, I cast a wide net. I met with the central characters in the book in their homes, at church, at a nail salon, on a college campus, at restaurants and coffee shops. With my researchers, Lauren Shapiro, a gifted young psychologist, and Alex Liu, an unrelenting reporter, we conducted interviews with people we found through word of mouth, on LISTSERVs, reddit, and various online communities. Nearly every interview was recorded on audiotape; the rest with videotape, written notes, or over Skype.

The interviews were intellectually and emotionally challenging. The ways people treat themselves are saddening, unnerving, and perplexing. One woman who appears in the dating chapter, Stephanie Nelson, a successful child psychologist with silky blonde hair and a style out of *Town & Country,* told me: "I don't think of myself as pretty. It's not who I am." She said this emphatically and without a hint of self-pity. I often thought: *Oh, but you are. How can you not see it?*

Overweight and obese people have not cornered the market on insecurity and self-hatred, but, the psychological literature tells us, they carry an outsize burden.

After my first interview with Sammee Matthews, the BBW striptease promoter in Las Vegas who had been sexually abused as a child and whose livelihood now depended on her extreme size, I cried and shook. She was so alive, so full-up with pain, and I desperately wanted her to know that she was worthy of love. It was hard to see how she could heal.

The scientific literature and interviews with leaders in the fields of psychology, sociology, and medicine guided my efforts : Dana, Eric, Dina, Ron, Rob, Sammee, and the other men and women who appear in these pages are not unconnected anecdotes. They are examples of emerging trends. There are other trends that fascinated me but were beyond the limits of the story I could tell here. Race and ethnicity and sexual orientation mediate the collision of weight and sex in important ways, and both are subjects worthy of their own inquiries.

If you go to a bookstore or library and look at the indexes of books about intimacy, dating, marriage, and personal relationships, you are not likely to find the words *obesity* or *weight*. At the same time, writings about obesity and weight gain—both in the popular press and in academia—largely exclude any discussion of sex or human relationships. And yet obesity and sex are physical and psychological phenomena; they are utterly personal and exquisitely shared (obesity cannot be disguised after all). This book is my attempt to knit these two disparate research worlds together and to record the real lives of ordinary people at the intersection. Clearly, there are obese and overweight people who are happy and fulfilled and feel deeply connected in their relationships—emotionally and sexually. But for many teenagers and adults, young and old, obesity *is* altering intimacy: The sexual self is cooling; desires once thought driven by instinct are faltering; moments of pleasure are intruded upon. Being squeamish or incredulous about these changes has consequences. It is my hope that the stories in this book—bravely shared and candidly told—engender a respectful but vigorous debate about obesity's toll on human connectedness and the ways men and women can find a way back to each other.

Acknowledgments

I am deeply indebted to the women and men who allowed me to ask profoundly personal questions and shared their inner worlds: Dana Englehardt and her husband, Larry; Eric Leckbee and his wife; Sammee Matthews; Regina and Peter Nunes; April Flores and her beloved Carlos Batts; Ron and Karen Katz; Dina Legg and her husband, Gene (who proposed in the most memorable way); Rob Gaughan; Stephanie Nelson; Carlos Romero; Tisha Combs; Catherine Brinkman; and the dozens of others who shared their still-unfolding journeys.

For some, those journeys started with Bill Hartman, an effervescent and caring psychologist. He has long witnessed the impact of obesity in people's personal lives, and I'm grateful he agreed to be one of my earliest guides. There were many others: Barbara Metcalf, Dr. John Rabkin, Darcy Hansen, Jack Mazerak, Dr. Naznin Dixit, Dr. Carlton Gorton, Dr. John Hall, Drew Jackson, Erin Shirley, Jacinda Roach, Dr. Erin Cummins, Lynn Schneider, Tiffani Grant, Eli Kassis, Julie Hammerstein, Joyce Mitchell, Kali Martin, Lisa Medoff, Malia Sperry, Mark Oberg, Mickey McCabe, Michael Reece, Sonya Satinsky, Mariann Caprino, Dr. Scott Chudnoff, Dr. Pratibha Vermulapalli, Janice Lipsky, Dr. John Morton, Dr. Leah Millheiser, Dr. Michael Eisenberg, Dr. Alison Huang, Heidi Schelling, Alexandra Brewis Slade, Ashley Randall, Tricia Burke, Ronnie Kolotkin, Dr. Scott Kahan, Dr. John Foreyt, Holly Rose Fee, and Jennie Noll.

Dr. Edward Karpman, the medical director of the Men's Health Clinic at El Camino Hospital, and Dr. David Sarwer, professor of psychology in psychiatry and surgery at the Perelman School of Medicine at the University of Pennsylvania and director of clinical services at the Center for Weight and Eating Disorders, were incredibly generous with their time and expertise.

The process of finding people willing to be interviewed began with a radio piece for a series curated by the national editor at NPR News, Steve Drummond. Steve is a journalist's editor: He makes brave decisions and guides and invigorates reporters. I am forever grateful that he said *yes* to a piece about weight and sex and then made it better than I could have imagined.

I am grateful to have extraordinary colleagues and friends who have offered their advice and support: Joe Palca, David Folkenflik, Scott Hensley, Deb Franklin, Joe Neel, Anne Gudenkauf, Gisele Grayson, Peggy Girshman, John Fairhall, Diane Webber, Drew Altman, David Rousseau, Penny Duckham, Tina Hoff, Michael Krasny, Kat Snow, David Carr, Robin Marantz Henig, Bob Kocher, Leslie Fesenmyer, Jennifer Javornik, Becca Prager, Katie Prager, Nicolette Zarday, and Jessica Adams.

I could not have done this book without the steady guidance of my agent, Jim Levine, and many rounds of thoughtful and caring edits from Leslie Wells. Trisha Calvo championed the project early on, and Ursula Cary and the talented team at Rodale skillfully guided this book to print.

Gathering voices from around the country took a team of reporters and researchers, and I was blessed to work with Abigail Phillips, Maureen Langlois, and Erin Daly. Alex Liu, who writes the Science of Sin blog, is a trusted and adventurous reporter, and Lauren Shapiro is a gifted psychologist without whom this project would not have been possible. I am deeply indebted to all of them.

My parents, Ed and Betty Varney, instilled in me a curiosity about the world, and it has been the greatest gift. Jake McKinley came up with what is perhaps the best alternative book title ever, *The Passion of the Heavy,* and blesses us with his infectious laughter. Fountain Varney Whitaker had the patience to let his mother write at playgrounds and during swim lessons and nourished me with his love. And to Jesse McKinley, whose love is sublime and unending.

ENDNOTES

CHAPTER 1

1. The CDC and American Medical Association guidelines for pediatric weight classification and terminology differ. Researchers relying on CDC data sets usually use the CDC definitions. Girls who are greater than or equal to the 95th percentile are at risk for overweight; those who are greater than or equal to the 5th percentile or less than or equal to the 85th percentile are defined as normal; and those below the 5th percentile are considered low BMI. Those greater than or equal to the 99th percentile are considered extremely obese.

2. D. D. Freeman et al., "Racial/Ethnic Differences in Body Fatness among Children and Adolescents," *Obesity* 16, no. 5 (2008): 1105–11.

3. Gamble et al., "Obesity and Health Risk of Children in the Mississippi Delta," *Journal of School Health* 82, no. 10 (October 2012): 478–83.

4. A. J. Steene-Johannessen et al., "Waist Circumference Is Related to Low-Grade Inflammation in Youth," *International Journal of Pediatric Obesity* 5, no. 4 (2010): 313–19.

5. Jonathan Bor, "The Science of Childhood Obesity," *Health Affairs* 29, no. 3 (2010): 393–97.

6. *Journal of the American Medical Association.* See Robert Wood Johnson Foundation Childhood Obesity Fast Facts. http://www.rwjf.org/en/topics/rwjf-topic-areas/health-policy/childhood-obesity/childhood-obesity-fast-facts.html.

7. Centers for Disease Control and Prevention. See Robert Wood Johnson Foundation Childhood Obesity Fast Facts. http://www.rwjf.org/en/topics/rwjf-topic-areas/health-policy/childhood-obesity/childhood-obesity-fast-facts.html.

8. C. L. Ogden et al., "High Body Mass Index for Age among U.S. Children and Adolescents, 2003–2006," *Journal of the American Medical Association* 299, no. 20 (2008): 2401–5; C. L. Ogden et al., "Prevalence of High Body Mass Index in U.S. Children and Adolescents, 2007–2008," *Journal of the American Medical Association* 303, no. 3 (2010): 242–49; C. L. Ogden et al., "The Epidemiology of Obesity," *Gastroenterology* 132, no. 6 (2007): 2087–102.

9. See Robert Wood Johnson Foundation Childhood Obesity Fast Facts. http://www.rwjf.org/en/topics/rwjf-topic-areas/health-policy/childhood-obesity/childhood-obesity-fast-facts.html.

10.   *New England Journal of Medicine.* See Robert Wood Johnson Foundation Childhood Obesity Fast Facts. http://www.rwjf.org/en/topics/rwjf-topic-areas/health-policy/ childhood-obesity/childhood-obesity-fast-facts.html.

11.   C. Y. Wang et al., "Health and Economic Burden of the Projected Obesity Trends in the USA and the UK," *Lancet* 378 (2011): 815–25.

12.   See note 3, above.

13.   F. M. Biro et al., "Pubertal Assessment and Baseline Characteristics in a Mixed Longitudinal Study of Girls," *Pediatrics* 126, no. 3 (September 2010): 583–90.

14.   S. E. Anderson et al., "Relative Weight and Race Influence Average Age at Menarche: Results from Two Nationally Representative Surveys of U.S. Girls Studied 25 Years Apart," *Pediatrics* 111, no. 4 (April 2003): 844–50.

15.   F. M. Biro et al., "Pubertal Correlates in Black and White Girls," *Journal of Pediatrics* 148, no. 2 (February 2006): 234–40.

16.   F. M. Biro et al., "Pubertal Assessment Method and Baseline Characteristics in a Mixed Longitudinal Study of Girls," *Pediatrics* 126, no. 3 (September 2010): 583–90.

17.   This is the "Critical Weight Hypothesis" first described in 1971 by Rose Frisch and Roger Revell.

18.   S. E. Anderson et al., "Relative Weight and Race Influence Average Age at Menarche."

19.   J. A. Graber et al., "Is Pubertal Timing Associated with Psychopathology in Young Adulthood?" *Journal of the American Academy of Child and Adolescent Psychiatry* 43 (2004): 718–26; C. Hayward et al., "Psychiatric Risk Associated with Early Puberty in Adolescent Girls," *Journal of the American Academy of Child and Adolescent Psychiatry* 36 (1997): 255–62.

20.   J. Deardorff et al., "Early Puberty and Adolescent Pregnancy: The Influence of Alcohol Use," *Pediatrics* 116 (2005): 1451–56.

21.   J. A. Graber et al., "Is Pubertal Timing Associated with Psychopathology in Young Adulthood?"

22.   C. N. Markey, "Invited Commentary: Why Body Image Is Important to Adolescent Development," *Journal of Youth and Adolescence* 39, no. 12 (2010): 1387–91.

23.   M. J. Merten, K. A. S. Wickrama, and A. Williams, "Adolescent Obesity and Young Adult Psychosocial Outcomes: Gender and Racial Differences," *Journal of Youth and Adolescence* 37 (2008): 1111–22.

24.   "Obesity and Cancer Risk," www.cancer.gov/cancertopics/factsheet/Risk/obesity.

25.   For more on this, see: K. A. Bogle, "The Shift from Dating to Hooking Up in College: What Scholars Have Missed," *Sociology Compass* 1/2, (2007): 775–88; J. R. Garcia and C. Reiber, "Hook-Up Behavior: A Biopsychosocial Perspective," *Journal of Social, Evolutionary, and Cultural Psychology* 2 (2008): 192–208.

26.   R. Boynton-Jarrett et al., "Childhood Abuse and Age at Menarche," *Journal of Adolescent Health* 52, no. 2 (February 2013): 241–47.

27.   C. T. Halpern, R. B. King, S. L . Oslak, and J. R. Udry, "Body Mass, Dieting, Romance, and Sexual Activity in Adolescent Girls: Relationships Over Time," *Journal of Research on Adolescence* 15, no. 4 (November 2005): 535–59.

28.   W. D. Manning, P. C. Giordano, and M. A. Longmore, "Hooking Up: The Relationship Contexts of "Nonrelationship" Sex," *Journal of Adolescent Research* 21, no. 5 (September 2006): 459–83.

29.   J. Mendle, E. Turkheimer, and R. E. Emery, "Detrimental Psychological Outcomes Associated with Early Pubertal Timing in Adolescent Girls," *Developmental Review* 27, no. 2 (June 2007): 151–71.

30.   J. J. Sabia and D. I. Rees, "The Effect of Body Weight on Adolescent Sexual Activity," *Health Economics* 20 (2011): 1330–48. See also "Sexual Health of Adolescents and Young Adults in the United States," The Henry J. Kaiser Family Foundation, http://kff.org/ womens-health-policy/fact-sheet/sexual-health-of-adolescents-and-young-adults-in-the-united-states/.

31.   Centers for Disease Control and Prevention, Morbidity and Mortality Weekly Report, "Sexual Experience and Contraceptive Use Among Female Teens—United States, 1995, 2002, and 2006–2010," 61, no. 17 (May 4, 2012): 297–301, http://www.cdc.gov/mmwr/ preview/mmwrhtml/mm6117a1.htm?s_cid=mm6117a1_e.

32.   J. Sobal and M. Bursztyn, "Dating People with Anorexia Nervosa and Bulimia Nervosa: Attitudes and Beliefs of University Students," *Women and Health* 27, no. 3 (1998): 73–88; J. Sobal et al., "Attitudes About Weight and Dieting among Secondary Students," *International Journal of Obesity* 19 (1995): 376–81.

33.   J. D. Latner et al., "Stigmatized Students: Age, Sex, and Ethnicity Effects in the Stigmatization of Obesity," *Obesity Research* 13 (2005): 1226–58; J. D. Latner and A. J. Stunkard, "Getting Worse: The Stigmatization of Obese Children," *Obesity Research* 11 (2003): 452–56; D. Neumark-Sztainer et al., "Weight-Teasing among Adolescents: Correlations with Weight Status and Disordered Eating Behaviors," *International Journal of Obesity and Related Metabolic Disorders* 26 (2002): 123–31; D. Neumark-Sztainer, M. Story, and L. Faibisch, "Perceived Stigmatization among Overweight African-American and Caucasian Adolescent Girls," *Journal of Adolescent Health* 93 (2003): 1342–48. For a sad and disturbing look into teasing of obese Mexican-American girls, see the supplemental information for S. A. Taylor et al., "A Qualitative Study of the Day-to-Day Lives of Obese Mexican-American Adolescent Females," *Pediatrics* 131 (2013): 1132–38 and supplemental SI1–SI16.

34.   C. T. Halpern et al., "Body Mass Index, Dieting, Romance, and Sexual Activity in Adolescent Girls: Relationships over Time," *Journal of Research on Adolescence* 15, no. 4 (2005): 535–59.

35.   J. Cawley, K. Joyner, and J. Sobal, "Size Matters: The Influence of Adolescents' Weight and Height on Dating and Sex," *Rationality and Society* 18, no. 1 (February 2006): 67–94; C. T. Halpern, J.R. Udry, B. Campbell, and C. Suchindran, "Effects of Body Fat on Weight Concerns, Dating, and Sexual Activity: A Longitudinal Analysis of Black and White Adolescent Girls," *Developmental Psychology* 35, no. 3 (1999): 721–36; D. J. Kallen and A. Doughty, "The Relationship of Weight, the Self Perception of Weight, and Self Esteem with Courtship Behavior," *Marriage and Family Review* 7, no. 1/2 (1984): 93–114; M. J. Pearce, J. Boergers, and M. J. Prinstein, "Adolescent Obesity, Overt and Relational Peer Victimization, and Romantic Relationships," *Obesity Research* 10 (2002): 386–93.

36.   "Percent of Children (10–17) Who Are Overweight or Obese," The Henry J. Kaiser Family Foundation, http://www.kff.org/other/state-indicator/overweightobese-children/.

37.   "Overweight and Obesity Rates for Adults by Race/Ethnicity," The Henry J. Kaiser Family Foundation, http://www.kff.org/other/state-indicator/adult-overweightobesity-rate-by-re/.

38.   C. Wang et al., "Low Testosterone Associated with Obesity and the Metabolic Syndrome Contributes to Sexual Dysfunction and Cardiovascular Disease Risk in Men with Type 2 Diabetes," *Diabetes Care* 34, no. 7 (July 2011): 1669–75.

39.   A. C. Petersen, "Adolescent Development," *Annual Review of Psychology* 39 (1999): 583–607.

40.   R. N. Ellis, B. Rogoff, and C. Cromer, "Age Segregation in Children's Social Interactions," *Developmental Psychology* 17, no. 4 (1981): 399–407.

41.   S. M. Dornbusch et al., "Sexual Development, Age, and Dating: A Comparison of Biological and Social Influences Upon One Set of Behaviors," *Child Development* 52 (1981): 179–85.

42.   J. Cawley (2006) found that obese adolescents are about half as likely to initiate dating as healthy-weight adolescents are. In an earlier study in 2001, Cawley also found that heavier girls, but not heavier boys, were less likely to have dated. Earlier studies found similar results (Halpern et al. 1999; Kallen and Doughty 1984—see above). See also Mir M.Ali et al., "Racial Differences in the Influence of Female Adolescents' Body Size on Dating and Sex" Economics & Human Biology, 12 (January 2004): 140–52.

43.   R. M. Puhl and J. D. Latner, "Stigma, Obesity, and the Health of the Nation's Children," *Psychological Bulletin* 133, no. 4 (2007): 557–80. Puhl and Latner found that weight-based teasing and victimization, not simply a child's body weight, is what leads to unfavorable outcomes for overweight adolescents. This extends to physical and psychological health and dating opportunities.

44.   D. Carr et al., "Bigger Is Not Always Better: The Effect of Obesity on Sexual Satisfaction and Behavior of Adult Men in the United States," *Men and Masculinities* 16, no. 4 (October 2013): 1–26.

45.   B. Roscoe, M. S. Diana, and R. H. Brooks, "Early, Middle, and Late Adolescents' Views on Dating and Factors Influencing Partner Selection," *Adolescence* 22 (1987): 59–68; S. Jackson and H. Rodriguez-Torne, eds., *Adolescence and Its Social Worlds* (Hillsdale, NJ: Lawrence Erlbaum Associates, 1993), pp. 95–119.

46.   B. B. Brown, "'You're Going Out with Who?' Peer Group Influences on Adolescent Romantic Relationships," in *The Development of Romantic Relationships in Adolescence*, W. Furman, B. B. Brown, and C. Feiring, eds. (New York: Cambridge University Press, 1999), 291–329; S. E. Cavanagh, "The Social Construction of Romantic Relationships in Adolescence: Examining the Role of Peer Networks, Gender, and Race," *Sociological Inquiry* 71, no. 5 (2007): 1395–1408.

47.   R. E. Sieving et al., "Friends' Influence on Adolescents' First Sexual Intercourse," *Perspectives on Sexual and Reproductive Health* 38, no. 1 (2006): 13–19.

48.   A. S. Masten et al., "The Structure and Coherence of Competence from Childhood Through Adolescence," *Child Development* 66 (1998): 1635–59; Susan Harter, *The Construction of the Self: A Developmental Perspective* (New York: The Guilford Press, 1999); J. A. Connolly and R. Konarski, "Peer Self-Concept in Adolescence: Analysis of Factor Structure and Associations with Peer Experience," *Journal of Research on Adolescence* 4 (1994): 385–403; A. F. Kuttler, A. M. La Greca, and M. J. Prinstein, "Friendship Qualities and Social Emotional Functioning of Adolescents with Close, Cross-Sex Friendships," *Journal for Research on Adolescence* 9 (1999): 339–66; D. L. McDonald and J. P. McKinney, "Steady Dating and Self-Esteem in High School Students," *Journal of Adolescence* 17 (1994): 557–64.

49.   W. Furman and L. Shaffer, "The Role of Romantic Relationships in Adolescent Development," in P. Florsheim, ed., *Adolescent Romantic Relations and Sexual Behaviors: Theory,*

Research, and Practical Implications (Mahwah, NJ: Lawrence Erlbaum, 2003), pp. 3–22; W. Furman and E. Wehner, "Romantic Views: Toward a Theory of Adolescent Romantic Relationships," in R. Montemayor, G. R. Adams, and T. P. Gullota, eds., *Personal Relationships During Adolescence*, vol. 6 (Thousand Oaks, CA: Sage, 1994), pp. 168–195; S Shulman, "Conflict and Negotiation in Adolescent Romantic Relationships," in P. Florsheim, ed., *Adolescent Romantic Relations and Sexual Behaviors: Theory, Research, and Practical Implications* (Mahwah, NJ: Lawrence Erlbaum, 2003), pp. 109–35; S. D. Madsen and W. A. Collins, "The Salience of Adolescent Romantic Experiences for Romantic Relationship Qualities in Young Adulthood," *Journal of Research on Adolescence* 21, no. 4 (2001): 789–801; I. Seiffge-Krenke, "Testing Theories of Romantic Development from Adolescence to Young Adulthood: Evidence of a Developmental Sequence," *International Journal of Behavioral Development* 27 (2003): 519–31.

50.   J. Cawley, K. Joyner, and J. Sobal, "Size Matters: The Influence of Adolescents' Weight and Height on Dating and Sex," *Rationality and Society* 18, no. 1 (2006): 67–94.

51.   M. Kirkman, D. Rosenthal, and A. M. A. Smith, "Adolescent Sex and the Romantic Narrative: Why Some Young Heterosexuals Use Condoms to Prevent Pregnancy but Not Disease," *Psychology, Health, and Medicine* 3, no. 4 (1998): 355–70.

52.   S. Averett, H. Corman, and N. Reichman, "Effects of Overweight on Risky Sexual Behavior of Adolescent Girls," National Bureau of Economic Research Working Paper Series. Working Paper 16172 http://www.nber.org/papers/w16172; J. J. Sabia and D. I. Rees, "The Effect of Body Weight on Adolescent Sexual Activity," *Health Economics* 20 (2011): 1330–48.

53.   Y. A. Cheng and N. Landale, "Adolescent Overweight, Social Relationships and the Transition to First Sex: Gender and Racial Variations," *Perspectives on Sexual and Reproductive Health* 43, no. 1 (2011): 6–15.

54.   A. Y. Akers et al., "Exploring the Relationship among Weight, Race, and Sexual Behaviors among Girls," *Pediatrics* 124, no. 5 (2009): e913–e920. Akers et al. analyzed data from nearly 7,200 high school girls and did not find a statistically significant relationship between high BMI and sexual activity. But the study could not control for confounding factors, including family structure. Akers et al. found that girls who perceived themselves as overweight has less sexual experience.

55.   D. Neumark-Sztainer et al., "Psychosocial Concerns and Health-Compromising Behaviors among Overweight and Nonoverweight Adolescents," *Obesity Research* 5, no. 3 (1997): 237–49. Social isolation protected heavy youth from the more reckless decisions that teenagers inevitably make: to smoke cigarettes and to abuse alcohol and drugs. A study from 1997, for example, found that obese girls drank less alcohol, and obese boys were less likely to use marijuana compared with healthy-weight adolescents. Those obese teens may have been exiled into social obscurity, but at least their weight kept them away from risky behaviors.

56.   M. I. Pearce, J. Boergers, and M. J. Prinstein, "Adolescent Obesity, Overt and Relational Peer Victimization, and Romantic Relationships," *Obesity Research* 10 (2002): 386–93.

57.   Deborah L. Tolman, *Dilemmas of Desire: Teenage Girls Talk about Sexuality* (Cambridge, MA: Harvard University Press, 2002).

58.   Y. Cheng, "Weight Status and Sexuality Development from Adolescence to Young Adulthood: A Dissertation in Sociology and Demography" (dissertation, Pennsylvania State University, 2008), http://udini.proquest.com/view/weight-status-and-sexuality-goid:807444097/.

59.   M. Villers, "Sexual Behavior in Obese and Overweight Adolescent Female Students," (paper, 58th Annual Clinical Meeting of the American College of Obstetricians and

Gynecologists, San Francisco, CA, 2010); S. Averett, H. Corman, and N. Reichman, "Effects of Overweight on Risky Sexual Behavior of Adolescent Girls," National Bureau of Economic Research Working Paper Series, No. 16172 (July 2010).

60.   http://abcnews.go.com/Health/childhood-obesity-call-parents-lose-custody/ story?id=14068280; July 2011 article on childhood obesity in the *Journal of the American Medical Association*, coauthored by Harvard University child obesity expert Dr. David S. Ludwig; http://jama.jamanetwork.com/article.aspx?articleid=1104076. About 2 million U.S. children have a BMI at or beyond the 99th percentile.

61.   M. B. Ratcliff et al., "Risk-Taking Behaviors of Adolescents with Extreme Obesity: Normative or Not?" *Pediatrics* 127 (2011): 827–34. The prevalence of extreme obesity is higher among black children (4.3 percent) than Hispanic (2.9 percent) and white children (2.1 percent), and the vast majority of them will continue to be obese when they become adults.

62.   Responses from Asian teens are often excluded from national surveys because it is difficult to reach statistical significance given the small subpopulation and the fact that some of the largest national surveys give four options for race: white, black, Hispanic, and other.

63.   F. W. Heiland and M. A. Ali, "Racial Differences in the Influence of Female Adolescents' Body Size on Dating and Sex 2010" (lecture); See also note 65.

64.   A. Y. Akers et al., "Exploring the Relationship among Weight, Race, and Sexual Behaviors among Girls," *Pediatrics* 124, no. 5 (2009): e913–e920; see also note 65.

65.   A. D. Neumark-Sztainer et al., "Ethnic/Racial Differences in Weight-Related Concerns and Behaviors among Adolescent Girls and Boys: Findings from Project EAT," *Journal of Psychosomatic Research* 53, no. 5 (2002): 963–74; A. Feingold, "Gender Differences in Effects of Physical Attractiveness on Romantic Attraction: A Comparison across Five Research Paradigms," *Journal of Personality and Social Psychology* 59, no. 5 (1990): 981–93; N. Nollen et al., "Correlates of Ideal Body Size among Black and White Adolescents," *Journal of Youth and Adolescence* 35, no. 2 (2006): 276–84.

66.   M. R. Cunningham et al., "'Their Ideas of Beauty Are, on the Whole, the Same as Ours': Consistency and Variability in the Cross-Cultural Perception of Female Physical Attractiveness," *Journal of Personality and Social Psychology* 68, no. 2 (1995): 261–79.

67.   M. Story et al., "Ethnic/Racial and Socioeconomic Differences in Dieting Behaviors and Body Image Perceptions in Adolescents," *International Journal of Eating Disorders* 18, no. 2 (1995): 173–79.

68.   S. H. Thompson, R. G. Sargent, and K. A. Kemper, "Black and White Adolescent Males' Perceptions of Ideal Body Size," *Sex Roles* 34, no. 5 (1996): 391–406.

69.   Y. A. Cheng and N. Landale, "Adolescent Overweight, Social Relationships and the Transition to First Sex: Gender and Racial Variations," *Perspectives on Sexual and Reproductive Health* 43, no. 1 (2011): 6–15.

CHAPTER 2

1.   Barbara Natterson-Horowitz and Kathryn Bowers, "Our Animal Natures," *New York Times,* June 9, 2012, http://www.nytimes.com/2012/06/10/opinion/sunday/our-animal-natures.html?pagewanted=all&_r=0.

2.   Diane Ackerman, *A Natural History of Love* (New York: Random House, 1994), p. 262.

3.   "According to Stone (1980), changes in economic production and labor markets, together with public health measures, helped to encourage young persons to marry for love. Families had less sway over the choices of young people as production moved away from the family and into the factory, and as life expectancy increased, so did the emotional investment a spouse was willing to make in his or her partner. In some cultures where partners are still chosen by a young person's family, love is still not seen as a requisite for marriage." Erica Owens, "The Sociology of Love, Courtship, and Dating," in C. Bryant and D. Peck, eds., *21ˢᵗ Century Sociology* (Thousand Oaks, CA: Sage Publications, Inc., 2007), p. 266.

4.   Centers for Disease Control and Prevention, "Adult Obesity Facts," http://www.cdc.gov/obesity/data/adult.html.

5.   K. M. Flegal, M. D. Carroll, C. L. Ogden, and L. R. Vurtin, "Prevalence and Trends in Obesity Among US Adults, 1999–2008," *Journal of the American Medical Association* 303, no. 3 (2010): 235–41.

6.   C. Levi-Strauss, *Les Structures Elementaires de la Parente [The Elementary Structure of Kinship]* (The Hague, Netherlands: Mouton, 1967).

7.   D. M. Buss and D. P. Schmitt, "Sexual Strategies Theory—An Evolutionary Perspective on Human Mating," *Psychological Review* 100 (1993): 204–32.

8.   M. Mikulincer, V. Florian, and G. Hirschberger, "The Existential Function of Close Relationships: Introducing Death in the Science of Love," *Personality and Social Psychology Review* 7, no. 1 (2003): 20–40. For more on adult attachment patterns, see P. R. Shaver and M. Mikulincer, "Adult Attachment Strategies and the Regulation of Emotion," in J. Gross, ed., *Handbook of Emotion Regulation* (New York: The Guilford Press, 2007), pp. 446–63.

9.   J. Greenberg, T. Pyszczynski, and S. Solomon, "The Causes and Consequences of a Need for Self-Esteem. A Terror Management Theory," in R. F. Baumesiter, ed., *Public and Private Self* (New York, NY: Springer-Verlag, 1986), pp. 189–92.

10. S. L. Gortmaker et al., "Social and Economic Consequences of Overweight Adolescence and Young Adulthood," *New England Journal of Medicine* 329, no.14 (1993): 1008–12; D. Conley and R. Glauber, "Gender, Body Mass, and Socioeconomic Status: New Evidence from the PSID," *Advances in Health Economics and Health Service Research* 17 (2006): 253–75; S. Avertett et al., "For Better or Worse: Relationship Status and Body Mass Index," *Economics and Human Biology* 6, no. 3 (2008): 330–49; S. Mukhopadhyay, "Do Women Value Marriage More? The Effect of Obesity on Cohabitation and Marriage in the USA," *Review of Economics of the Household* 6, no. 2 (2008): 111–26.

11. http://www.elainehatfield.com/ch104.pdf.

12. J. S. Wiggins, N. Wiggins, and J. C. Conger, "Correlates of Heterosexual Somatic Preferences," *Journal of Personality and Social Psychology* 10, no. 1 (1968): 82–90. doi: 10.1037/h0026394.

13. Werner J. Cahnman, "The Stigma of Obesity," *Sociological Quarterly* 9, no. 3 (June 1968): 283–99. doi:10.1111/j.1533-8525.1968.tb01121.x.

14. Harris had coauthored what might be the best-titled academic article ever: M. B. Harris, R. Harris, and S. Bochner, "Fat, Four-Eyed, and Female: Stereotypes of Obesity, Glasses, and Gender," *Journal of Applied Social Psychology* 12, no. 6 (1982): 503–16. doi: 10.1111/j.1559-1816.1982.tb00882.x.

15.   The great majority of students were white (91 percent); 7 percent were black; 0.5 percent were Asian; and 1 percent were Hispanic.

16.   M. S. Clark and J. R. Mills, "A Theory of Communal (and Exchange) Relationships," in P. A. M. Van Lange, A. W. Kruglanski, and E. T. Higgins, eds., *Handbook of Theories of Social Psychology* (Thousand Oaks, CA: Sage Press, 2012): pp. 232–50.

17.   M. W. Widerman and S. R. Hurst, "Body Size, Physical Attractiveness, and Body Image Among Young Adult Women: Relationships to Sexual Experience and Sexual Esteem," *Journal of Sex Research* 35 (1998): 272–81. doi: 10.1080/00224499809551943. The authors found college-age women who were heavier were less likely to be involved in a romantic relationship and were less likely to have sexual experiences even when the women were interested in sex and had positive attitudes about sexual relationships. This was similar to Halpern et al.'s findings in 2005 of high school age girls: For each one-point increase in BMI, the likelihood of being in a romantic relationship decreased by 6 to 7 percent.

18.   R. W. Brislin and S. A. Lewis, "Dating and Physical Attractiveness: Replication," *Psychological Reports* 22, no. 3 (June 1968): 976.

19.   E. Goffman, "On Cooling the Mark Out: Some Aspect of Adaptation to Failure," *Psychiatry* 15 (1952): 456.

20.   L. S. Taylor, A. T. Fiore, G. A. Mendelsohn, and C. Cheshire, " 'Out of My League': A Real-World Test of the Matching Hypothesis," *Personality and Social Psychology Bulletin* 37, no. 7 (2003): 942–54. doi: 10.1177/0146167211409947/.

21.   See, for example, J. Mckillip and S. L. Redel, "External Validity of Matching on Physical Attractiveness for Same and Opposite Sex Couples," *Journal of Applied Social Psychology* 13 (1983): 328–37.

22.   M. Rosenfeld and R. Thomas, "Searching for a Mate: The Rise of the Internet as a Social Mediary," *American Sociological Review* 77, no. 4 (2012): 523–47. By 2009, the Internet had become the third most likely way that heterosexual couples met each other.

23.   Taylor et al., " 'Out of My League' ": 947.

24.   S. M. Kalick and T. E. Hamilton, "The Matching Hypothesis Reexamined," *Journal of Personality and Social Psychology* 51 (1986): 673–82.

25.   S. Mukhopadhyay, "Do Women Value Marriage More? The Effect of Obesity on Cohabitation and Marriage in the USA," *Review of Economics of the Household* 6 (2008): 111–26. doi: 10.1007/ s11150-007-9025-y; J. H. Cawley, K. Joyner, and J. Sobal, "Size Matters: The Influence of Adolescents' Weight and Height on Dating and Sex," *Rationality & Society* 18, no. 1 (2006): 67–94; J. Sobal, "Social Consequences of Weight Bias by Partners, Friends, and Strangers," in K. D. Brownell, R. M. Puhl, M. B. Schwartz, and L. Rudd, eds., *Weight Bias: Nature, Consequences, and Remedies* (New York, NY: Guilford Press, 2005), pp. 150–64.

26.   P. C. Regan, "Sexual Outcasts: The Perceived Impact of Body Weight and Gender on Sexuality," *Journal of Applied Social Psychology* 26 (1996): 1803–15.

27.   G. Hitsch, A. Hortacsu, and D. Ariely, "What Makes You Click?—Mate Preferences in Online Dating," January 2010, http://home.uchicago.edu/~ghitsch/Hitsch-Research/ Guenter_Hitsch_files/Mate-Preferences.pdf.

28. M. E. Eisenberg, D. Neumark Sztainer, and K.D. Lust, "Weight-Related Issues and High-Risk Sexual Behaviors Among College Students," *Journal of American College Health* 54, no. 2 (2005): 95–101. Eisenberg et al. found that among young female college students, those with higher BMIs were more likely to engage in casual sex and to have multiple partners.

29. Holly R. Fee, "Obesity and Nonrelationship Sex: Are Obese Young Adults Hooking Up?" Center for Family and Demographic Research, 2013. http://www.bgsu.edu/organizations/cfdr/file130808.pdf. Morbidly obese women were 52 percent more likely to hook up than men.

30. E. Prohaska and J. A. Gailey, "Achieving Masculinity through Sexual Predation: The Case of Hogging," *Journal of Gender Studies* 19, no. 1 (March 2010): 13–25.

31. J. A. Gailey and A. Prohaska, "Knocking Off a Fat Girl: An Exploration of Hogging, Male Sexuality and Neutralizations," *Deviant Behavior* 27 (2006): 31–49; A. Prohaska and J. A. Gailey, "Fat Women as "Easy Targets": Achieving Masculinity through Hogging," in E. D. Rothblum and S. Solovay, eds., *The Fat Studies Reader* (New York: New York University Press, 2009), pp. 158–66.

32. S.-Y. Park et al., "Do Third-Person Perceptions of Media Influence Contribute to Pluralistic Ignorance on the Norm of Ideal Female Thinness?" *Sex Roles* 57, no. 7–8 (October 2007): 569–78. http://link.springer.com/article/10.1007%2Fs11199-007-9284-3#page-1.

33. P. Regan, "Sexual Outcasts: The Perceived Impact of Body Weight and Gender on Sexuality," *Journal of Applied Social Psychology* 26, no. 20 (1996): 1803–15.

34. M. Snyder and J. A. Haugen, "Why Does Behavioral Confirmation Occur? A Functional Perspective on the Role of the Target," *Personality and Social Psychology Bulletin* 2 (1995): 963–74. http://psp.sagepub.com/content/21/9/963.full.pdf+html.

35. P. Regan, "Sexual Outcasts," 1805.

36. Ibid.,1812.

37. Holly R. Fee and Michael R. Nusbaumer, "Social Distance and the Formerly Obese: Does the Stigma of Obesity Linger?" *Sociological Inquiry* 82, no. 3 (August 2012): 356–77. doi: 10.1111/j.1475-682X.2012.00420.x.

38. M. Schmidt, "Obesity in Young Men, and Individual and Combined Risks of Type 2 Diabetes, Cardiovascular Morbidity and Death Before 55 Years of Age: A Danish 33-Year Follow-Up Study," British Medical Journal Open 3, no. 4 (2013): e002698. doi:10.1136/bmjopen-2013-002698.

39. "In the last decade, as rates of overweight and obesity in Americans have risen, obesity has become one of the most significant health problems for emerging adults, as well as perhaps the greatest predictor of health problems in later adulthood. While emerging adults may have lower rates of overweight and obesity than older adults, approximately three-quarters of emerging adults are overweight or obese (National Center for Health Statistics, 2005), which carries serious implications. For example, being mildly or moderately overweight at ages 20–22 is a significant predictor of obesity by ages 35–37 (McTigue, Garrett, & Popkin, 2002) and being seriously overweight or obese elevates the risk of heart disease, diabetes, high cholesterol, hypertension, and some types of cancer (National Center for Health Statistics, 2005). The high rates of overweight and obesity seen among emerging adults may be due, in part, to a lack of physical activity. Research has demonstrated a significant decrease in physical activity during the transition from adolescence to young adulthood (GordonLarsen, Nelson, & Popkin, 2004),

which in turn is independently associated with obesity in young adulthood (Tammelin, Laitinen, & Näyhä, 2004). Furthermore, findings from a population-based, longitudinal cohort study show an inverse relationship between fitness in emerging adulthood and risk factors for cardiovascular disease such as hypertension and diabetes in middle age, even after controlling for body mass index (Carnethon, Gidding, Nehgme, Sidney, Jacobs, & Liu 2003)." J. L. Tanner, J. J. Arnett, and J. E. Leis, "Emerging Adulthood: Learning and Development during the First Stage of Adulthood," in M. C. Smith and N. DeFrates-Densch, eds., *Handbook of Research on Adult Learning and Development* (New York: Routledge, 2009), pp. 34–67.

CHAPTER 3

1.   W. R. Harlan et al., "Secular Trends in Body Mass in the United States, 1960–1980," *American Journal of Epidemiology* 128 (1988): 1065–74.

2.   J. P. Koplan and W. H. Dietz, "Caloric Imbalance and Public Health Policy," *Journal of the American Medical Association* 282, no. 16 (October 27, 1999): 1579–81.

3.   U.S. Department of Health and Human Services, "The Surgeon General's Call to Action to Prevent and Decrease Overweight and Obesity 2001" (2001). http://surgeongeneral.gov/library/calls/obesity/CalltoAction.pdf.pdf.

4.   K. D. Brownell and T. A. Wadden, "Etiology and Treatment of Obesity: Understanding a Serious, Prevalent, and Refractory Disorder," *Journal of Consulting and Clinical Psychology* 60, no. 4 (1992): 505–17.

5.   David B. Allison and Monica L. Baskin, eds., *Handbook of Assessment Methods for Eating Behaviors and Weight Related Problems*, 2nd ed. (Thousand Oaks, CA: Sage Publications, 2009), p. 34.

6.   R. L. Kolotkin and R. D. Crosby, "Psychometric Evaluation of the Impact of Weight on Quality of Life-Lite Questionnaire (IWQOL-Lite) in a Community Sample," *Quality of Life Research* 11 (2002): 157–71.

7.   R. L. Kolotkin et al., "Assessing Impact of Weight on Quality of Life," *Obesity Research* 3, no. 1 (January 1995): 49–56.

8.   Albert Moll, *Untersuchungen über die Libido sexualis* (Adamant Media Corporation/ Elibron Classics, 2004).

9.   W. McDougall, *Introduction to Social Psychology,* 8th ed. (Boston: John W. Luce & Company, 1914): pp. 1–18.

10.   B. Caballero, "The Global Epidemic of Obesity: An Overview," *Epidemiologic Review* 29, no. 1 (2007): 1–5; L. Breslow, "Public Health Aspects of Weight Control," *American Journal of Public Health* 42 (1952): 1116–22; U.S. Department of Health, Education, and Welfare, *Obesity and Health* (Washington, DC: U.S. Public Health Service, 1966), report no. 1485.

11.   I. Brown and J. Thompson, "Primary Care Nurses' Attitudes, Beliefs, and Own Body Size in Relation to Obesity Management," *Journal of Advanced Nursing* 60 (2007): 535–43.

12.   I. Brown, "Nurses' Attitudes Towards Adult Patients Who Are Obese: Literature Review," *Journal of Advanced Nursing* 53 (2006): 221–32.

13.   L. A. Neighbors et al., "Weighing Weight: Trends in Body Weight Evaluation Among Young Adults, 1990 and 2005," *Sex Roles* 59 (2008): 68–80.

14.   R. M. Puhl and C. A. Heuer, "The Stigma of Obesity: A Review and Update," *Obesity* 17 (2009): 941–64.

15.   E. U. Chen and M. Brown, "Obesity Stigma in Sexual Relationships," *Obesity Research* 13 (2005): 1393–97.

16.   V. Swami and M. J. Tovee, "Does Hunger Influence Judgments of Female Physical Attractiveness?" *British Journal of Psychology* 97 (2006): 353–63.

17.   G. J. Duncan, B. Wilkerson, and P. England, "Cleaning Up Their Act: The Effects of Marriage and Cohabitation on Licit and Illicit Drug Use," *Demography* 43 (2006): 691–710.

18.   R. Lund et al., "Cohabitation and Marital Status As Predictors of Mortality—An Eight Year Follow-Up Study," *Social Science & Medicine* 55 (2002): 673–79; H. Liu and C. Reczek, "Cohabitation and U.S. Adult Mortality: An Examination by Gender and Race," *Journal of Marriage and Family* 74, no. 4 (August 2012): 794–811.

19.   L. A. Neighbors and J. Sobal, "Weight and Weddings: Women's Weight Ideas and Weight Management Behaviors for Their Wedding Day," *Appetite* 50 (2008): 550–54.

20.   B. Rauschenbach, J. Sobal, and E. A. Frongillo Jr., "The Influence of Change in Marital Status on Weight Change over One Year," *Obesity Research* 3 (1996): 319–27; J. Sobal, B. Rauschenbach, and E. A. Frongillo, "Marital Status Changes and Body Weight Changes: A US Longitudinal Analysis," *Social Science & Medicine* 56 (2003): 1543–55; S. Averett, A. Sikora, and L. M. Argys, "For Better or Worse: Relationship Status and Body Mass Index," *Economics and Human Biology* 6 (2008): 330–49; L. Dinour et al., "The Association between Marital Transitions, Body Mass Index, and Weight: A Review of the Literature," *Journal of Obesity* 2012 (2012): 294974.

21.   J. Sobal, K. Hanson, and E. A. Frongillo, "Gender, Ethnicity, Marriage Status and Body Weight in the United States," *Obesity Research* 17 (2012): 2223–31.

22.   Andrew J. Cherlin, "In the Season of Marriage, a Question. Why Bother?" *New York Times* (April 28, 2013): SR7.

23.   T. A. Falba and J. L. Sindelar, "Spousal Concordance in Health Behavior Change," *Health Services Research* 43 (2008): 96–116; R. W. Jeffery and A. M. Rick, "Cross-Sectional and Longitudinal Associations between Body Mass Index and Marriage-Related Factors," *Obesity Research* 10 (2002): 809–15.

24.   J. Hebebrand et al., "Epidemic Obesity: Are Genetic Factors Involved via Increased Rates of Assortative Mating?" *International Journal of Obesity and Related Metabolic Disorders* 24, no. 3 (2000): 345–53; P. Jacobsen, J. S. Torgerson, L. Sjöström, and C. Bouchard, "Spouse Resemblance in Body Mass Index: Effects on Adult Obesity Prevalence in the Offspring Generation," *American Journal of Epidemiology* 165, no. 1 (2007): 101–8.

25.   The NS and P. Gordon-Larsen, "Entry into Romantic Partnership Is Associated with Obesity," *Obesity* 17 (2009): 1441–47.

26. S. L. Averett, A. Sikora, and L. M. Argys, "For Better or Worse: Relationship Status and Body Mass Index," *Economics & Human Biology* 6 (2008): 330–49.

27. J. Sobal, B. S. Rauschenbach, and E. A. Frongillo Jr., "Marital Status, Fatness and Obesity," *Social Science & Medicine* 35 (1992): 915–23.

28. For more on the degree to which the self-esteem and moods of overweight people are affected by weight-related stigma in relationships, see D. M. Quinn and J. Crocker, "Vulnerability to the Affective Consequences of the Stigma of Overweight," in *Prejudice: The Target's Perspective,* J. K. Swim and C. Stangor, eds. (San Diego, CA: Academic Press, Inc., 1998), 125–43.

29. C. Bove and A. Sobal, "Body Weight Relationships in Early Marriage. Weight Relevance, Weight Comparisons, and Weight Talk," *Appetite* 57 (2011): 729–42.

30. Meltzer et al., "Marital Satisfaction Predicts Weight Gain in Early Marriage," *Health Psychology* 32 (2013): 824–27.

31. P. Lundborg, P. Nystedt, and B. Lindgren, "Getting Ready for the Marriage Market? The Association between Divorce Risks and Investments in Attractive Body Mass among Married Europeans," *Journal of Biosocial Science* 39 (2007): 531–44.

32. Averett et al., "For Better or Worse."

33. D. Boyes and J. D. Latner, "Weight Stigma in Existing Romantic Relationships," *Journal of Sex and Marital Therapy* 35 (2009): 282–93; A. L. Meltzer and J. K. McNulty, "Body Image and Marital Satisfaction: Evidence for the Mediating Role of Sexual Frequency and Sexual Satisfaction," *Journal of Family Psychology* 24 (2010): 156–64; V. Sheets and K. Ajmere, "Are Romantic Partners a Source of College Students' Weight Concern?" *Eating Behaviors* 6 (2005): 1–9.

34. V. Sheets and K. Ajmere, "Are Romantic Partners a Source of College Students' Weight Concern?" *Eating Behaviors* 6 (2005): 1–9.

35. S. J. Billman and J. D. Ware, "Marital Satisfaction of Wives in Untreated Sleep Apneic Men," *Sleep Medicine* 3 (2002): 55–59; D. Carr and A. Friedman, "Body Weight and the Quality of Interpersonal Relationships," *Social Psychology Quarterly* 69 (2006): 127–49; C. N. Markey and P. M. Markey, "Romantic Relationships and Body Satisfaction among Young Women," *Journal of Youth and Adolescence* 35 (2006): 271–79.

36. G. A. Gonzaga, B. Campos, and T. Bradbury, "Similarity, Convergence, and Relationship Satisfaction in Dating and Married Couples," *Journal of Personality and Social Psychology* 93 (2007): 34–48.

37. R. M. Puhl and K. D. Brownell, "Confronting and Coping with Weight Stigma: An Investigation of Overweight and Obese Individuals," *Obesity* 14 (2006): 1802–15.

38. Boyes and Latner, "Weight Stigma in Existing Romantic Relationships."

39. E. Butler, V. J. Young, and A. K. Randall, "Suppressing to Please, Eating to Cope: The Effect of Overweight Women's Emotion Suppression on Romantic Relationships and Eating," *Journal of Social and Clinical Psychology* 29 (2010): 599–623.

40. T. J. Burke et al., " 'You're Going to Eat *That*?' Relationship Processes and Conflict Among Mixed-Weight Couples," *Journal of Social and Personal Relationships* (July 9, 2012): 1–22.

41. Boyes and Latner, "Weight Stigma in Existing Relationships." Women with higher BMIs reported that their relationships are more likely to end.

CHAPTER 4

1.   Richard K. Lee et al., "Central Obesity as Measured by Waist Circumference Is Predictive of Severity of Lower Urinary Tract Symptoms," *British Journal of Urology International* 110 (2012): 540–45. For men with large waists, the data are especially strong: An analysis of 409 middle-aged and older men treated at the Institute of Bladder and Prostate Health at New York–Presbyterian Hospital/Weill Cornell found that 74.5 percent of men with the biggest waists reported erectile dysfunction, compared with 50 percent of men with midsize waists and 32 percent of men with smaller waists. Men reported problems with ejaculation along a similar pattern.

2.   Abdulla, D. Daya, and T. Davies, "Buried Penis: An Unrecognized Risk Factor in the Development of Invasive Penile Cancer," *Canadian* Urological *Association Journal* 6, no. 5 (October 2012): E199–E202.

3.   R. Sturm and A. Hattori, "Morbid Obesity Rates Continue to Rise Rapidly in the United States," *International Journal of Obesity* 37 (June 2013): 889–91.

4.   A. Pestana et al., "Management of 'Buried' Penis in Adulthood: An Overview," *Plastic and Reconstructive Surgery* 124, no. 4 (October 2009): 1186–95.

5.   Abdulla, Daya, and Davies, "Buried Penis: An Unrecognized Risk Factor in the Development of Invasive Penile Cancer."

6.   J. Casale et al., "Concealed Penis in Childhood: A Spectrum of Etiology and Treatment," *Journal of Urology* 162 (1999): 1165–68, http://dx.doi.org/10.1016/S0022-5347(01)68114-X; C. F. Donatucci and E. F. Ritter, "Management of the Buried Penis in Adults," *Journal of Urology* 159 (1998): 420–24, http://dx.doi.org/10.1016/S0022-5347(01)63939-9.

7.   For more on how obesity reduces testosterone levels in men see, F. Saad et al., "Testosterone as Potential Effective Therapy in Treatment of Obesity in Men with Testosterone Deficiency: A Review," *Current Diabetes Reviews* 8 (2012): 131–43.

8.   C. Wang et al., "Low Testosterone Associated with Obesity and the Metabolic Syndrome Contributes to Sexual Dysfunction and Cardiovascular Disease Risk in Men with Type 2 Diabetes," *Diabetes Care* 34 (2011): 1669–75.

9.   I. Andersen, B. Heitman, and G. Wagner, "Obesity and Sexual Dysfunction in Younger Danish Men," *Journal of Sexual Medicine* 5 (2008): 2053–60. Given the varying sexual norms across countries, I've mostly referenced studies conducted in the United States. I have included foreign studies that look at the physiological mechanisms that underlie obesity and sexual functioning.

10.   A. Tchernof and P. Despres, "Pathophysiology of Human Visceral Obesity: An Update," *Physiology Review* 93 (2013): 359–404.

11.   Y. Matsuzawa, "The Role of Fat Topology in the Risk of Disease," *International Journal of Obesity* 32, Supplement 7 (2008): S83–92.

12.   Tchernof and Despres, "Pathophysiology of Human Visceral Obesity: An Update."

13.   M. Diaz-Arjonilla et al., "Obesity, Low Testosterone Levels and Erectile Dysfunction," *International Journal of Impotence Research* 21 (2009): 89–98.

14.   S. Loves, J. Ruinemans-Koerts, and H. de Boer, "Letrozole Once a Week Normalizes Serum Testosterone in Obesity-Related Male Hypogonadism," *European Journal of Endocrinology* 158 (2008): 741–47.

15.   M. L. Andersen et al., "The Association of Testosterone, Sleep, and Sexual Function in Men and Women," *Brain Research* 1416 (2011): 80–104.

16.   S. Budweiser et al., "Sleep Apnea Is an Independent Correlate of Erectile and Sexual Dysfunction," *Journal of Sexual Medicine* 11 (2009): 3147–57.

17.   A. Yassin and G. Doros, "Testosterone Therapy in Hypogonadal Men Results in Sustained and Clinically Meaningful Weight Loss," *Clinical Obesity* 3, nos. 3–4 (June 2013): 73–83; F. Saad et al., "Testosterone as Potential Effective Therapy in Treatment of Obesity in Men with Testosterone Deficiency: A Review," *Current Diabetes Reviews* 8, no. 2 (March 2012): 131–43.

18.   Centers for Disease Control and Prevention, "Diabetes Report Card 2012: National and State Profile of Diabetes and Its Complications," http://www.cdc.gov/diabetes/pubs/reportcard/diabetes-incidence.htm[cdc.gov];G. L. Beckles and C. Chou, "Diabetes—United States, 2006 and 2010," *Morbidity and Mortality Weekly Report* 62, no. 3 (2013): 99–104.

19.   "Low Testosterone," American Diabetes Association, www.diabetes.org/living-with-diabetes/complications/mens-health/sexual-health/low-testosterone.html.

20.   R. Schiel and U. A. Muller, "Prevalence of Sexual Disorders in a Selection-Free Diabetic Population," *Diabetes Research and Clinical Practice* 44 (1999): 115–21.

21.   R. Rosen et al., "Erectile Dysfunction in Type 2 Diabetic Men: Relationship to Exercise Fitness and Cardiovascular Risk Factors in the Look AHEAD Trial," *Journal of Sexual Medicine* 6 (2009): 1414–22.

22.   S. Dhindsa et al., "Testosterone Concentrations in Diabetic and Non-Diabetic Obese Men," *Diabetes Care* 33, no. 6 (2010): 1186–92.

23.   M. Barron et al., "Sex-Specific Effects of High-Fat Diet on Indices of Metabolic Syndrome in 3xTg-AD Mice: Implications for Alzheimer's Disease," *PLoS ONE* 8, no. 10 (2013): e78554. doi:10.1371/journal.pone.0078554.

24.   Endocrine Society, "Obesity Leads to Brain Inflammation, and Low Testosterone Makes It Worse," *ScienceDaily* June 17, 2013, www.sciencedaily.com/releases/2013/06/130617172833.htm.

25.   A. Thompson et al., "Erectile Dysfunction and Subsequent Cardiovascular Disease," *Journal of the American Medical Association* 294 (2005): 2996–3002.

26.   C. Gazzaruso et al., "Relationship between Erectile Dysfunction and Silent Myocardial Ischemia in Apparently Uncomplicated Type 2 Diabetic Patients," *Circulation* 110 (2004): 22–26.

27.   W. A. Bluemntals et al., "Is Erectile Dysfunction Predictive of Peripheral Vascular Disease?" *Aging Male* 6 (2003): 217–21.

28.   Peter Jaret, "First Come Erectile Ills, Then Heart Trouble," *New York Times,* March 1, 2008.

29.   R. Kolotkin, X. Zunker, and T. Ostbye, "Sexual Functioning and Obesity: A Review," *Obesity* 20, no. 12 (December 2012): 2325–33.

30.   T. Travison et al., "The Natural Progression and Remission of Erectile Dysfunction: Results from the Massachusetts Male Aging Study," *Journal of Urology* 177 (2007): 241–46;

Endocrine Society, "Overweight Men Can Boost Low Testosterone Levels by Losing Weight," *ScienceDaily*, June 25, 2012.

31. J. L. Hannan et al., "Beneficial Impact of Exercise and Obesity Interventions on Erectile Function and Its Risk Factors," *Journal of Sexual Medicine* 6, supplement 3 (March 2009): 254–61.

32. S. La Vignera et al., "Physical Activity and Erectile Dysfunction in Middle-Aged Men," *Journal of Andrology* 3, no. 2 (2012): 154–61.

33. Yassin and Doros, "Testosterone Therapy in Hypogonadal Men Results in Sustained and Clinically Meaningful Weight Loss."

34. J. L. Kristeller and R. A. Hoerr, "Physician Attitudes Toward Managing Obesity: Differences among Six Specialty Groups," *Preventative Medicine* 26 (1997): 542–49; M. R. Hebl and J. Xu, "Weighing the Care: Physicians' Reactions to the Size of a Patient," *International Journal of Obesity and Related Metabolic Disorders* 25 (2001): 1246–52.

35. Gary D. Foster et al., "Obesity and Its Treatment," *Obesity Research* 11 (2003): 1168–77.

36. Jane Brody, "A Label Calls Attention to Obesity," *New York Times*, July 2, 2013. People who are obese are at an increased risk of developing cancers of the colon, breast, endometrium, esophagus, pancreas, kidney, thyroid, and gallbladder.

37. R. Kolotkin et al., "Obesity and Sexual Quality of Life," *Obesity* 14 (2006): 472–79.

38. Ibid.

39. E. O. Laumann, A. Paik, and R. C. Rosen, "Sexual Dysfunction in the United States: Prevalence and Predictors," *Journal of the American Medical Association* 281 (1999): 537–44.

40. H. Rellini et al., "The Relationship between Women's Subjective and Physiological Sexual Arousal," *Psychophysiology* 42 (2005): 116–24.

41. For more on diabetes and female sexual functioning see P. Enzlin et al., "Diabetes Mellitus and Female Sexuality: A Review of 25 Years' Research," *Diabetic Medicine* 15 (1998): 809–15.

42. S. T. Linday et al., "Sexuality Among Middle-Aged and Older Adults with Diagnosed and Undiagnosed Diabetes," *Diabetes Care* 33 (2010): 2202–10.

CHAPTER 5

1. http://favstar.fm/users/julia_sandsxxx

CHAPTER 6

1. R. Sturm and A. Hatori, "Morbid Obesity Rates Continue to Rise Rapidly in the United States," *International Journal of Obesity* 37, no. 6 (2013): 889–91.

2.   G. C. van Hout et al., "Psychosocial Functioning following Bariatric Surgery," *Obesity Surgery* 16, no. 6 (2006): 787–94.

3.   Negative body image is positively associated with body mass index. See D. B. Sarwer, T. A. Wadden, and G. D. Foster, "Assessment of Body Image Dissatisfaction in Obese Women: Specificity, Severity, and Clinical Significance," *Journal of Consulting Clinical Psychology* 66, no. 4 (1998): 651–54.

4.   G. D. Foster, T. A. Wadden, and R. A. Vogt, "Body Image in Obese Women Before, During, and After Weight Loss Treatment," *Health Psychology* 16, no. 3 (1997): 226–29; G. F. Adami et al., "Body Image and Body Weight in Obese Patients," *International Journal of Eating Disorders* 24, no. 3 (1998): 229–306; J. M. Dixon, M. E. Dixon, and P. E. O'Brien, "Body Image: Appearance Orientation and Evaluation in the Severely Obese: Changes with Weight Loss," *Obesity Surgery* 12, no. 1 (2002): 65–71; D. B. Sarwer, J. K. Thompson, and T. F. Cash, "Body Image and Obesity in Adulthood," *Psychiatric Clinics of North America* 28 (2005): 69–78.

5.   Van Hout et al., "Psychosocial Functioning following Bariatric Surgery."

6.   Ibid.

7.   M. H. Zeller et al., "Two-Year Trends in Psychosocial Functioning after Adolescent Roux-en-Y Gastric Bypass," *Surgery for Obesity and Related Diseases* 7, no. 6 (2011): 727–32.

8.   D. B. Sarwer et al., "Changes in Quality of Life and Body Image after Gastric Bypass Surgery," *Surgery for Obesity and Related Diseases* 6, no. 6 (2010): 608–14.

9.   William Hartman, "Psychological Issues in Obesity & Weight Loss: Body Image & Sexual Functioning" (presentation, Weight Management Program, San Francisco, California).

10.   M. A. Camps, E. Zervos, S. Goode, and A. S. Rosemurgy, "Impact of Bariatric Surgery on Body Image Perception and Sexuality in Morbidly Obese Patients and Their Partners," *Obesity Surgery* 6, no. 4 (1996): 356–60.

11.   D. S. Bond et al., "Significant Resolution of Female Sexual Dysfunction after Bariatric Surgery," *Surgery for Obesity and Related Diseases* 7, no. 1 (2011): 1–7.

12.   *Journal of Sexual Medicine* 9, Supplement 5 (December 2012): 327.

13.   R. L. Kolotkin et al., "Two-Year Changes in Health-Related Quality of Life in Gastric Bypass Patients Compared with Severely Obese Controls," *Surgery for Obesity and Related Diseases* 5, no. 2 (March/April 2009): 250–56.

14.   J. Sobal, B. S. Rauschenbach, and E. A. Frongillo, "Obesity and Marital Quality: Analysis of Weight, Marital Unhappiness, and Marital Problems in a U.S. National Sample," *Journal of Family Issues* 16, no. 6 (1995): 746–64.

15.   L. C. Porter and R. S. Wampler, "Adjustment to Rapid Weight Loss," *Families, Systems & Health* 18, no. 1 (2000): 35–54.

16.   J. W. Pearce, M. D. LeBow, and J. Orchard, "Role of Spouse Involvement in the Behavioral Treatment of Overweight Women," *Journal of Consulting and Clinical Psychology* 49, no. 2 (1981): 236–44.

17.   www.iub.edu/~kinsey/resources/FAQ.html#frequency.

18.   R. B. Stuart and B. Davis, *Slim Chance in a Fat World* (Champaign, IL: Research Press, 1978).

19.   V. E. Blank, M. J. Herman, A. Kunis, and W. J. Vitale, "Jealous Husband Threatens Diet," *Obesity and Bariatric Medicine* 10: 104–8.

20.   R. B. Stuart and B. Jacobsen, *Weight, Sex, and Marriage: A Delicate Balance* (New York: The Guilford Press, 1994); Norton and prospective analyses support this position; see L. Fischman-Havstad and A. R. Marston, "Weight Loss Maintenance as an Aspect of Family Emotion and Process," *British Journal of Clinical Psychology* 23 (1984): 265–71.

21.   V. Felitti, "Childhood Sexual Abuse, Depression, and Family Dysfunction in Adult Obese Patients: A Case Control Study," *Southern Medical Journal* 86 (1993): 732–36.

Index